FORDHAM UNIVERSITY LIBRARY

Rose Hill Campus

This book is due not later than the date on slip. For each book kept overtime there is a fine for each day.

FACULTY MEMBERS MUST RETURN ALL BOOKS AT THE CLOSE OF THE SPRING SEMESTER

MONOGRAPH SERIES
UNITED STATES CATHOLIC HISTORICAL SOCIETY

UNITED STATES CATHOLIC HISTORICAL SOCIETY

President
VICTOR L. RIDDER

President-Elect
FRED R. BEAUDRY

Vice President
RT. REV. MSGR. FLORENCE D. COHALAN

Secretary
RT. REV. MSGR. JOHN J. HARRINGTON

Assistant Secretary
HUGO F. RICCA

Treasurer
PAUL G. REILLY

Editors of Publications
RT. REV. MSGR. EUGENE V. CLARK

Directors

ROBERT F. CONNERY
JOHN V. CONNORTON
JOHN F. CURRY III
GEORGE B. FARGIS
CHARLES HERBERMANN
JOSEPH G. E. HOPKINS
VERY REV. MSGR. JAMES P. MAHONEY

GARRY MCEOIN
RT. REV. MSGR. JAMES A. REYNOLDS
BEN REGAN
HON. HAROLD A. STEVENS
VERY REV. MSGR. GEORGE TIFFANY

UNITED STATES CATHOLIC HISTORICAL SOCIETY

MONOGRAPH SERIES
XXVII

FATHER VARELA
Torch Bearer from Cuba

by

JOSEPH AND HELEN McCADDEN

NEW YORK
THE UNITED STATES CATHOLIC
HISTORICAL SOCIETY
1969

Copyright © 1969
THE UNITED STATES CATHOLIC
HISTORICAL SOCIETY

OFFICE OF THE SECRETARY OF THE SOCIETY
ST. JOSEPH'S SEMINARY, YONKERS, NEW YORK

FÉLIX VARELA (c. 1837)

FÉLIX VARELA (c. 1850)

CONTENTS

Prólogo—by Reverend Raúl del Valle vii

Prologue: The Church of New York in Father Varela's Time
—by Right Reverend Florence D. Cohalan xi

Foreword—by Right Reverend Eugene V. Clark xvi

Acknowledgments xvii

CHAPTER		PAGE
I.	He Teaches His Cubans to Think	1
II.	He Charts the Way to Freedom	38
III.	He Serves as a Priest in New York	72
IV.	He Creates the Church of the Transfiguration	99
V.	The Flame Burns Low	124
VI.	His Torch Becomes a Beacon	146

Bibliography 174

Index 187

PRÓLOGO

En la galería de cubanos ilustres, que es notablemente copiosa, figuran hombres excepcionales por su grandeza de alma y por su acendrado patriotismo. Entre ellos sobresale en primera línea la noble figura del Padre Félix Varela.

Con razón el Padre Varela ocupa un lugar preeminente entre los patricios cubanos. Sacerdote, filósofo, educador, parlamentario, escritor y publicista, descuella entre sus compatriotas de una manera singular, por haber sido el iniciador ideológico de la lucha por la libertad e independencia de Cuba. Sería imposible escribir la historia cabal de la nación cubana y de las luchas por la independencia de la Perla de las Antillas, sin hacer referencia adecuada a la obra patriótica del Padre Varela. En realidad, en él se encuentran las raíces de la nacionalidad cubana y de las luchas por la independencia de la Patria. Primero, como maestro de filosofía y de derecho constitucional en el Seminario de San Carlos de La Habana, el ilustre sacerdote sembró en el corazón de sus discípulos, que formaron una pléyade admirable, sentimientos de amor a la verdad, a la justicia, a la libertad, y a las tradiciones e intereses patrios. Más tarde, al comienzo de su destierro en los Estados Unidos proclamó abiertamente desde las páginas de *El Habanero* su mensaje independentisto, que fué como una clarinada patriótica para despertar la conciencia dormida de la juventud cubana.

Por causa de sus ideas políticas, y en particular por su fidelidad al ideal de la independencia de Cuba, el Padre Varela fué perseguido y tuvo que vivir en el destierro casi durante la mitad de su vida, desde su llegada a New York en diciembre de 1823 hasta su muerte en febrero de 1853. Probablemente le hubiera sido fácil obtener un indulto de repatriación, de haberse sometido servilmente al despotismo colonial imperante en la Isla. Pero aquel inquebrantable sacerdote cubano, de cuerpo frágil pero de temple acerado, prefirió vivir con dignidad la agonía de su destierro hasta el fin de su vida, dando así a la juventud cubana un ejemplo magnífico de entereza de ánimo, de integridad política y del más noble patriotismo.

El Padre Varela llevó siempre a Cuba, su única y adorada Patria, en la mente y en el corazón. Sin embargo, su ardiente amor a

Cuba no fué en modo alguno obstáculo para que también amara a los Estados Unidos, que generosamente le dió la bienvenida en momentos angustiosos de su vida, cuando huía de la furia implacable de Fernando VII, al recobrar éste sus poderes absolutos para tiranizar al pueblo español y a lo que quedaba de las colonias de América. Lejos de vivir de espaldas a la sociedad norteamericana, el Padre Varela trató de comprenderla y de servirla con lealtad y nobleza. Sin dejar de sentirse cubano en ningún momento, no permitió que lo dominara la amargura del destierro, ni dejó tampoco pasar el tiempo esterilmente. Así pues, una vez que hubo echado las bases ideológicas de la independencia de Cuba, (que sólo habría de lograrse con el correr de los años gracias a los sacrificios heroicos del pueblo cubano), el Padre Varela se entregó por entero al ministerio sacerdotal en medio de la sociedad que le había dado generosa hospitalidad.

En New York el Padre Varela encontró un campo vastísimo para su celo sacerdotal. La diócesis de New York, creada en 1808, comprendía entonces todo el Estado de New York y parte del de New Jersey. El catolicismo no tenía en aquella época ni sombra del prestigio y de la pujanza que tiene en nuestros días. Practicamente todo el territorio de la Unión Norteamericana era tierra de misiones. En 1825, cuando el Padre Varela recibió las licencias ministeriales del Obispo Connolly, había en la diócesis de New York solamente unos 35,000 católicos y una docena de sacerdotes esparcidos por el inmenso territorio de la diócesis. La mayoría de la población católica estaba compuesta de inmigrantes y de gente humilde y sencilla, en su mayoría de origen irlandés, alemán, francés y español. Por añadidura, el ambiente estaba dominado por una clase de protestantismo fanáticamente anticatólico. El panorama era en verdad desolador desde el punto de vista religioso. Pero para un sacerdote de fe profunda y de ardiente celo apostólico como el Padre Varela, aquella desoladora situación no era sino un acicate punzante que lo obligaría a redoblar sus esfuerzos por la gloria de Dios y la salvación de las almas.

En Cuba el Padre Varela se había destacado como filósofo ecléctico, orador elocuente y maestro ideal para la juventud. En New York ganaría fama como hombre abnegado, escritor acucioso, apologista admirable, y sobre todo, como sacerdote, lleno de fervor y de caridad cristiana.

La vida y el ejemplo del Padre Varela no pertenecen exclusivamente a la historia del pueblo cubano. El vivió casi la mitad de su vida en los Estados Unidos, y dejó una estela luminosa en la historia del catolicismo norteamericano. En realidad fué uno de los apóstoles—tal vez el más benemérito de todos—que libraron las batallas iniciales, llenas de dificultades y peligros, por plantar la semilla de la fe católica en el corazón de la nación norteamericana. Al morir en 1853 después de haber sido Vicario General de la diócesis de New York durante 25 años, gozaba fama de santo y era venerado y querido por todos como se quiere y venera a un sacerdote sin par.

La memoria del Padre Varela forma parte del patrimonio espiritual del catolicismo norteamericano, y por tanto debe de divulgarse su vida y su pensamiento entre el clero y los fieles católicos de los Estados Unidos. Desgraciadamente, hoy la figura de Varela apenas es conocida por un reducido grupo de eruditos entre los católicos norteamericanos. Faltaba una biografía bien escrita en inglés, como esta que han escrito los doctores Joseph James McCadden y Helen Matzke McCadden, para revindicar la memoria del Padre Varela y darlo a conocer a la opinión pública. En este sentido los doctores McCadden han venido a llenar un gran vacío en la bibliografía del catolicismo norteamericano, y de paso han prestado un gran servicio a la Iglesia, al revivir la memoria de este santo e ilustrado sacerdote.

Los doctores J. J. McCadden y H. M. McCadden han escrito una obra digna de encomio por su amplitud, ponderación, estilo y documentación histórica. En muchos aspectos, sobre todo en lo que se refiere al apostolado sacerdotal del Padre Varela en los Estados Unidos, los doctores McCadden revelan datos y circunstancias ignoradas, o sólo superficialmente conocidas, aún entre los cubanos familiarizados con la vida de nuestro egregio compatriota. Además, desde el punto de vista de la crítica histórica y de la documentación académica, esta es a mi juicio la mejor biografía que se ha escrito sobre el Padre Varela.

La vida del Padre Varela tiene para las generaciones de hoy no sólo un interés histórico, sino también un interés humano y religioso de gran actualidad. En sus ideas filosóficas y políticas, en su pensamiento teológico y social, y en sus métodos de apostolado, el Padre Varela fué un genuino precursor del movimiento de renovación católica del siglo XX, que ha culminado felizmente en el Concilio Vaticano II y en el movimiento ecuménico que anima a la Iglesia en nuestros días. Uno de los aciertos de esta excelente obra de los doctores McCadden está precísamente en haber señalado ciertamente el liberalismo del pensamiento vareliano, en el cual se armonizan perfectamente dentro de la más genuina ortodoxia católica, la ciencia y la religión, la libertad y el orden, la tradición y el progreso.

Este es un libro que honra a Cuba y al catolicismo norteamericano. Cuba comparte con los Estados Unidos la memoria del Padre Félix Varela. La vida de este santo y sabio sacerdote debe ser conocida por todos los que se interesen en descubrir las raíces de la cultura cubana y del catolicismo en los Estados Unidos.

Rev. Raúl del Valle
New York
20 de mayo de 1967

PROLOGUE: THE CHURCH IN NEW YORK IN FATHER VARELA'S TIME

If we are to appreciate properly the services rendered to the Catholic Church in New York by Father Varela, we must have some knowledge of its background and its condition when he came, and also its position in relation to the growth of both the Church and the United States. With the exception of a brief interlude under James II, the Catholics in this area lived a subterranean existence for a century and a half before the Revolution. The tremendous growth of both America and the Church in this country since then tends to blind us to the slow pace of their beginning and to the fact that no one living then could have foreseen how greatly both were to develop. The growth of the Church is even more surprising than that of the country and statistically it is more impressive. Since 1790 the population of the United States has multiplied by fifty and the Catholic population by over fifteen hundred. In these circumstances it requires a real effort of the imagination to visualize the conditions under which the pioneer Catholics and their immediate successors labored and suffered for the Faith.

In 1763 the Holy See asked Bishop Challoner of London for a report on the condition of Catholics in the Thirteen Colonies. He replied that in only two of them, Maryland and Pennsylvania, could the Catholic religion be practiced openly and even in them it was severely curtailed. There were twelve priests and about sixteen thousand Catholics in Maryland and about half as many of each in Pennsylvania. There was neither priest nor church in the remaining eleven and only scattered handfuls of Catholics were known of in them. When Rome proposed establishing a Vicariate Apostolic here in 1765, Charles Carroll of Carrollton, later the sole Catholic signer of the Declaration of Independence, implored the Pope not to do so lest it result in further persecution.

The Revolution ultimately brought happier times for Catholics, though in the beginning there was not much reason to suppose it would. The religious toleration granted to the French Canadians by the Quebec Act, 1774, made effective anti-British and anti-Catholic propaganda for the Patriots; and the French Alliance with the Americans inflamed the Tories. However, the principles proclaimed by the Revolution, the indespensable help supplied by Catholic France and Spain, and the insignificance of the Catholic body here created a new climate for Catholics after 1783. The Revolution made it necessary to replace the Royal Charters with State Constitutions. The New York State Constitution of 1777 granted religious toleration to Catholics but required all applicants for naturalization to renounce papal jurisdiction in ecclesiastical as well as in civil matters. When the Federal Constitution was adopted, this provision was restricted to office holders in New York State and Catholics were barred from office on the state level until 1806. The law barring priests from entering the state, passed in 1700, was repealed in 1784. In that same year, in October, the first resident priest since the fall of James II arrived. He was Father Charles Whelan, an Irish Capuchin who had served as a Chaplain in the French fleet during the Revolution.

Father Whelan formed a Catholic congregation of about 200 in New York City, which had a population of about 30,000. About 20 Catholics were regular communicants. Since New York was the national capital, which it remained until 1790, some of the Catholics were drawn from the foreign legations and consulates. These were French, Dutch, Spanish, German and Portuguese members of his small flock but the majority were Irish. The first necessity was a church and St. Peter's on Barclay Street, the first Catholic Church in the city and state, was opened on November 4, 1786. It was built on land bought from Trinity Church and largely with funds from Spain and Mexico.

In 1789 Pope Pius VI erected the diocese of Baltimore which contained the entire United States. The first Bishop, John Carroll, estimated that there were about 30,000 Catholics in a population of about 4,000,000. Half of these lived in or near Baltimore, and 3000 of these were Negroes. New York State had about 1500 Catholics and New York City about 200, New Jersey had about 700. In 1808 this immense diocese, larger than all Western Europe, was divided into five. The diocese of New York contained the entire state of New York and the northern half of New Jersey, an area of about 55,000 square miles which then contained two Catholic churches. Today the same area contains 10 dioceses, 2002 parishes and about 7,500,000 Catholics.

When the first resident Bishop of New York, John Connolly, O. P., arrived on November 25, 1815, he found three churches and four priests in the diocese. There was not one religious house, Catholic school or charitable institution. Two of the churches, St. Peter's and the old Cathedral (1815), were in the City and heavily in debt. The third, St. Mary's in Albany (1793), was the only Catholic church between New York and Detroit. The population of New York City was increasing rapidly and had grown from 33,000 in 1790 to 100,000 in 1815. The Catholics had increased from 200 to about 15,000. The recent ending of the Napoleonic Wars had released the flood of immigration that was to last until World War I.

The growth of New York State kept pace with that of the city, and both surpassed the national average. In 1790 New York, with 340,120, was the fifth state in population, being surpassed by Massachusetts, North Carolina, Pennsylvania and Virginia. It was third in 1800, with 589,051. It took first place in 1820 with 1,372,812. The opening of the Erie Canal in 1825 confirmed the preeminence New York was to hold for nearly a century and a half. From 1830 to 1860 New York State contained one seventh of the national population. From 1790 to 1850 that population increased by a third every ten years, and during much of that time the population of New York City increased at five times the national rate. In the same period over two million square miles were added to the national territory.

Political developments kept pace with material growth. When Father Varela came here in December 1823, during the presidency of James Monroe, the Union had 21 states, only two of which, Missouri and Louisiana, were west of the Mississippi. When he died in February, 1853, Millard Fillmore was President, there were 30 states, and California was in the Union. The population had grown from 9.6 million in 1820 to 23.1 million in 1850. Catholic growth was impressive too. The 30,000 of 1790 had reached 70,000 by 1807 and about 500,000 by 1829, when the First Provincial Council of Baltimore met. By 1853 there were about 2,000,000 Catholics. There were 11 dioceses in 1823 and 31 in 1853. Later that year 10 more, the largest number yet erected here in a single year, were added.

The growth of the Church in New York followed much the same

pattern as the rest of the country, outside the South. Under Bishop Connolly (1815-1825) and Bishop Dubois (1826-1842) and well into the administration of Bishop Hughes (1842-1864), New York was an immense, unwieldy, poverty-stricken missionary diocese. The greatest asset was a rapidly growing population which was unable to staff or support the institutions it required. There was an acute and chronic shortage of personnel and money. Bishop Connolly's major achievement was the bringing of the Sisters of Charity to New York in 1817. He built thirteen churches in ten years, but when he died the Catholic population had multiplied by five and proportionately things were worse than before. None of his churches was built in the city, which waited twenty-nine years for a second church and forty for its third. By 1834 there were seven churches on Manhattan Island, all situated south of Fourteenth Street.

The outstanding figure in New York Catholic history in the XIX Century was John Hughes, fourth Bishop and first Archbishop of New York. He was a vigorous leader and competent administrator whose episcopate was a time of rapid growth. It saw a steady improvement in the social and economic position of many of his flock. It saw too the most violent anti-Catholic movements in the history of New York to date. The improved positions of the Catholics enabled him to undertake the tasks his predecessors could not carry through; the founding of the seminary at Fordham, of Fordham College, Manhattanville, Mt. St. Vincent's, St. Vincent's Hospital, the parochial school system, the new Cathedral and many others, too numerous to mention. When he came he found 40 priests, 80 churches, and 200,000 Catholics in a total population of about 2,700,000. When he died four dioceses, Albany, Brooklyn, Buffalo, and Newark, had been carved out of New York, reducing it to its present area, 4717 square miles. The Archdiocese had 150 priests, 89 churches and chapels, 10,000 pupils in Catholic schools and about 500,000 people.

It would have been foolish not to expect a reaction against the Church when it became evident that the Catholic body here was increasing at an astonishing rate. The Nativist Movement, which began by 1820 and lasted through and long after Father Varela's time, was a major influence in the lives of the Catholics here then and it had lasting effects on the Church. Although it aimed in the first instance at the Irish, because they were Catholic and Irish and poor, it aimed later, with diminishing intensity, at each successive immigrant group. It is important to remember that it never succeeded in limiting immigration or in undermining the legal position guaranteed to all citizens by the Constitution. It gave rise unwittingly and indirectly to the Catholic School System, the Church's major contribution to the country to date, the survival of which is now our greatest practical concern.

Though many things have changed in the Church and the United States since Father Varela's time, there are certain constants. One is that the Catholics, now firmly rooted here, are the largest and most unpopular minority in the country, a fact unlikely to be modified substantially by the Ecumenical Movement. Another is that on the national scene the Church still suffers from a shortage of personnel and money. This shortage probably will become more acute.

The changes have been more numerous and spectacular. It is tempting to wonder which would have surprised Father Varela most. Two seem especially noteworthy. First, the decline in the strength and doctrinal orthodoxy of organized Protestantism. How much this development has helped or hurt the Catholic Church and the country is not easily decided. The second is the change in the source of the attacks on the church. Since 1963 attacks on the Church herself, her doctrine and moral teaching, her law, her institutions and her customs have come mainly from within the fold and often from within the sanctuary and the religious life. No one can estimate correctly now the duration and cost of this development. It seems certain already that it will make many feel that in some ways Archbishop Hughes and Father Varela and their associates really had an easier time than their present day successors.

RIGHT REV. FLORENCE D. COHALAN

FOREWORD

The United States Catholic Historical Society is pleased to add to its monograph series, this study of Father Varela by Joseph and Helen McCadden.

It is clearly a labor of affection based on an extraordinary familiarity with the records and literature of their subject. Their bibliography is a major asset for students of the period. The Society is pleased to offer its members and libraries of the country this rich mine of material in the form of a careful review of Father Varela's career as a priest, philosopher, teacher and patriot.

No one would admit more readily than the authors that each of the titles above, not to mention the subject's personal virtue, could easily sustain a full study. But this volume happily opens the door to all students and admirers of Father Varela. We all look forward to a day when Cuban scholars, relieved of tragedy at home, and other Americans who rejoice in Cuban accomplishment, will pursue the fascinating course of this great Cuban's life, thoughts and ideals.

Father Raúl del Valle kindly contributed a Spanish prologue offering his own evaluation. Monsignor Florence Cohalan responded to our request to supply our readers with a brief study of the situation of the Catholic Church in New York when Father Varela arrived in New York. We are most grateful to both writers for their expert assistance.

This volume is the first in our Series to follow the publication of our INDEX of all the published works of the United States Catholic Historical Society. This study by the McCaddens is indexed and will, we hope, at a later date, be entered into the next publication of our general INDEX.

We are, as ever, grateful to the members and benefactors of our Society who make these publications possible.

Eugene V. Clark, Ph.D.
Editor of Publications
U.S.C.H.S.

ACKNOWLEDGMENTS

For their generous cooperation in making materials available for this manuscript, the authors thank especially the librarians and respective staffs of the Manuscript Division and the Hispanic Foundation in the Library of Congress; the New York Public Library; the Historical Society of Pennsylvania; the Hispanic Society of America; the St. Augustine Historical Society, Florida; St. Joseph's Seminary in Yonkers; the American Catholic Historical Society of Philadelphia; the Archives of the Catholic University of America; and the Archives of the Archdiocese of Baltimore.

They are indebted also to the following individuals for information, encouragement, and other assistance: to Reverend Raúl del Valle, a Cuban priest now stationed in New York, who graciously wrote the *Prólogo*; to Dr. Herminio Portell Vilá, noted Cuban historian, of Washington, D.C.; to Dr. Bartholomew F. Fair of Overbrook, Penna.; to Very Reverend Monsignor George E. Tiffany, Reverend Robert B. O'Connor, and Doctor Henry J. Browne, for opening to them the varied collections at St. Joseph's Seminary; to Reverend William P. Mulcahy, M.M., for giving access to the parish records of the Church of the Transfiguration, New York City; to Sister Gemma Marie Del Duca, S.C., of Seton Hill College, Greensburg, Penna.; to Reverend Michael V. Gannon, Director of the Mission of Nombre de Dios, St. Augustine; to Mrs. Doris C. Wiles, historian, of St. Augustine; to Most Reverend Eduardo Martínez Dalmau, Bishop of Teuzi; to Dr. Gustavo Amigó Jansen, S.J., of El Salvador, for the text of his writings on Father Varela; to Reverend Horatio Núñez, of Elizabeth Seton College, Yonkers; to Brother Berchmans Eduardo, F.C.S., and Mr. Guillermo P. Romagosa, of Manhattan College; and to Reverend William Francis Blakeslee, C.S.P., who reintroduced Father Varela to twentieth-century English-language readers.

This monograph has benefited greatly from editorial suggestions by Right Reverend Monsignor John Tracy Ellis and Father del Valle, who read the manuscript, and from the patient guidance of Right Reverend Monsignor Eugene V. Clark, editor of United

States Historical Society publications, who also has furnished a Foreword.

The only previous book-length biographies of Félix Varela are those by José Ignacio Rodríguez and Antonio Hernández Travieso, both in Spanish. Doctor Rodríguez also wrote the first (and for many decades the only) article in English on Varela; and the voluminous collections of the José Ignacio Rodríguez Papers are a mine of information.

Also eminently useful to this study have been the publications of the University of Havana, which during recent years has issued numerous scholarly works on Varela and has reprinted with commentaries most of the books that he wrote in his native tongue. The University has also issued Spanish translations of articles by him published in North American periodicals.

None of Varela's writings in Spanish, however, have as yet appeared in English: the excerpts in the present volume were translated by the authors.

The original of the Frontispiece (c. 1837) is an oil painting in the Office of the Historian of the City of Havana; the c. 1850 likeness is from a widely-known daguerreotype used in the 1878 edition of Rodríguez' *Vida del presbítero don Félix Varela*. Both illustrations were obtained through the kindness of Father del Valle.

This work is an attempt to recall to North American neighbors of Cuba the brilliant and venerated Cuban who served as a devoted missionary in old New York. A definitive life of Father Varela awaits the free access in more peaceful times to literary treasures housed in his native land, and the possible discovery of heretofore missing primary source materials.

—Joseph James McCadden
Helen Matzke McCadden
May, 1968

FATHER FÉLIX VARELA: TORCHBEARER FROM CUBA

CHAPTER I

He Teaches His Cubans to Think

Soldiering seemed the destiny of the man-child, born on November 20, 1788, whom Fray Miguel Hernández, O.P., chaplain of His Most Catholic Majesty's regiment stationed in Havana, baptized exactly one week later in the church dedicated to the Holy Angel Guardian. The infant's people were Spaniards, residing in the colony because military orders assigned them there. His father, Lieutenant Francisco Varela y Pérez, native of Tordesillas in Old Castile, had served as paymaster of the militia and runner of human cargoes on slave ships from the Canaries. The mother, María Josefa, born in Santiago de Cuba, was daughter to Lieutenant Colonel Bartolomé Morales y Remírez, a Castilian, commander of the regiment, and to Doña Rita Josefa Morales.

The blood of his family ran to battle. Don Bartolomé and his forbears had for their Most Catholic King fought in the Moorish wars, and his son, Bartolomé Morales y Morales, maintaining the family tradition, became second lieutenant in the Third Battalion of Cuba. Both Francisco and Colonel Bartolomé bore decorations for valor from the hands of His Majesty Charles III of Spain.

The new member of the Church Suffering bore the name of Félix Francisco José María de la Concepción Varela y Morales. Posterity was to know him as *El Padre Félix Varela y Morales*, or, in English-speaking circles, simply as Father Varela. He was third child to his parents, their first and only son. The grandfather, Don Bartolomé Morales, and Doña Rita Morales served as godparents.[1] One month after his birth, Spain lost her energetic king, Charles III, and fell under the irresponsible rule of Charles IV and his licentious Queen.

---

[1] The infant had both a grandfather and an uncle named Bartolomé Morales; he also had both a grandmother and an aunt named Rita Morales. The baptismal certificate does not distinguish as to which Rita was godmother. For the certificate, see José Ignacio Rodríguez, *Vida del presbítero don Félix Varela*. (*Vida*). All references below are to the 2nd (1944) edition.

María Josefa was not granted to see her boy thrive. Her obscure flame burned out before the lad was four. The Morales kin took charge of her offspring, and Félix became the focus of an admiring circle of females—his elder sisters, María de Jesús and Cristina, and two maiden aunts, María and Rita Morales. Francisco Varela, who had become a captain of fusiliers by royal order in 1789, remarried speedily, begot another son, Manuel, and followed Josefa to an early grave. Manuel would become a prominent tobacco merchant of Havana; Félix, his homeland's mightiest thinker; but of their father it is not recorded whether his Spanish bones were interred in Cuba or in His Majesty's colony of East Florida or in some distant, unknown port.

Félix Varela y Morales was an orphan by the age of six. His grandfather, Don Bartolomé, promoted by the King to the rank of Brevet Colonel on August 2, 1791, was made Commander of the Third Battalion of the Regiment of Cubans garrisoned in St. Augustine, capital of the Spanish colony of East Florida; and the thick-walled, slit-windowed, deep-dungeoned Castle of San Marcos in that city became Félix Varela's childhood home.

Florida, ceded to England as a prize of war in 1763 and returned to Spain when the thirteen American colonies won their freedom in 1783, was administered from Madrid through Havana. St. Augustine, oldest white settlement in North America, had seen four decades of Spanish civilization before the founding of Jamestown; it had been flourishing for half a century when the Plymouth Pilgrims set sights toward the New World. But the twenty years of British-American occupation had left its ancient Spanish culture a shambles. There were still the four main parallel streets, the alleys too narrow for carriages, the secretive Spanish dwellings of yellowed coquina, the massive fortress with its muddy moat. The Spanish residents, however, had fled, and their Catholic Indian converts had been dispersed or murdered. The British and their savage allies had destroyed the mission chapel at Tolomato; they pillaged the shrine of Nuestra Señora de la Leche (Our Lady of the Milk): they quartered soldiers in the Franciscan convent; and in San Marcos itself they had defaced the chapel paintings and used the holy place as a barracks. When East Florida reverted to Spain, there were British-American residents and Negroes and

Indians; but, except for a settlement of refugee Minorcans, Catholicism was practically erased. To minister to the Minorcans and the garrison and the returning Spanish settlers, Charles III sent two Irish priests trained in Salamanca, Fathers Thomas Hassett and Michael O'Reilly. The clerics established a school and salvaged stone from the rubble of the ruined chapels to erect a shrine to St. Augustine's patron saint. An ancient mission bell, inscribed "Sancte Joseph, Ora Pro Nobis. D 1682," and the cross from La Leche linked the new Church of St. Augustine (later a Cathedral) to pre-British days. The bell, one of four in the Moorish cupola, has been called the oldest in the United States.[2]

Trying to recapture its century-old Spanish heritage, St. Augustine had in the 1790's the misty, impermanent air of an Old World culture transplanted without its roots. With its scant 2,000 souls, it was hub city of a swampy, mosquito-infested wilderness peopled by Indians and refugees and renegades. Over it brooded the Castle, where lived Don Bartolomé and his dependents—its gloomy mazes a-murmur with ghosts of besiegers repulsed, of slow-starved defenders, of prisoners tormented, of skeletons immured in dungeon walls, of freebooters and footsoldiers and commanders pawns in the kings' games of war. The forced labor of Appalachian Indians during 60 years had erected the fortress, and some 140 Mexican convicts had been imported in 1755-56 to reinforce and enlarge it. Its walls astounded military engineers because cannon balls became imbedded in their coquina surface without shattering it.

The lad Varela found it dizzying to look down from the battlements of San Marcos into the murky encompassing ditch. The towering bastions were named for St. Peter, St. Paul, St. James, and other holy men; but there was little sanctity in the sepulchral vaults, with their chains and instruments of torture. The vauntings of the menfolk—of forays against Indians, of slave raids, of American guerilla attacks, of bloody encounters with the British— troubled him. Slipping into the town, he witnessed other cause for pain: in the wide plaza before St. Augustine's church, black men were sold like cattle. To his keen, receptive spirit steeped by

---

[2]George R. Fairbanks, *The History and antiquities of the City of St. Augustine, Florida,* p. 174.

Father O'Reilly in Christian idealism, the inconsistencies of aggressive Spanish militarism and soul-seeking Spanish Catholicism became glaringly apparent.

Yet the grimness of life about him did not sear the boy, for in the inner circle of his family love protected him. Don Bartolomé, who sat in the councils of war in Florida and, for a time in 1796, served as Acting Governor, was aged enough to shun personal ambition: he declined the onerous post of Governor. Preferring to watch his dreams fulfilled in his descendants, he took pride in his precocious ward, while Doña Rita cherished young Félix as her own. Handsome the lad was not—slight, sallow, long-featured, with high forehead and shining dark eyes already myopic from over-study; but he had gifts of the soul, being gracious of speech, quick of mind, and warm of heart.

Despite the remoteness of the colonial outpost, Félix was fortunate in his educational opportunities. Spanish missionaries were also teachers; and the earliest school for white children in the present United States had been opened in St. Augustine in 1606, one year before the English cavaliers settled at Jamestown. The British occupation of 1763-83 had wiped out education along with churches and convents; and King Charles, patron of learning, had selected Father Hassett for the East Florida vicariate because of his reputation for success with Catholic instruction in Philadelphia. The idea of universal government-sponsored education had not yet rooted in the young North American republic when, in 1786, Hassett founded a school in reading, writing, arithmetic, and religion, free to all regardless of color and compulsory for white youths. For the government of schools, the priest devised a set of rules more enlightened and humane than prevailed for the next half-century in most of the former British colonies. One of his classroom devices became prevalent in Spanish-speaking American schools: a boy, on being excused to leave the room, must strike a pendulum suspended from the ceiling—and he must be back before the pendulum stopped swinging.[3] Young Varela needed no menacing pendulum to hold him in class; for he was avid of learning.

About the time that the lad's guardian brought him to St.

---

[3] Joseph B. Lockey, "Public Education in Spanish St. Augustine," pp. 147-68.

Augustine, Father Francisco Traconis, master of Father Hassett's school, obtained permission to return to Havana. Thereupon, Father Michael O'Reilly was pressed into service as teacher. O'Reilly was eminently qualified: he was zealous, understanding, and learned; besides Latin and theology, he was versed in English, Spanish, French, Greek, mathematics, and music. He was already serving as chaplain to the troops and to the hospital, and the added burden of the school bore heavily on his health. In 1795, on Hassett's promotion to canon of the cathedral in New Orleans, O'Reilly took his place as vicar of East Florida. He had the church to complete; he had untold trouble in getting priests to staff the original school and a second institution for English-speaking lads which he opened in 1802;[4] yet he found time to explain the mysteries and satisfy the doubts of his most apt pupil, the young Varela.

From Father O'Reilly, the boy learned Latin and religion and music, and more of the wonders of creation than ever catechism recited. When he roamed the beaches and the swampy Matanzas, he saw in sandy shore and flashing wave and teeming tropical forest the hand of the life-giving Spirit. Of all God's works, only man seemed in need of improvement.

Félix knew himself consigned from birth to His Majesty's service, but his inner light beckoned elsewhere. When his time for enlistment drew near, he carried his qualms to the Padre. The sword, he had noted, could only destroy. He wanted to build. He joyed to see barbarous Indians transformed into radiant Christians on the Feast of Nativity.

There are two kinds of soldiers, explained O'Reilly. Some win fame and glory in physical combat, like his own brother, General Felipe O'Reilly, distinguished servant of Catherine of Russia and Charles III of Spain. Others, like his humble self, fight for the Lord, seeking their treasures in the hearts of men, their medals in the hereafter. Both kinds of warriors may be equally brave, and each has his appointed task—the one to conquer, the other to civilize. For himself, Father Michael preferred to do battle in poverty for the King of Kings.

Now the lad was almost fourteen. On the fringe of manhood,

---
[4]Michael J. Curley, *Church and state in the Spanish Floridas, 1783-1822*, pp. 220, 231, 265f, and 307ff.

his head crammed with all that Michael O'Reilly could teach, he stood at attention as Don Bartolomé, Commandant of San Marcos, bade him put aside the books and the idle watchings of youth and prepare for a man's career. The achievements of his fusilier sire and the influence of his grandfather would assure him of preferment in the military life. He was a Morales. In spite of his skimpy stature, he could qualify for a cadetship.

But the slight youth, the never unruly, the always compliant, showed stubborn as he confronted his awesome kinsman. With the abrupt surprising boldness of the thoughtfully shy, he declared: "I wish to be a soldier of Jesus Christ."

The commander of the Castle of San Marcos was incensed. The religious life was adequate for women, if they had no husbands to protect them. Two of Bartolomé's daughters, Rita and María, were safe in St. Teresa's, the Convent of the Discalced Carmelites in Havana. A Morales man, however, must carry arms.

Yet Félix bore his thin shoulders erect, his prominent eyes held steady. "I do not wish to kill men," he explained. "I wish rather to save their souls."[5]

Don Bartolomé knew steel when he saw it. It was before him that day, in the fragile frame of his cherished grandson. The boy, he decided, had been too much on his own, too long cosseted by adoring womenfolk and a dotard Irish priest. He would send him to relatives in Havana. Enrolled in the ancient Seminary of San Carlos, he could have his fill of theology and syllogism. When awakening manhood urged, he well might clamor for the lustier ways of the soldier's life.

Before he took sail for Havana, Félix Varela shared with Don Bartolomé a poignant loss. Doña Rita, the lad's *madrina* (godmother), was laid to rest in the walled Spanish Catholic cemetery with the Indian name—Tolomato. "My second mother," he called her, his best beloved, and could not know, in his weeping, that he would one day lie in honor in the same consecrated ground.

He grieved to leave the old soldier thus doubly stricken. But he

---

[5]*N.-Y. Freeman's jrnl. and Catholic register*, Mar. 19, 1853. Quoted by Rodríguez in *Vida*, and by Hernández Travieso in *El padre Varela*, p. 13; but Hernández Travieso in an earlier work, *Varela y la reforma filosófica en Cuba*, p. 66, n. 4, questions whether Félix would have spoken thus to his grandfather. (*Reforma filosófica*).

was young. From the island of his birth, the bells of his future clanged.

* * * * *

It was a heady atmosphere to which Bartolomé, unknowing, sent the young Félix in Havana. For an alert, intellectual youth, the military routine of the outpost of San Marcos, broken only by forays against troublesome neighbors, must inevitably fade into sordid memory.

A wind of change had been stirring the Island of Cuba—a wind that blew from Spain. The strong currents of unsettling thought that swept away an established civilization in France had caused tremors in the Iberian Peninsula. They did not unsettle the Faith nor, while Charles III reigned, did they rattle the throne; but they did shake into being a new interest in science, a growing concern for the betterment of man's material condition, an eagerness toward economic and social reform; and they quickened an educational renascence which had begun two centuries earlier.

There had been more vigor in Spanish Catholic thought than Anglo-Protestant historiographers with their stereotypes of the Inquisition, the Index, and the angels-on-the-point-of-a-pin charade once taught men to believe. The University of Salamanca, dating back to 1230, rivaled those of Bologna, Paris, and Oxford, and had the added distinction of introducing Arabic learning to the West.

Traditional scholasticism had been revitalized and updated in the fifteenth and sixteenth centuries by Spain's golden-age philosophers, among whom principally were Domingo Báñez, Gabriel Vásquez, Luis Vives, Luis de Molina, and Melchior Cano.[6] Shining lights were Vitoria and Suárez.

Francisco de Vitoria, the sixteenth-century Salamancan jurist, qualifies as the father of modern international law. The Jesuit, Francisco Suárez, earned a particular place in the history of world thought, stressing as he did the natural rights of man and the responsibility of monarchs: his doctrine that kingly power derived

---

[6]Bañez, 1528-1604, native of Medina del Campo, Dominican theologian; Vaśquez, 1549-1604, born in Cuenca, Jesuit; Vives, 1492-1540, layman born in Valencia; Molina, born in New Castile, 1535, died 1600, Jesuit; and Cano, 1509-1566, native of Cuenca, Dominican.

from the people caused James I of England to order the burning of his *De defensione fidei (Defending the faith)*, and his teachings on international law influenced the thinking of Grotius in *De iure belli ac pacis (The law governing war and peace)*.[7] In Suárez's expounding of the equality of all men in the sight of God, modern-day writers see the genesis of democratic institutions.[8]

The Spanish nation heard the rumblings of the Age of Science in the voluminous writings of Benito-Gerónimo Feijóo y Montenegro (sometimes spelled Feyjóo; 1676-1764), a native of Galicia, Spain, and a Benedictine scholar and abbot whose essays echoed the most advanced thinking of his time. Feijóo, a disciple of Francis Bacon and of the father of modern anatomy, Marie François-Xavier Bichat (1771-1802), called attention to Spain's prevailing educational stagnation—there was much he would eliminate and, in a world of new scientific and sociological awareness, much that he would add.

A recent Italian source describes Feijóo as "the greatest Spanish figure of the eighteenth century, by reason of his erudition and his critical spirit," whose works "constitute an immense encyclopedia of knowledge, in a Spain decadent in the sphere of thought."[9] A twentieth-century French authority speaks thus of Feijóo:

> A freeman of the Republic of Letters, that is what he called himself, and the name becomes him. . . . A man of encyclopedic knowledge, Feijóo was theologian, historian, man of letters, and scientist. He was an admirer of Bacon and Newton, who ranked in his eyes as the oracles of experimental truth. Descartes he regarded as a genius, a rash one, but a genius all the same, and he would break a lance in his support whenever occasion offered.[10]

As a Spaniard, Feijóo attacked the irresponsibility of the nobility, the use of torture and other abuses of justice. As a churchman, he deplored the spurious Aristotelianism, the stand-pat-ism, the superstition and childish observances that made religion seem

---

[7]Francis of Vitoria (Vittoria, Victoria), born in Navarre 1480, died 1546, Dominican; Suárez, 1548-1617, native of Granada.
[8]Cf. Moorhouse F. X. Millar, *Unpopular essays in the philosophy of history*, pp. 65-77.
[9]*Enciclopedia filosofica*, Istituto por la Collaborazione Culturale, 2: 303f.
[10]Paul Hazard, *European thought in the eighteenth century*, p. 88.

opposed to the march of science. As a world citizen, he decried blinding nationalism and favored better communication of nations toward the goal of world peace. A universal man, Feijóo covered from his monk's cell the fields of natural and political science, literature, philosophy, psychology, and esthetics, and reforms in church music suggested by him were later adopted by papal action.

The prodding of Feijóo's persistent pen spurred Spaniards, at home and in the colonies, to open their minds to progress; while men like Dr. Martin Martínez, author of *Filosofía esceptica,* and Dr. Antonio Gómez Pereira alerted their nation to the Baconian advances in empirical scientific method.

Charles III, ruler of Spain from 1759 to 1788, and his minister the Count of Aranda, friend of Voltaire and disciple of the Encyclopedists, gave practical expression to the new spirit, putting into operation the recommendations of thinkers like Feijóo. The reign had opened with a tragic and costly error—the expulsion of the Jesuits from His Majesty's dominions; then came assaults on the other religious orders; but, as he matured in wisdom, Charles sponsored many improvements for the benefit of his people: he circumscribed the powers of the Inquisition, opened schools, and encouraged agriculture, commerce, manufacture, and communications. He also—sobered, no doubt, by Britain's troubles with her fractious American colonies—displayed an unprecedented concern for the welfare of his subjects in the far-flung Spanish Empire.

In Cuba, where Feijóo was read in the Seminary, the changes took momentum with the arrival in 1790 of Don Luis de las Casas y Aragorri as captain-general, or military governor. Las Casas (1745-1800), like Aranda, had caught fire from the *philosophes* of the French Enlightenment and their Spanish counterparts; and the six years of his administration mark a milestone in the island's history.

Las Casas instituted in Havana the *Sociedad Económica de Amigos del País*—the Royal Patriotic Society—an organization of reform-minded young patriots which built a tradition of accomplishment down into the present era. Its prime purpose was to found schools; it acted also to promote agriculture, trade, literature, science, the fine arts, and good government. This Society came to embody the most advanced thought in Cuba, which it channeled into constructive measures. Because of the freedom permitted them through the *Sociedad,* the young intellectuals of Cuba did not then find themselves impelled to revolution.

Under Las Casas, Havana achieved its first public library; its first enduring newspaper, the *Papel Periódico* (1790), which became *El Diario de La Habana;* the *Guide for Strangers* (*Guía de Forasteros*); and the extensive Casa de Beneficencia, an establishment for the needy and the infirm,[11] whose buildings were completed in 1794. Las Casas authorized bridges, public walks, and roads, including the impressive Calzada del Horcón and the Calzada de Guadaloupe; he paved the streets of Havana, improved the Plaza de Toros, relieved sufferers from floods and hurricanes, removed restraints on trade, and introduced the cultivation of indigo. He reduced delays in the administration of justice; he erected a convent, a colosseum, and an institute of natural philosophy, botany, chemistry, and mathematics.[12] When he left Cuba in 1796, the plaudits of its admiring citizens were his god-speed.

The upheaval of old ways on this island was resumed at the turn of the century, when Spain relaxed the immigration restrictions and for the first time surrendered her exclusive monopoly on the trade of her colonies. Cuba's population of some 600,000 was about 60% white or free colored and 40% slave; a spurt in the importation of slaves—100,000 coming in from 1790 to 1805—while it pleased owners of the rich plantations, brought active opposition not only from those who deemed it morally wrong but also from political philosophers who knew that it augured a deep-seated sickness in the economy.

The destruction of the Haitian sugar industry by slave revolts, and the demands for sugar from the newly independent United States, were causing Cuba, which had formerly produced also coffee, tobacco, cattle, and other export items, to become a one-product state. Although the island was largely agricultural, commerce filled the ports of Havana and Santiago de Cuba, and there

---

[11]Cf. Espasa's *Encicl. univ. ilus. europ.-amer., s. v.* "Beneficencia." (Espasa). The Casa de Beneficencia in Havana has endured into the present era as an orphanage.
[12][Richard Burleigh Kimball], *Cuba and the Cubans,* pp. 32-33.

was a growing interest in journalism, law, and the sciences. Top government posts, like high church benefices, were subject to His Majesty's pleasure, but hope was burgeoning for parliamentary representation of colonial peoples in Madrid—a hope that would see brief fruition in the Constitution of 1812 and again in 1822. Along with the internal changes went a constant national unrest engendered by world events; a military mobilization in 1807 from fear of an English invasion, a disturbance caused by the unwelcome arrival of French refugees from Haiti, repeated rumors of trouble from rebellious Caribbean states, and island-wide protestations of loyalty to the Spanish monarchy whose abdication Napoleon forced in 1808. Cuba declared a state of war against the French Emperor; and, since he held control of the Mother Country, the island invited trade with other nations.

The military governor of Cuba during this unsettled period was the Marqués de Someruelos; but the moving spirit behind progress in Havana was its second bishop, Don Juan José Díaz de Espada y Fernández de Landa. His predecessor, Bishop José de Tres-Palacios, a native of Salamanca and a doctor of its famous theological university, was a traditionalist who frowned on the secularizing tendency of Las Casas' innovations; but scarcely had Espada been consecrated Bishop when he applied for membership in the Patriotic Society and was with one accord chosen Director.

Staunchly Catholic, the Spanish-born Espada also subscribed to the liberal enthusiasms of his day—to the extent that his opponents called him a Mason, an iconoclast, a freethinker in the robes of a cleric. He was dedicated to the improvement of public health; and to this purpose, with the aid of Someruelos, he established Havana's first walled cemetery. He drained marshes, reclaiming the area now graced by the Campo de Marte. He urged fathers of families to have their children vaccinated, and in a famous pastoral ordered his parish priests to further the Jenner crusade for immunization against small-pox. He sought to adapt to Cuba the avant-garde educational movements of the day—the Lancaster, or monitorial, system, and the Pestalozzian as well. Espada gave Havana a Lancasterian teacher-training institute; and he enabled the Reverend Doctor Juan Bernardo O'Gavan

(O'Gaban) y Guerra[13] to study at the model Pestalozzian Institute which the Queen's favorite, Manuel Godoy, had established in Madrid. He contributed generously to the Beneficencia and to the college of St. Frances de Sales, and he endorsed the efforts of the Patriotic Society to multiply public schools.

Bishop Espada also introduced numerous ecclesiastical reforms. He reprinted and annotated the synodal decrees of 1682 regulating ecclesiastical discipline. He restricted the religious processions of students, which were often marred by licentiousness. He forbade excessive ringing of churchbells in memory of the dead. He eliminated from the streets numerous shrines and crucifixes which marked the route of processions or the locale of assassinations. He redecorated the ornate churrigueresque cathedral in Havana (erected as the Church of St. Ignatius, 1724), removing old statues and introducing an imposing high altar of Carrara marble and magnificent frescoes and sculpture in the prevailing neo-classical mode. There have been those who lament Espada's destruction of the city's treasures of medieval religious art; but his renovating of thought in colleges and university, all under ecclesiastical rule, earned him a general paean of praise. Espada was the prelate of Cuba's private early-nineteenth-century *aggiornamento*—the patron of the island's most brilliant intellectual period.

Félix Varela was confirmed in the Faith by the righteous traditionalist, Bishop José de Tres-Palacios. But his spiritual and intellectual stimulus came from Bishop Espada y Landa.

* * * * *

When the nineteenth century opened, Cuba was educationally more advanced than most sections of the United States. In her church-sponsored schools, children of all classes, rich and poor, colored and white, were instructed together, and without charge; while in North America parents were expected to pay for education, charity pupils were segregated as inferiors, and even the brotherly Quakers, pioneers in public education, maintained separate schools, under separate benevolent societies, for "Africans."

---

[13] Joaquín Francisco Pacheco, *O'Gavan*. Salvador Muro y Salazar, Marqués de Someruelos, b. Madrid 1754, d. 1813, governed Cuba for the unprecedented term of 14 years.

For higher learning, Havana also had provision. Attached to the Cathedral was the Royal and Conciliar College and Seminary of San Carlos and San Ambrosio, which, until the expulsion of its Jesuit founders in 1767, had been called San Ignacio. This oldest college in Cuba represented the union of two separate Jesuit institutions dating back respectively to 1669 and 1724. At San Carlos, students received free and thorough instruction in Latin language and literature, logic, mathematics, rhetoric, ethics, theology, metaphysics, natural philosophy, and law. The University of Havana, established in 1728 after 40 years of planning and petitioning, was conducted by Dominicans. Although College and University collaborated—many students, like Félix Varela, took courses in both—yet they were, in Espada's time, diverging intellectually. San Carlos was infiltrated by the new thought, while the University remained strictly Aristotelian. Both institutions, however, were authoritarian in method: all instruction was in Latin, and most learning was by memorization and rote recitation of theses.

Espada had gathered under his leadership a coterie of brilliant, independent thinkers: among them, the *habanero* Father José Agustín Caballero (1771-1835), eclectic philosopher, editor of *El Diario,* and translator of the works of Condillac; Father Juan Bernardo O'Gavan y Guerra (1782-1838), descendant of an Irishman who had fled from Oliver Cromwell to a Spanish haven; another *habanero,* Dr. Tomás Romay y Chacón (1769-1849), medical doctor of some eminence who presided over the Junta Central de Vacuna (Vaccination Society) and engaged in pioneer studies on yellow fever; and Colonel Manuel Tiburcio de Zequeira y Arango, a co-editor of *Papel Periódico,* military governor of Río Hacha and Santa Marta, and the first poet to emphasize the patriotic Cuban theme.[14] The thought-waves at San Carlos were electric with their influence.

The young Varela, having been prepared effectively in Latin and the elements of religion and philosophy, was promptly admitted to San Carlos, first as day student, then as candidate for the

---

[14]José A. Presno, "Homenaje a la Memoria del Doctor Tomás Romay," *Universidad de la Habana,* 15 (Nov.-Dec. 1937): 18-31. Zequeira, or Sequeira, was a native of Havana (1760-1846).

priesthood. By 1804, when he was in his sixteenth year, he was pursuing superior studies in college and university toward the degree of Bachelor of Arts. Records indicate that he studied the traditional Aristotelian texts at the university; while in the College of San Carlos he came under the stimulating instruction of O'Gavan, who taught physics and ethics, and of Agustín Caballero, professor of logic and metaphysics.

As a candidate for the Bachelor's degree, Varela defended a series of propositions in the great hall of the University at 8:30 a.m. on August 1, 1806. His theses concerning the nature of ideas and of the soul, the influence of the mechanical order on physical perceptions, the Copernican theory of the movement of the sun, and the origin of species indicate how far his education had ranged from medieval scholasticism. The concepts he expounded belonged less to St. Thomas Aquinas than to Descartes, who exalted independent thought; and he acknowledged his debt to Feijóo and to Paulo Zaquía.[15] Already Varela displayed the eclectic tendency which was to be the hallmark of his philosophy. The existence of innate ideas he, like Locke, could not accept—but on the importance of meditation and reasoning he agreed with the Cartesians. His numerous courses on Aristotle at the University had satisfied curriculum requirements; but the glimpses of modern-era thought from Fathers O'Gavan and Caballero at San Carlos formed his real inspiration.

After attaining the Bachelor's status, Varela, in his nineteenth year, received the first tonsure and the permission of Bishop Espada to wear clerical habit. There followed in quick succession the four minor orders and the subdiaconate; and in 1808 he graduated from the College and Seminary as a Bachelor of Theology. The ideas he propounded on this occasion are significant: (1) That "Christ died of His very own free will;" and (2) That "it suffices for the Sacrament [of the Eucharist] that the priest fulfill the external rite willingly and seriously, whatever may be the evil disposition hidden within him . . . and even though he privately mock at the Sacrament and contemn it." Félix Varela believed

---

[15]For the documents he presented for his degree and the theses he defended, see Antonio Hernández Travieso, "Expediente de Estudios Universitarios del Presbítero Félix Varela," pp. 392-93, 397-98.

that the Son of Man had deliberately chosen to sacrifice Himself for the salvation of mankind, and that this offering was repeated daily on the altars of His churches. Like the Master he served, Varela then and throughout his career labored to liberate his fellowmen from the weight of ignorance and oppressive sin;[16] and although he was to open the vast area of learning through observation and sense experience to Cuban students, he would never cede his faith in the indispensable dominance of the Mystical Spirit over physical matter.

The new Bachelor of Theology was a young man in a hurry— as though forewarned that his years in Cuba would be short. Under the aegis of Bishop Espada, he began his career as teacher, instructing in Latin and rhetoric the younger students at San Carlos. He also set his hand to writing, one of his earliest works being a play, *El Desafío* (*The Duel*), which became a repertory item for later generations of students. He also continued his studies, preparing for the event of his ordination. For recreation, he played the violin. He was an accomplished performer and found release and solace in the deep harmonies of Beethoven. He inaugurated classes in music and in 1811 helped to found the Philharmonic Society of Havana, the first of its kind in Cuba.

Twice, when vacancies occurred on the faculty at San Carlos— in Latin and in theology—he presented himself as candidate in the competitive examinations. The openings went to older, more experienced men, but for Varela the opportunity thus to publicize his views served good purpose, and of the brilliance of his performance the Bishop took note.

The young theologian was ordained a deacon late in 1810. During the following year, he petitioned Bishop Espada to admit him to the priesthood, although because of his youth a special dispensation would be required. His reason for importuning was cogent: Don Bartolomé, returned from St. Augustine, was aged and infirm, and Félix considered that the old soldier's forbearance had earned him the right to witness his grandson's consecration. Accordingly, on December 21, 1811, before the great marble altar of the Cathedral in Havana, Bishop Espada ordained Félix Varela.

---

[16]*Reforma filosófica*, pp. 67-71, cites Varela's courses and the propositions he defended.

The new priest said his first Mass in the church attached to the Convent of St. Teresa, where his sister and one of his Morales aunts were nuns and his other aunt, María, was prioress under the name of Mother Natividad de María; and he offered thanks that Bartolomé Morales had been spared to see him solemnly enrolled as a soldier of the Lord.[17]

Bishop Espada had his own reasons for hastening the ordination of his protégé. He needed him on the faculty of San Carlos as replacement for Dr. O'Gavan, to whom honors were accruing thick and fast.

Urged by the Patriotic Society, the Bishop in 1808 had financed O'Gavan's studies at the Pestalozzian Institute in Madrid. The *Memoria* containing the priest's report of this trip drew the ire of the Inquisition in Mexico, which expurgated his enthusiastic references to "the profound Locke" and "the admirable Condillac." But censorship did not prevent O'Gavan from being confirmed by the Marquis of Someruelos as Provisor (or Vicar General) to Bishop Espada in the diocese of Havana; and it probably contributed to his election to represent Santiago de Cuba in the revolutionary Spanish Cortes that met at Cádiz in 1810. In this Cortes, which denounced the Inquisition and wishfully promulgated the short-lived Constitution of 1812, O'Gavan served as secretary and vice-president. "I glory," he said, "to have contributed with my feeble voice to the suppression of a tribunal [the Inquisition] whose system I consider incompatible with the Constitution of the monarchy."[18]

When Wellington liberated Spain from the French and restored the throne of Madrid to Ferdinand VII, persecution struck many of the leaders of the Cortes; but O'Gavan, an humble and affable priest, was permitted to return to a tumultuous reception in Havana. In 1815, the government in Madrid made him Magistrate of the Royal Court in Cuba, the first ecclesiastic to hold this office. Continuing to serve as financial secretary and diocesan right-hand to Espada, Dr. Juan Bernado O'Gavan y Guerra was occupied with heavier matters than teaching.

---

[17] *El padre Varela*, p. 49.
[18] Max Henríquez Ureña, *Panorama histórico de la literatura cubana*, 1: 124-26.

The promotion of O'Gavan opened the way for a shakeup at San Carlos which Espada long had contemplated. Combining the chair of logic and metaphysics with that of physics and ethics, the Bishop appointed to the consolidated professorship of philosophy his newly ordained priest, Don Félix Varela y Morales.

The College and Seminary of San Carlos had at this time a total faculty of eight. Almost without exception, the teachers were secular priests and native Cubans, and most of them, like Varela, were under thirty years of age. Bishop Espada had a staff to his own liking. The professors at the University—older men, order priests, conservative scholastics—might berate; the Holy Office in Mexico might censor; but he was determined to bring San Carlos abreast of the intellectually advancing times.

"Take the broom and sweep away all that is not useful." To his most recent appointee, the 23-year-old professor of philosophy, ethics, and physics, Espada gave, in substance, this injunction.[19] Caballero and O'Gavan had opened trails. Varela was to lead the thought of Cuba boldly out of the tradition-bound past and into the limitless vistas of the nineteenth century.

* * * * *

During the decade from 1812 to 1822, Félix Varela earned the title of Cuba's foremost philosopher and most illustrious teacher. He not only revolutionized the teaching of philosophy at the College —he added whole new fields of study. His creativity and effective energy were prodigious. He lectured, he wrote, he orated and— most important—he thought deeply and well. He virtually lived in his classroom, his laboratory, and his study. Leisure, he wrote in his *Apuntes acerca de la distribución del tiempo*, must be used in worthwhile activity. Like Leibnitz, he believed that "he who loses an hour, loses a piece of life."[20] He caused learning to become vital and pertinent and fashionable in Havana. When he assumed the chair of philosophy, there were 39 students in all at San Carlos. In 1821, some 200 jostled for admission to Varela's course in constitutional law.

Moreover, his disciples and his letters and his books spread his

---

[19]*Vida*, p. 13; *El padre Varela*, p. 53.
[20]Roberto Agramonte, "El Padre Varela," p. 66.

influence in everwidening circles after he left his native land. His inspiration carried on through José de la Luz y Caballero (his most famous disciple) and the journalist José Antonio Saco to the teacher poet Rafael María de Mendive, who in turn tutored José Martí ("El Apóstol" to modern Cubans). Today, students and admirers of Félix Varela's works abound in the Cuba of Fidel Castro and in the exile groups in Miami and New York.

The period of Varela's tenure as professor was an epoch of travail throughout Latin America. The urge for freedom, stimulated by the example of the United States and by intellectual impulses from Western Europe, found opportunity in the disintegration of the Spanish Bourbon monarchy. The mother country, along with much of continental Europe, had long been cowering in the giant shadow of the little man from Corsica. In 1812, while the Intruder-King, Joseph Bonaparte, clung precariously to power in Madrid and the heir to the Spanish throne sat in fawning captivity in the chateau of Valençay, a rebellious Cortes at Cádiz proclaimed a constitutional monarchy. Spanish subjects in the dominions were to have equal representation with those in the Peninsula, and there ensued general rejoicing. Inhabitants of St. Augustine erected a monument to the Constitution of 1812 in the public square. Juntas in the colonies placed their hopes in Ferdinand VII, siding with him against his inept father and his shameless mother; but they suffered a rude awakening when, released by the tottering Napoleon, Ferdinand abolished the Cortes, persecuted its members, and disavowed its accomplishments, revealing himself as a ruler both self-centered and vindictive.

Following the lead of Francisco Miranda, "the George Washington of South America," and of Simón Bolívar and other *criollo* patriots, much of Latin America threw off the colonial yoke during this period. Britain and the United States, nothing loath to see Spanish power crumble, abetted the revolutions with propaganda, money, commercial and political haggling, and volunteer manpower. Hard-pressed King Ferdinand sold Florida to its northern neighbor in 1819; and his armies were unable to prevent the new states of Mexico, Central America, and northern and western South America from asserting their independence. When the President of the United States, with a nudge from England, proclaimed the

Monroe Doctrine in 1823, he premised his declaration on the need to prevent other European countries from feasting on the moribund Spanish-American empire.

Of all her vast American holdings, only Cuba and Puerto Rico remained loyal to Spain throughout the nineteenth century. In Cuba this faithfulness was partly inspired by fear. The gruesome internecine strife and racial reprisals which *liberté* and *égalité*, with the guillotine as their emblem, had unleashed when nearby St. Domingue became the black kingdom of Haiti had caused Cuban *criollos* to cherish their Iberian ties. The Marqués de Someruelos gave small comfort to would-be French settlers, and he condoned the summary hanging of a luckless emissary from King Joseph Bonaparte. An abortive slave uprising in 1812 led by the free Negro José Antonio de Aponte was put down with a severity lurid with recollections of the Haitian holocaust. When a brief spell of independence for the eastern, Spanish-speaking sector of Santo Domingo ended in bloody conquest by Haiti, Cuban *criollos* were the more inclined to question the blessings of freedom. More than half the population of their island was slave or free Negro; and the spirit of the times did not breed moderation among men who revolted against injustice.

But not fear alone kept Cuba tranquil. In the first decades of the nineteenth century, the island was marching forward without serious internal upheavals. The policies of governors like Las Casas and Someruelos and of the Spanish-born Bishop Espada buttressed Cuba's continuing loyalty to the mother country. These dignitaries met the radical young intellectuals of Havana more than half-way, giving their island the benefits of progress without the scourge of civil strife. Not until later in the century, when the repressive measures of Ferdinand VII and Queen Isabella II closed the avenues to hope, did a vigorous underground flourish, favoring in one direction annexation to the United States and in the other complete insular independence.

Félix Varela, youngest but most influential professor in the College and Seminary of San Carlos, did not at first concern himself with politics, although in the tradition of his time he must as a philosopher consider all knowledge, social science included, as within his province. Bishop Espada had bestowed on him full scope to share in his homeland's intellectual resurgence. His job was to renovate thought, so that educated *habaneros* might work intelligently for the betterment of their island. His following was to extend beyond his own time and place, through much of Latin America and deep into the twentieth century, but this would be an unsolicited bonus.

The cardinal principle of Félix Varela's philosophy was his eclecticism—he claimed the right for himself and for every other thinking individual to re-examine the philosophers of the past and eliminate and adapt on the basis of present relevance. As Father Michael O'Reilly had constructed the Church of St. Augustine with a combination of new stone and materials from old chapels, so he would build his intellectual system, applying in his selection the test: "Is it necessary? Is it sound? Is it beneficial?"

Faith to him was not the blind acceptance of another's synthesis, whether ancient or contemporary; it was rather a belief in the nature of man and in the God from Whom all creation arose and to Whom all mankind tended. Using the word-patterns of his day, Varela protested that wisdom about this world came not from memorizing syllogisms but rather from observing and studying the material world and from using the mind to understand man and his universe.

God had given man eyes to see, ears to hear, a brain to reason with. Let him not blank his powers in the mechanical prating of thoughts of men long dead. Let him rather employ his talents to increase the sum of living knowledge.

Varela conceded historical status to Aristotle who, since his introduction to Spain by Arab and Jewish thinkers, had become the reigning philosopher of the Christian Middle Ages, and who served as prime prophet at the University of Havana and in most other Catholic seminaries. The dominance of St. Thomas Aquinas over Catholic philosophy was not reestablished until later, at the time when he was proclaimed Master of All Scholastic Doctors, 1879, and Universal Patron of Schools and Universities, 1880, in pronouncements by Pope Leo XIII.

It is difficult for the modern student, accustomed to free discussion, open inquiry, experimentation, and the inductive method, to comprehend the hold which those who adhered to the findings of

Aristotle had on much of education even into the nineteenth century. The authoritative Greek had covered so much of human knowledge—logic, philosophy, psychology, ethics, biology, astronomy, politics, literature, esthetics, and was regarded as correct in so many of his conclusions that for centuries it seemed needful but to assimilate the writings of Aristotle to become a learned man. The medieval Christian's acceptance of Greek metaphysics and techniques and the Renaissance humanist's glorification of classical culture both helped to solidify the Aristotelian hold on the studious mind.

Then there burst on the European scene the newly translated works of the Peripatetic leader, and this gigantic addition to the literature only emphasized how easily all his writings could be dovetailed together and mortised into a glorious synthesis of inherited learning. Each scholar-teacher (*Scholasticus*) then tried his hand at synthesis (*Summa*) or at personal commentating; some of them went back to Plato, but the overwhelming number embraced Plato's most eminent disciple, wherefore the disciple—Aristotle—vaulted to such exclusive eminence as to win the unmistakable name of *Philosophus* (*The Philosopher*). Soon the field became crowded with *Summae,* and thinkers turned to commentating on each other instead of on *Philosophus.*

The inheritance bequeathed, then, to the century of Varela was not that of the golden age of scholasticism but rather of what has been called not its demise but its decadence. Scholasticism had become isolated from the ongoing world by layers of formalism.

Revolt came slowly, with the rebels showing varying degrees of disagreement with the intellectual establishment. Francis Bacon, for example, whom Varela credited with breaking the medieval routine of synthesis and commentary, accepted Aristotle's ideal of the universal scholar and emulated him likewise in studying nature at first hand. Modern science had its beginnings when men stopped conning Aristotle's conclusions and set to learning directly (as he himself had done) from the world about them, using their own powers of observation and reason and producing inventions unknown to the Greeks. This was the form of liberation—independent investigation and acceptance of the new physical discoveries—which Félix Varela championed for the youth of Cuba.

Varela classified as the "three sects" of Aristotelianism the schools of Thomas Aquinas, Duns Scotus, and William of Ockham. More than 21 centuries after the death of the overpowering Stagirite, Varela found it necessary to declare that the works of the encyclopedic Greek represented but one tremendous step, and certainly not the ultimate peak, in man's understanding of his world. He acclaimed Galileo, Francis Bacon, and the Spanish doctor, Antonio Gómez Pereira, for rejecting *el yugo aristotélico* and initiating the True Philosophy.[21] He praised Newton, Leibnitz, and the German philosopher and mathematician, Christian Wolff (1679-1754), for their contributions to scientific thought. He extolled the mathematician-priest, Pierre Gassendi, for reviving the atomic theory and the democratic principles of Epicurus and striving to adapt that serene Greek philosopher to Christian thought. But the principal glory in restoring philosophy to its rightful place as a living science he conceded to Descartes, who had warred to the death on Aristotelianism and erected, "insofar as the circumstances of his times permitted," an excellent system.[22]

Being a genuine eclectic, a selector of what seemed to him true and useful, Varela did not subscribe wholly to the beliefs of any one philosopher; and, unlike Locke and Descartes and Destutt, Count of Tracy,[23] from all of whom he garnered, he avoided the dazzling but debatable central premise. Acknowledging much to admire in Locke and in Descartes, he rejected the extreme *"tabula rasa"* assumptions of the one and the "innate ideas" of the other, finding that learning comes from both sense perception and thought processes. He culled ideas alike from the sensualist neo-Epicureanism of Gassendi and the Cartesian intellectualism which Gassendi attacked; from the positivism of Condillac,[24] which led

---

[21]Félix Varela y Morales, *Lecciones de filosofía,* 1961 ed., 1: 20ff. Gómez Pereira: Espasa insists this is his real name, not Antonio Gómez Pereira; born, Medina del Campo c. 1500.
[22]Varela, *Instituciones de filosofía ecléctica,* 1952 ed., 1: 23.
[23]Pierre Gassendi, of Provence, 1592-1655, philosopher, scientist, mathematician, clergyman, friend of Descartes, staunch Catholic. Antoine César Victoire Charles Destutt, Comte de Tracy, b. 1754 in Bourbonnais, France, admirer of Voltaire, senator after the French Revolution.
[24]Étienne Bonnot de Condillac, of Grenoble (1714 or 1715-1780), popularizer of Locke's philosophy, Abbé of Mureaux, tutor of the Duke of Parma (grandson of Louis XV), member of French Academy.

some unwarily into agnosticism; and from the dogmas of the Church Fathers who were the very foundation of the Faith.

Varela fought fanaticism and superstition as vigorously as he did atheism, considering them reverse faces of ignorance. His resultant philosophy was not, as might be presumed, a hodge-podge; it was a reasoned, reasonable interpretation, stemming from the Catholic culture of Spanish America but taking nourishment from the progressive European thought of the day. Avoiding the flamboyant, it was bold mainly in its rejection of outdated finalities, in its declaration of independence for thought, in its rebellion against the stagnation of commentator-digesting commentators, in its openness to the discoveries of science. A century later, the historian Juan Álvarez, though caviling at Varela's partiality for Condillac, named him as the Cuban "most worthy of the name of philosopher."[25]

Since time-honored texts had doubtful utility in Félix Varela's forward-looking instruction, he set out at once to produce his own. In the first year of his professorship (1812), he published a series of propositions for defense by his students—among them, his guiding principle: "The best philosophy of all is the eclectic, in which we do not swear by the word of any one man, but are led by reason and experience, learning from all but clinging pertinaciously to no one."[26] It is interesting, in his *Propositiones Variae*, that he used the scholastic Latin and the scholastic format of proposition, demonstration, minor proof, opposition, and reply, with the syllogistic *ergo's, quod's, enim's,* and *sed's,* to establish the thesis with which he would overthrow scholasticism.

In another pamphlet printed the same year, Varela listed 226 propositions for discussion, ranging from metaphysics, logic, and moral philosophy to contemporary chemistry, physics, and astronomy. An enlarged and improved edition appeared in 1813.

Don Pedro Valera y Jiménez, Archbishop of Santo Domingo and Primate of the Indies,[27] observed on a visit to Cuba the teaching of the Bishop of Havana's protégé; he asked Varela to

---

[25]*Cath. Encycl.,* 7: 154a.
[26]Freely translated from Varela's original Latin as quoted by José Manuel Mestre y Domínguez, *De la filosofía en La Habana,* pp. 78-79.
[27]Santo Domingo is claimed as the cradle of Christianity in the New World, being the first metropolitan see established in America.

prepare a text in the new philosophy for his ecclesiastical seminary. The result was a two-volume *Institutiones philosophiae eclecticae ad usum juventutis,* entirely in Latin and covering logic and metaphysics; it was dated Havana, 1812.[28] This was Varela's first major printed work.

Although the substance of the Latin *Institutiones* showed radical innovations, the tone of medieval scholasticism remained—in the use of the universal Latin, and in the classifications of thought, the propositions to argue, the rules to learn, the premises, the studied ratiocination, the conclusions attained—in short, the deductive approach.

The following year, Varela made the first breach in the scholastic format. All higher instruction in Cuba up to this time was transmitted in Latin, the common medium of Western scholars and scientists. Varela was an accomplished master and teacher of the language of Cicero. However, he realized that, for education to achieve the prevalence which the era demanded, the intermediate hurdle of the classical idiom must be abolished. Therefore in 1813, with the consent of Bishop Espada, he began conducting classes in the vernacular; not, as he stressed, merely for the sake of innovation, but for the wider dissemination of knowledge. Latin served a purpose as the international language of the learned; but the new ideas and the new sciences would affect the world of Everyman, who must be enabled to understand them.

The *Institutiones* was republished in 1813 in Spanish with supplements on mathematics and physics. Its two volumes constituted, says Rodríguez, the first philosophical treatise ever printed in that language in any part of the world.[29] Both the Latin and the Spanish versions were, after numerous imprints, republished by the University of Havana in 1952.

During 1814, Father Varela produced two additional books in Spanish, summarizing the courses at San Carlos in chemistry, botany, zoology, physiology, mathematics, metaphysics, ethics, and even drawing. These were followed by *Elenco (Outline)*, 1816;

---

[28]For a summary in English of Varela's writings and orations during his Cuban period, cf. Rodríguez, "Father Felix Varela, Vicar General of New York from 1837 to 1853." ("Father Felix Varela").
[29]*Ibid.,* p. 467.

Lección Preliminar; and *Apuntes Filosóficos* (*Philosophical Notes*); and the three editions of *Miscelánea Filosófica* (Havana 1819, Madrid 1821, and New York 1827). The *Miscelánea* contained extracts from Destutt de Tracy on the human understanding; essays on grammar, poetry, the ideology of Francis Bacon Baron Verulam, Viscount of St. Alban's (1561-1626), the art of translation, and the influence of emotions on thought, the importance of historical synthesis, the merits of inductive and deductive reasoning, the influence of nomenclature, and the means of making a scientific career more attractive to youth; also, more philosophically, a series of notes on the guidance of the human spirit, on "the Latin language ideologically considered," and on scholasticism in its causes, forms, and effects. The 1827 edition contained also Varela's oft-quoted essay on the various faces of Patriotism—the self-seeking, the jingoistic, the imprudent, and the genuine.

The culmination of Varela's philosophical writings in Cuba was his *Lecciones de filosofía,* a three-volume work which Rodríguez tells us was "for many years the text-book in logic, metaphysics, ethics, natural philosophy, and chemistry in the colleges of Cuba, Mexico, and other countries of Spanish origin."[30] It first appeared in Havana in 1818-19 and subsequently went through numerous editions in the Americas and Europe, four of them personally revised and enlarged by the author—at Philadelphia in 1824 and New York in 1828, 1832, and 1841. The University of Havana republished it in April 1961, two years after the revolutionary Castro regime seized power in Cuba.

The *Lecciones,* like all his major works after the *Institutiones,* is written in the vernacular. In it he abandons entirely the syllogistic style. The chapters constitute a series of reasoned essays. On the flyleaf is a theme from Condillac: "I write solely for the ignorant. Since they do not speak the language of any science, they can the more easily understand mine, which is more to their capacity than any other, having been taken from nature, which will speak to them as I do."

A random selection of section-headings from Volume 1 indicates the range and slant of Varela's thought: "On the Means of Cor-

---

[30]*Ibid.,* p. 468.

recting Intellectual Processes;" "On Talent, Genius, Judgment, and Good Taste;" "Observations on Books and Method of Study;" "On the Good Use of Reason and on Its Opposites, Fanaticism and Pedanticism;" "On the Life of the Body, the Action of the Spirit on the Body and the Means of Knowing It;" "On the Variety of Human Propensities;" "On the Light of Reason and Natural Right;" "On the Relations of Man with Society;" "On the Nature of Society and of Patriotism;" "The Knowledge Which Man Has of His Creator and His Consequent Obligations."

Deploring on the one hand the cruel excesses of religious fanatics and, on the other, the murderous license of unbelievers in Revolutionary France, the temperate Cuban closes his volume with an ejaculation: "Would that these lessons might contribute in some manner to protect the young as well from ridiculous fanaticism as from dismal irreligion! Could they but inspire them to love for a religion which will make them happy and for a fatherland which in them—yes, in them—places all its hope!"[31]

Varela took vigorous issue with those who claimed a conflict between religion and science. Philosophy and religion, he said, were nothing if they were not true; and therefore they must take into account the truths uncovered by the natural and physical sciences. The liberation from the devotees of Aristotle predicated a switch from merely intellectual exercises to learning through observation and scientific investigation. Students who had gleaned knowledge only from lectures and books must now be introduced to laboratory techniques. To understand their world, they must study it, not deducing from established premises but concluding, upward, from assembled, verified data.

Since no other competent teacher was available, it fell on Félix Varela to set up the courses in experimental physics and chemistry which his approach to learning demanded. He personally initiated the first courses in modern science in Cuba, assembling the equipment, constructing much of the apparatus with his own hands, testing the chemical formulae before hazarding them with his students, collecting on field trips specimens mineralogical, botani-

---

[31] Fifth ed., repub. Havana, 1961, 1: 305.

cal, and biological. One of his pupils, José Manuel Valerino, illustrated the text on physics which he prepared.

The instructor, learning along with his students the techniques and axioms of the new sciences, failed not to communicate his enthusiasm to them. Tirelessly he walked among them, peering with them into microscopes, helping them perform chemical miracles, exhorting them to challenge ancient conclusions and to observe for themselves. These students later attested the thrilling experience of learning for the first time, not from the printed page but from the world about them.

Varela was the born teacher, completely dedicated, constantly surrounded by youths whom he sparked to thought and serious purpose. The "Spanish-American Socrates," one author has named him—from the diversity of his followers and his electric effect upon them.[32] Long after fate had taken him from them, they remembered; they kept in touch; they lived by his teachings and passed them on to their children's children.

"Regenerator of Cuban thought"—thus would later generations of his countrymen honor the memory of Father Varela. The catalog of his students included many who would achieve fame in Cuba or, like their master, in enforced exile. Nicolás Manuel de Escobedo, his first amanuensis in the preparation of lectures, who became an outstanding jurist and orator; José Valerino, artist and illustrator; Felipe Poey y Aloy, lawyer, natural history specialist, and first president of the Anthropological Society; the political firebrand, Gaspar Betancourt Cisneros; the priest-philosopher Francisco Ruiz; Cristóbal Madan, who entered commerce and championed Cuban causes in New York; Manuel González del Valle, professor of philosophy; José María Casal, advocate, editor, and writer: such are the men to whom Félix Varela handed the torch.

Most distinguished among Félix Varela's disciples were two whose names rank with his in the annals of Cuban thought, and therefore in the history of the Americas. José Antonio Saco, an orphan much buffeted by fate, took up the causes championed by his mentor and won fame as a journalist and political reformer and

---

[32] *El padre Varela*, p. 129.

especially as the author of a monumental *History of Slavery*. José de la Luz y Caballero, nephew of Father José Agustín Caballero, shares the spotlight with Varela in Cuban philosophy and education. Although he abandoned the religious life after minor orders, he devoted his talents to the welfare of others, and particularly to the enlightenment of youth. More than any other, Luz transmitted to younger minds the fruitful lessons of Félix Varela. He tutored Rafael Mendive and many of the freedom fighters of 1868; and these became the inspiration of José Martí.

"Whenever we think in the Island of Cuba," wrote Luz, "we think with veneration and love of him who first taught us to think."[33] This statement so aptly expressed the influence of Varela as "master teacher, master philosopher, master intellectual, and master revolutionary"[34] that it has, in contracted form, among Cubans generally, become universally associated with his name: "the first who taught Cubans to think, Father Félix Varela."

* * * * *

Bishop Espada y Landa was using his position as prelate to further the physical and intellectual, as well as the spiritual, well-being of his flock; and his protégé, Félix Varela, soon advanced into participation in the national life. While revitalizing the processes of learning from his chair at San Carlos, he was also telling the people from the public rostrum that they must now take a hand in state policy and exhorting the ruling classes to greater civic responsibility.

Varela, we are told, was, despite his unprepossessing appearance and gentle demeanor, a stirring speaker. His style was eloquent: not bombastic or flowery, but direct, lucid, a forceful communication of well-reasoned, constructive, warmly held, and sometimes momentous convictions. "He possessed," says one biographer, "the soul of an artist, the heart of a saint, the tongue of an orator."[35]

He came to public attention shortly after his ordination with a

---

[33]*Vida*, p. 89.
[34]Emilio Roig de Leuchsenring, *Ideario cubano Félix Varela, precursor de la revolución libertadora cubana*, Colección histórica cub. y amer., 12, Havana, Municipio, 1953, p. 7. (*Ideario cubano*). Cf. also Sergio Cuevas Zequeria, "El Padre Varela, Contribución a la Historia de la Filosofía en Cuba," *Rev. de la Facultad de letras y ciencias*, 2, no. 3, May 1906: 217-20.
[35]William Francis Blakeslee, C.S.P., "Felix Varela—1788-1853," p. 29.

sermon delivered in a populous sector of Havana. Cuba, a colony governed despotically since the days of the *conquistadores* by governors sent from Madrid, was choosing its first delegates to the Spanish Cortes under the Constitution of 1812. It was an unprecedented privilege for Cubans to vote in a Spanish election; and the Bishop ordered the celebration of the Mass of the Holy Spirit to invoke divine guidance. This was the year—1812—of the Aponte rebellion in Cuba; of Francisco Miranda's imprisonment after brief military successes in Venezuela; of hostilities between Britain and the United States over impressment of seamen; of Wellington's defeat of the French at Salamanca; of the flouting of Joseph Bonaparte and Ferdinand VII by the self-appointed junta at Cádiz. But Father Varela, in his pre-electoral exhortation, bespoke faith in the power of a conscientious electorate. From now on, the people must rule; and they had it in their power to curb injustice and war. "Seek ye only truth and peace" was his theme. He urged the congregation against self-interest, superstition, and the impiety which bred violence, and reminded them that the self-control and the active virtue of citizens are the true bulwark of the state.[36] His words well suited the solemn occasion. The *Diario del Gobierno de la Habana* and other periodicals printed them with acclaim, and from then on there were few occasions of note which did not feature an oration by the young professor from San Carlos.

The Royal Patriotic Society, originated for civic-minded young men by Las Casas, noted Varela's progressive ideas and his energies bent to the common good, and on January 24, 1817, it officially voted him into membership. His initiatory address as preserved in the Society's records and reproduced by Rodríguez dealt with "the influence of ideology on society and the means of correcting its application;"[37] but it was really a plea for universal education.

"It is a dictate of nature," he said, "for all men to aspire to the enlightenment of their understanding. It is a precept of society that those who are charged with public instruction should seek all means to make themselves capable of so arduous a function." The members of the Royal Society, because of their position in the

---

[36] *Vida,* pp. 27-28, reprints the sermon and describes its effect.
[37] *Ibid.,* pp. 35-60.

social system, had a particular duty to direct their talents to the common good. "It is for you to teach men to think from their earliest years; or, better, to remove the obstacles to their thinking." He proposed specific means to the achievement of this goal and urged the Society to devise others, keeping always in mind "the importance which man's thinking bears in the common weal."[38]

The Patriotic Society assigned him to its most important committee, the Section on Education. He induced the Society to sponsor at San Carlos a course on Fundamental Sciences and Arts, covering mathematics, art, chemistry, natural history, botany, and anatomy. He participated in the founding of primary schools. Seeking to improve the status of the vernacular in public instruction, he wrote critiques of the *Spanish Grammar* of Father Laguardia and the *Elements of the Spanish language* by Don Mariano Velázquez de la Cadena. He composed a set of reading selections for elementary schools, which the Society printed and disseminated. This work, whose numerous editions were quickly exhausted, consisted of maxims and reflections on private and social conduct, under such headings as Prudence, Charity, Fortitude, Anger, Vengeance, Sadness, Restlessness, Joy, Beneficence, Modesty, Despair, and Temperance—their counsel adding up to a plea for moderation, optimism, and love for one's fellow-men. These brief essays found their way eventually into the *Progressive Spanish reader,* published in New York by Appleton (1856) and authored by Professor Agustín José Morales, cousin of Varela and faculty member of the New York Free Academy, later known as the College of the City of New York, and now a part of the City University of New York.

In December 1818, the Royal Society of Friends of the Fatherland, in consideration of Félix Varela's assistance in its patriotic endeavors, designated him *Socio de Mérito,* Honor Associate. It was not considered necessary to vote on this decision— the distinction was bestowed by acclamation.

* * * * *

Inexorably, the soldier of God was moving into participation in the history of his native isle and of the shaky Spanish Empire to

---

[38]*Idem;* freely translated from quotations on pp. 35 and 40.

which it belonged. In three major politically-oriented addresses, in 1818 and 1819, he illuminated for the people of the dependency of Cuba the principles of good government and the realities of their own situation.

The first of these talks was occasioned by a death.

Don José Pablo Valiente y Bravo, *intendente* of Havana in the time of Las Casas, died in Spain late in 1817. During his stay in Cuba (1792-1799), Valiente had contributed to progress in the island, correcting abuses in taxation and the public service and the administration of law, building wharfs, promoting commerce, stabilizing the currency, and supporting educational and charitable institutions. For his beneficence, the Royal Patriotic Society had taken him to its bosom, bestowing on him, as it later did on Félix Varela, its highest honor.

On word of this distinguished administrator's demise, the municipality of Havana organized in conjunction with the clergy a solemn religious memorial, at which Varela was principal speaker. The *Elogio* delivered by the priest-philosopher on this occasion, March 10, 1818,[39] is considered by some as his finest oration. In it he praised the meritorious public official, outlining Valiente's services to Cuba as *intendente* and, later, as a member of the Council of the Indies. Valiente, the orator said, was a man who sacrificed his private interests for those of the people; he guided with wise counsel the ship of state through dangerous circumstances; he fostered trade and agriculture and letters; he represented the rights of colonials in the Cortes; and, when need arose, during the disgrace of the Spanish monarchy, he stood up to the oppressors "like Dion to Dionysius."[40] Withal, he was a champion of peace, knowing that a wise man gains nothing by force—that the understanding is so powerful that if it cannot convince, all other recourses are useless.

"A consul of the people, a man wise and cultured"—in these terms Varela epitomized the virtues of Valiente, and implicitly set an ideal for his own career and for Cuba's rising generation.

Varela could laud the late *intendente* wholeheartedly: he ad-

---

[39]*Vida*, pp. 53-61.
[40]Dion, a Syracusan and follower of Plato, expelled the tyrant Dionysius the Younger from Syracuse on the island of Sicily *c.* 356 B.C.

mired the man, endorsed his achievements, and would one day emulate his opposition to royal injustice. At the close of 1818, however, a less appealing assignment fell to his lot, when the Royal Society requested him to deliver an address in praise of King Ferdinand VII of Spain.

It was only too well known that the monarch was no model, either as ruler or as family man; and Félix Varela, with his high concept of human dignity and public morality, must of necessity mistrust him. Ferdinand had intrigued against his own father with Napoleon; had walked fatuously into French captivity while Spain was surrendered to Joseph Bonaparte; had dissolved his Empire's first representative Cortes and scrapped its first democratic Constitution; had connived with the Holy Alliance to suppress the liberties of Spaniards. On the other hand, Ferdinand enjoyed a certain popularity in Spanish America, which had welcomed his accession after the shameful reign of Charles IV and the imperial anarchy of the Napoleonic era.

Cuba, especially, had reason for gratitude to Ferdinand VII.[41] Each of its towns and cities was represented at court by a *procurador,* who had the King's ear and could often obtain favors. Such a solicitor was the *habanero* Francisco de Arango y Parreño, who advised Ferdinand, in the tempest of Spanish-American rebellions, how to keep the Pearl of the Antilles loyal to Spain.[42] Ferdinand had exempted Cuba's Dr. O'Gavan from the general harassment of deputies to the Cortes of 1812—had even given him political and ecclesiastical preferment. In 1817, a royal decree abolished the tobacco monopoly in the island. The following year, the king opened the ports of Cuba to foreign (non-Spanish) commerce, removed duties from imports of gold and silver, and prescribed government measures to develop the port of Matanzas; soon the first steamboat, the *Neptune,* arrived in the island's waters, destined for the Matanzas-Havana run.[43] Most important, ideologically, was Ferdinand's treaty with Britain in 1817 for the abolition of the

---

[41]"Father Felix Varela," p. 469.
[42]Cf. Andrés de Arango, ed., *Obras del excmo. señor D. Francisco de Arango y Parreño, passim.* Francisco María de la Luz Arango y Parreño, lawyer, born and died in Havana (1765-1837).
[43]*El padre Varela* recounts benefits to Cuba under Ferdinand on pp. 159-63. Cf. also *Vida,* pp. 47-48.

slave trade. Cubans like Arango had been petitioning Madrid since 1790 to ameliorate the treatment of Negroes. The measure for suppression of the nefarious traffic was rightly credited to the quarter-century of agitation from Havana, although, unfortunately, the traffic continued illegally for many more years.

The directors of the Royal Economic Society saw, therefore, much cause for gratitude to Ferdinand VII, by the expression of which they might hope to elicit further favors. As to Félix Varela, he must voice their thanks without compromising his ideals.

Consequently the "eulogy" which the priest-philosopher delivered on December 12, 1818 pertains more to Cuba than to Ferdinand. It pulses with praise of the island country and of the lavishness with which nature has endowed her—in beauty, in climate, in resources, in inhabitants. This is to become a favorite, heartfelt theme with Varela—he loves his native isle and finds her so beautiful that she should always be happy. But laws, he proceeds, have kept her people, until recently, from enjoying the fulness of their natural blessings. Now, "at last, the voice of liberty, from the lips of a benefactor, can be heard in all parts. Plant your tobacco, sell it according to your own judgment, place a price on the fruits of your sweat, and be the judges of the value of your own goods. The law renounces a right which dishonors it. Under a most kind Prince, there is no place for oppression or monopolies."[44] Credit for this relief, adds Varela, must be given to the King, and also to Francisco de Arango of Havana, now in Madrid.

In masterful fashion, therefore, Varela gave the necessary bow to Ferdinand, even while he represented to the Cubans the treatment they should, by right, expect from their rulers in Madrid. To his speech, the King could take no exception; from it, the people must take great heart.

The death of Ferdinand's father, who before his abdication had reigned as Charles IV, occurred early in 1819. Varela was called

---

[44] A manuscript pamphlet of this oration is in Library of Congress, "José Ignacio Rodríguez Papers" (JIRP), Box 16, filed under "Vidal Morales;" headed, "Memorias de la Real Sociedad de la Habana. Núm. 25—Elogio de S. M. el Sr. D. Fernando 7º contraído solamente á los beneficios que se ha dignado conceder á la isla de Cuba ... leído en el Junta general el 12 de dic^e. de 1818 por el Pbro Don Félix Varela." Cf. also *Vida*, pp. 49-50.

upon for the funeral oration in the Cathedral of Havana, May 12, 1819. Here was the touchiest chore of all. Every one agreed that Charles was a weak, foolish man, a shadow king who had let his country go by default to Napoleon, a father at odds with his son, a husband who condoned his wife's adultery and showered honors of state on her brazen lover. His reign had been unfortunate for Spain and for Spaniards the world over. Yet one must not speak ill of the freshly dead.

"I do not eulogize a man—I plead for a King." So began the philosopher-priest.

> I petition the King of Kings, who saw fit to place the scepter in the hand of Charles. I ask Him to pity His servant and pardon his human frailties. As a man, he was subject to many trials and miseries. He tried to carry out the policies of the benevolent Charles III, his father, but the perfidy of those about him tainted his efforts. None the less, in a span of twenty years he achieved much: he promoted agriculture, communication, education, and the arts.
>
> I say of him what a wise orator said of the good Germanicus: 'He had one defect, and that was to be too good for a court so corrupt.'

Now at last, continued the orator, the evils that enmeshed the King are ended for him. In life he was sorely tried—may the Merciful Father in the hereafter permit him peace.[45]

One could have wept with Félix Varela over the fallen, inept ruler. Learned, astute, eloquent, the speaker was also a man of compassion. A plain little man, he had stood erect and looked into the eyes of the ruler of Spain's Empire and seen there a weak human being haunted by problems too spectral to handle—a ruler no bigger, really, than those whose public servant the Lord had made him.

Havana stood still that May morning of 1819 in sorrow for the monarch it had despised. *El Padre* with consummate speech had revealed the suffering fellow-man whom God had clothed in the royal purple.

* * * * *

If the people of Spain hoped Ferdinand might mature after his

---
[45]*Vida,* pp. 62-65.

father's death, they were doomed to disappointment. No words of praise for him came from the Iberian Peninsula—only anger at his self-seeking, petulant tyranny. The Inquisition was again in operation. The constituents of the Cortes of Cádiz perished in prison or plotted in exile. Education, suspected of breeding malcontents, languished from purposeful neglect. Widespread rebellions were mocking the might of Spain in Latin America. The royal treasury was empty—Florida had been sold to the United States for a pittance; the unpaid army was restive; the citizens grumbled for bread and justice and human dignity.

Revolt erupted in 1820. Captained by General Rafael del Riego, dissidents overwhelmed the capricious monarch. In March they forced him to restore the Constitution of 1812. The call went forth for a reconvening of the Cortes, which Ferdinand had terminated in 1814.

Havana heard the news with rejoicing—her civic leaders had been awaiting this event. At that distance, hope for representative government was possible, even under a Ferdinand VII. The Royal Society of Friends of the Country decided that young men must now be instructed in the science of self-government. Bishop Espada y Landa agreed that a course in constitutional law be initiated at San Carlos. He ordered Varela to compete for the new professorship. The priest, already burdened, and urging his lack of training in the subject, tried to beg off; but Espada overruled him.

Again, the open competitive examinations—there were three candidates—and again Félix Varela edified the public and the committee of judges. He was given a period of months to prepare for the new chair, for which there were neither teaching materials nor curriculum precedents available. Bishop Espada assigned Varela's able and devoted disciple, José Antonio Saco, to assume some of his earlier responsibilities at San Carlos.

After a half-year of intensive study, Varela produced the necessary textbook: *Observaciones sobre la constitución de la monarquía español*. His course in Political Economy and Constitutional Law, the first of its kind in Latin America, was initiated in the Great Hall of San Carlos in January 1821. It had 193 enrolled students; and a swarm of auditors strained at the open windows and doors to catch his words.

As recorded in the *Observaciones,* Varela's political aims were straightforward, democratic, and pacific. Unlike the Mexican priest-revolutionary, Miguel Hidalgo y Costilla, who rallied an insurgent army around the banner of Our Lady of Guadaloupe, Varela did not advocate, at that time, separatism; he never favored armed rebellion. He believed, as he had told the Royal Society in 1817, that right ideas, energetically disseminated, could triumph without the aid of muskets.

The course on the Spanish Constitution, founded by the Patriotic Society, sponsored by Bishop Espada, and organized and taught by Varela, was to train Cubans to participate in government. "I would call this chair," said Professor Varela, "the chair of liberty, of the rights of man, of national guarantees . . . the ground-work of the great edifice of our happiness, that which for the first time has reconciled among us the laws and Philosophy, that which curbs both fanaticism and despotism."[46]

Sovereignty and liberty, said Varela, were the foundation-stones of the constitutional system. Power comes from the people, who, having conferred some of it on their ruler for their own good, are duty-bound to obey the laws. But there are certain inviolable natural rights which the individual cannot cede, either to the king or to the dominant majority, for their loss would make him a slave. Power is limited by division; neither the monarch nor the Cortes may infringe on the rights and functions retained by the people and the municipal governments. The royal veto is no longer absolute. Thus is liberty guarded.

Sovereignty and government, he continued, must not be confused, for the second is the mere executor of the general will, in which the former resides. Equality, which is allied with liberty, falls into three classes: natural and social, which are necessarily accompanied by certain inequalities, since nature has not made all men alike, and legal, which accords all men the same rights before the law, be they rich or poor, ignorant or wise, powerful or weak. The Constitution has been so devised that all citizens may be represented, that their will may be performed and their rights protected. The well-being of the entire Spanish people depends largely

---

[46] Varela, "Discurso Inaugural," *Observaciones,* 1944 ed., p. 1.

on the disposition and effectiveness of the deputies and the monarch, who, should they glaringly fail in the performance of their functions, may be removed from power.

In opposing individual despotism, Varela warned also against the tyranny of the crowd. Unlike the mechanistic Thomas Hobbes (1585-1679), who taught that man has no rights independent of the State, Varela held that injustice could never become just because the multitude favored it; and that justice was not achieved merely because the laws and the State held a disposition toward it. Justice and the rights of individuals were absolutes, stemming from God and the nature of man: to them, the laws and the state, be it monarchy or republic, must conform. To achieve this natural justice would require a supreme effort at self-improvement by the people and their natural leaders.

If Varela, in his *Observaciones* and his lectures on government, set high the standards for constitutional government, he also sounded loud the call for cooperation by Cubans of all degrees and classes. As teacher of philosophy and science, he had encouraged them to rely on their own senses, their own reason. Now he was awakening them to political consciousness, to make of themselves responsible citizens. To quote a mid-twentieth-century Cuban historian:

> If José de la Luz Caballero said, justly, of Félix Varela that 'he was the first who taught us to think,' likewise Varela was the first intellectual Cuban who taught the intellectuals of his epoch and of future generations that they ought not isolate themselves criminally in the marble tower of their literary, artistic, or scientific speculations; but that, precisely because they were intellectuals, they had the greater duty to concern themselves with national problems in order to enlighten and lead their people; and Varela was also, in this sense, the first of our intellectual revolutionaries.[47]

To the philosopher from San Carlos, the world of learning had opened directly into the arena of political action; and the followers of Félix Varela were soon to demand that he lead them personally in the fight for the kind of government he had delineated for them.

---

[47] *Ideario cubano*, p. 7. For an account of the political upheavals which Spain suffered, 1821-26, see pp. v-xviii and 1-34 of vol. 1 of Antonio Perala, *Historia de la guerra civil.*

CHAPTER II

He Charts the Way to Freedom

Félix Varela was saying farewell to his beloved native land. His countrymen had chosen him as their spokesman in the Spanish Cortes. He had not wanted to stand for election, with his course on constitutional law in mid-session and importunate students and unwritten books pressing for his time. But Bishop Espada had commanded him. In this hour of crucial conflict between tyranny and representative government, the island needed him as champion in Madrid.

Obedient to his Bishop, Varela turned over his academic chairs: to Nicolás Manuel de Escobedo, his course on the constitution; to José Antonio Saco, the professorship of philosophy. Bishop Espada supplied him $2,500 for the voyage to Spain—a sum which was later refunded.[1]

Varela took sad farewell of his clustering followers, of his kinsfolk in Havana, of his colleagues in the Patriotic Society, of his beautiful native island:

> 'The love of fatherland is one of the principal obligations of Spaniards.' (Article 6 of the political Constitution).
>
> My heart attested to this article before my lips; it was written in the great book of Nature, and human nature taught it to me from the moment in which, placed among the number of its beings, I heard their voices. There are no sacrifices: honor, pleasure, all should be renounced in the service of the Fatherland. A son of illustrious Havana, educated here, I would disgrace the sentiments of the most constant and most generous of people, if apprehension of dangers could deter me.

There was a note of foreboding in his "Despedida"—his words caressed his loved ones as though there might be no tomorrow.

> Already it may be that the Arbiter of destinies, separating me from mortals, prepares for me a funeral mansion in the measureless waves; already the tyrants who would oppress Spain may be exerting all their power against the august Con-

---

[1] The bills and receipts are reproduced in Francisco González del Valle, "Páginas para la Historia de Cuba."

gress in which you have seen worthy to seat me—it matters not; a son of liberty, an American spirit, knows not fear.

My fellow-citizens, having given me the greatest of honors, you have imposed the most serious obligations. I will not be happy if I do not fulfill them.

In the interim, you have my prayers.[2]

Varela embarked on April 28, 1821, on the frigate *Purísima Concepción* (*Immaculate Conception*), captained by Pedro Gorostiola. He carried with him his violin; and, since several of the passengers were members of his Philharmonic Society, the voyage was brightened with music. After recovering from seasickness, El Padre played the violin and Fernando Adot the flute, and Adolfo Quesada, whose future held a brilliant musical career, accompanied them on the clavichord. Varela also entertained by reciting or improvising ten-line verses (*décimas*). His friend and disciple, the seminarian Francisco Ruiz, and two sons of Varela's uncle, Bartolomé Morales y Morales, traveled with him. His cousins were *en route* to visit an aunt in Seville; and one of them, Buenaventura Morales, kept a diary of the voyage and the overland travel—*Diario de Viaje, e Itinerario del Padre Varela*—which has been copiously excerpted in Rodríguez's *Vida*.

Also headed for Spain were two other delegates: Tomás Gener y Bohigas (1787-1835), a native of Barcelona who, after making his fortune as a provision merchant, had turned to public service in Matanzas, the important seaport on Cuba's north coast; and the scholarly young jurist, Leonardo Santos Suárez. Dr. Juan Bernardo O'Gavan y Guerra, veteran of the Cortes of 1812, was also elected, but his designation was contested because men of color had shared in the voting. A fourth delegate, José de la Cuevas, represented Santiago de Cuba.

Two armed vessels of war escorted the *Purísima Concepción* across the Atlantic.

It was a perilous mission. The dangers at sea, from storms and from privateers, were as nothing to the uncertainties that menaced the delegates in Spain. At the moment, Rafael del Riego's rebellious army held the upper hand over the capricious king in the

---

[2]Varela, "Despedida," *Diario del gobierno constitucional de La Habana*, Apr. 18, 1821; repr. in 1944 ed. of Varela's *Observaciones*, p. 155.

Peninsula—as Cubans called the Motherland—forcing His Majesty to tolerate the Cortes. Should the precarious balance be tipped, there was little doubt how Ferdinand would wreak his vengeance. None of the deputies would then be spared—neither those from Spain, nor the young men from the Island of Cuba.

Meanwhile, Félix Varela's *habaneros* would miss their wise young prophet, with his faith in the power of right thinking, his trust in the goodness of man, his counsel of service and self-control and open-mindedness. Already there was a seething—the merchants mistrusted the intellectuals, the Spanish-born feared explosion of *criollo* revolt, the Negroes were caught between longing and the habit of subjection, between the idealism of abolitionists and the white man's dread of loss and of reprisals. Already men were looking to the south and to the west, where Gran Colombia and Mexico had declared their freedom of Spain and were seeking other dominions to liberate. But Varela had cast his lot with constitutional government—with the Cortes in Madrid which, he hoped, would liberate his people from political oppression as he had liberated them from intellectual bondage.

Back home, Saco's opening lecture to the class which his master had founded outlined a course quite similar to Varela's, but the rhetoric was less temperate.

> Prostrate before the shades of Kepler and Newton, we will see fall the fateful blindfold with which imposters, liars, false interpreters of the Deity, have covered the eyes of the believing multitude; we will see disappear the shadows and unrealities which have been imposed on us as truth. Then, and only then, man will begin to be that which he was when he came from the hands of nature . . . here there are neither masters nor pupils, wise men nor ignorant, rich or poor, but sons of nature; sons all of illustrious America, we are equal—there is no other distinction than that which comes from merit and virtue.[3]

El Padre Varela might have chastened that Rousseau-esque outburst, had he not been 3,000 wind-driven miles away.

* * * * *

The slight young priest from Havana (he was not yet 33), with

---

[3]*Obras de Don José Antonio Saco*, by "Un paisano del autor," 2: 417f.

the luminous smile and the great, myopic brown eyes, quickly became at home in the land of his forbears. Liberal leaders welcomed this dynamic thinker from the Ultramar. He made contacts in Cádiz and Seville, then proceeded to the metropolis, Madrid. Here he became acquainted with his fellow-delegates and with leaders of the European intelligentsia. He published a revised second edition of his *Miscelánea Filosófica*. By the time the Cortes came to session, on the first of October, 1822, his views were well known and his talents held in esteem.

We are informed by a fellow-delegate that the energetic fervor with which he defended his convictions, the reasonableness and justice of his proposals, his charity of outlook, soon distinguished him among his compeers. He spoke and presented reports on a wide variety of topics: the disorders and impotence of Spain, naval power, military rule, conspirators against constitutional government, political prisoners, exemption of provincial inhabitants from the military draft, clerical rule, government of overseas provinces, the independence of American colonies, and the abolition of slavery.[4]

There was a pressing need for the Cortes to adopt a new policy toward the ultramarine provinces still affiliated with the mother country. If Spain was to have, from now on, a constitutional monarchy, the autocratic power of colonial governors, responsible heretofore only to the king, must be limited. It was not sufficient for their citizens to have representation in Madrid; they must share likewise in their home governments. On December 15, 1822, Félix Varela and two colleagues submitted to the Cortes a plea for a Commission to prepare a political and economic prospectus for provincial governments. Varela, along with Leonardo Santos Suárez, was appointed to this Commission; and in February of 1823 he offered a plan for the virtual autonomy of Cuba and other overseas possessions, embodying many of the principles which Britain later applied to her self-governing dominions. His report received the endorsement of the Commission and was recommended for adoption to the Cortes.

---

[4] Enrique Gay Calbó, "El Padre Varela en las Cortes Españolas de 1822 y 1823," p. 114. ("Las Cortes").

Varela foresaw dire results to Spain if justice was not extended to its colonies:

> It is necessary to disabuse ourselves. While offices in America are merely an object of scheming; while the inhabitants of these places see in the agents of government merely adventurers who come to make their fortune quickly without caring about the means they employ nor the esteem of a people to whom they will soon bid eternal farewell, a people whose complaints they fear not, because they reach the ears of government enfeebled and are soon lost in the great crowd of protectors against disgrace which the evil always find; and since these grievous ills have no other remedy than silent suffering, they will lead to desperation, and it will be impossible to secure peace, to remove the resentments and to cement friendly mutual relationships.

The Varela plan for ultramarine government was in reality a constitution, with a preamble and 189 articles, dealing with (1) the organization, powers, and responsibilities of municipal governments; (2) the organization, rights, and duties of provincial deputations; and (3) the choice and functions of governors and other officials. The elected deputies would be empowered to suspend, in their homeland, the execution of laws enacted by the Cortes which they considered prejudicial to their compatriots. Too often, Varela commented, statutes which seemed just in Madrid became waterlogged in their passage across the Atlantic. "The representatives," he recommended, "could also suspend a governor-general who failed in his duties toward the governed."[5]

Varela's *Project for Colonial Autonomous Government,* while it bore a resemblance in spirit to a memorial which his teacher, José Agustín Caballero, had prepared for the Cortes of Cádiz, was infinitely more detailed: it showed how the principles of self-government could be applied in practice and it gave cogent reasons for their adoption.

The *Diario de La Habana,* during the summer of 1823, reported the debates in the Cortes on Varela's *Project,* endorsing his views and denouncing those who opposed him.[6] Many reputed Spanish

---

[5] For text of Varela's "Proyecto," see his *Observaciones,* 1944 ed., pp. 181-87.

[6] José M. Chacón y Calvo, "El Padre Varela y la Autonomía Colonial," pp. 457-59. ("La Autonomía Colonial").

liberals, among them the "divine Argüelles," showed themselves reactionary where American problems were concerned. None the less, the report of the Commission on Colonial Government was being accepted, article by article, and might well have won final approval had the Cortes itself not come suddenly to an inglorious end. For over a century, Varela's proposals for autonomy were to lie buried in Spain's Archives of the Indies, until scholars of an independent Cuba, in honoring their pioneer social philosopher, resurrected them.

A second report which Varela drew up for the *Comisión de Ultramar* embodied recommendations on American independence. He did not hold with those who agitated for the breaking of Cuba's ties with the mother country; he consistently condemned armed rebellion, believing, as a true soldier of God, that the best weapons were those of the spirit. Yet he recognized the fact that much of the empire in America was irretrievably lost—that Spain was too feeble, militarily and politically and morally, to regain the lands which had declared themselves free. He proposed, therefore, that the new Spanish-American republics be invited to send delegates to meet on neutral ground with representatives of Spain, who would be empowered to treat with them on all matters, not excluding the recognition of their independence. To the ties of language, history, and culture, which could not be severed, let Spanish-speaking countries add treaties of friendship for economic progress and mutual betterment. Here, again, Varela was far ahead of his time, envisioning for Spain and her former dependencies a relationship such as our era has witnessed in Britain's Commonwealth of Nations.

American insurrectionists, Varela told his Spanish brethren, wish to affiance themselves to liberty. They have the advantage of immense territories and richly available manpower. If you subdued them, at enormous expense and effort, they would break loose again as soon as your armies were removed. They have little to fear from you if they regard you as oppressors, but much to hope if they regard you as friends and allies, or, better, as their brothers.[7]

---

[7]"Las Cortes," pp. 122-24.

To the reasonable propositions of Félix Varela, that His Majesty recognize gracefully the American *de facto* governments, the liberal constitutionalists, following the lead of Agustín Argüelles, declared that it was "unbecoming for Spain to speak of independence." The Cortes declined to vote on the matter.

Varela's third major legislative project during his year in the Cortes dealt with the abolition of slavery. Here was a subject on which he had felt strongly since, during his childhood in St. Augustine, his conscience had cried out against the slave auction in the church plaza. Christians were far from unanimous in condemning slavery; even in the republican United States, right down to the Civil War, there were clergymen, Catholic as well as Protestant, who defended the institution on moral and Biblical grounds. In Latin America, where racism was less deeply ingrained than in British territories, conservative clergy tended to side with the wealthy *haciendados,* to whom slave-owning seemed as necessary as to the Carolina and Virginia planters. But there had always been in the Spanish settlements, since the days of Bishop Bartolomé de Las Casas, contemporary of the *conquistadores,*[8] a murmur of religious protest against the subjugation of one human being by another. Of this latent Catholic concept, Father Félix Varela was a vocal exponent in the Cortes of 1822-23.

The inhabitants of Cuba were divided in their attitude toward slavery. Rodríguez tells us that, from 1790 on, *habaneros* at the court of Madrid had pressed for the outlawing of the slave trade, arguing that this government-sponsored traffic wrought injustice on human beings and damage to the basic economy of their island.[9] The *procurador* from Havana, Francisco de Arango y Parreño, was credited with inducing Ferdinand VII to enter in 1817 into the treaty with England for the outlawing of the slave trade. Yet when deputies at the Cortes of Cádiz offered plans for abolition in 1811, there was an outcry from Cuba. Sugar by this time was king on the island, and the growing and harvesting of cane seemed

---

[8]Casas, or as commonly in the United States, Las Casas, was born about 1474 in Seville and died 1566. His father, Franciscus, sailed on Columbus' second voyage. Bartolomé came to Cuba 1502, was ordained a Dominican priest 1510, and soon began a life-long campaign to improve the lot of Indians and Negroes in the Americas.
[9]*Vida,* p. 48, ftn.

to require cheap slave labor. Moreover, the slave population had increased so considerably during the previous two decades that the Spaniards and *criollos,* who were deeply distrustful of each other, both feared the effects of liberation. Meanwhile, Christian idealists at San Carlos and humanitarian intellectuals in the Royal Patriotic Society continued to plead against injustice.

For Félix Varela, representing his country's best thought in the Cortes, there was no middle ground on the question of slavery. It was wrong in itself, and it was harmful to his fatherland's way of life. Cuba, he declared, was destined by nature for greatness, but the presence of slavery stood in the way of achievement. The inhabitants of the island, he said, looked with horror at the enslavement of Africans which they found themselves compelled to countenance. Liberty for the Africans would coincide with the best interests of the proprietors and with the public security; yet the law, which alone could rectify the evils, had instead intensified them. Agriculture and the other arts had come to depend almost solely on slave labor, eliminating free workers from the economy. Should the slaves arise to demand by force the rights which had been denied them by law, they would be so preponderant in numbers as to be irresistible. "The white men of the Island of Cuba do not cease to congratulate themselves on having demolished the ancient despotism, recovering the sacred rights of free men. And do they ask that the natives of Africa be tranquil spectators of this jubilation? Fury and desperation oblige them to seek the alternatives of liberty or death!"

"Let us undeceive ourselves," the Varela *Memoria* to the Cortes went on. "Constitution, liberty, equality are synonymous; and their very names repudiate slavery and inequality of rights. In vain do we seek to reconcile these contradictions."[10]

Having established his case for abolition, Varela then showed, in a minutely detailed plan, how it could be accomplished without violation of the interests of proprietors and without disrupting the economy. The latest census, in 1817, had counted almost 315,000 whites to 240,000 Negroes, more than half of whom were slaves. With an average annual importation of 25,000 Africans since then,

---

[10]Excerpted from Varela's *Memoria* by Gay Calbó in "Las Cortes," pp. 118-19.

the color ratio was now about one to one. More than anything else, white Cubans feared the sort of bloody retribution which had accompanied the sudden political ascendancy of Negroes in nearby Haiti. Taking both vested interests and the public weal into account, Varela's plan not only called for the abolition of the slave trade; it also allowed for the reimbursement of owners, the breaking up of the vast sugar plantations, the diversification of the rural economy, and the gradual absorption of former slaves into the free community.

Cuban historians have pointed out that their country would have escaped much future heartache had Varela's plan been adopted.

> Father Varela, the Cuban deputy, many years before abolitionist ideas triumphed in the United States, planned to the most minute detail the emancipation of slaves in Cuba. . . . Neither France nor England, and less even the United States, well informed though the three nations were of the course of events in the Spanish Cortes, stirred themselves to aid the Cuban delegates in their efforts to extinguish in Cuba the institution of slavery, which Spain was to perpetuate for another two-thirds of a century . . . .
> The consequences of the abolition of slavery in 1822 would have been of extraordinary importance to Cuba, not only because the measure would have given a mortal blow to the gigantic development of the sugar industry then in progress, but also because it would have forced the division and subdivision of the country's arable land and established on a solid foundation a numerous rural population growing what was needed for its own subsistence, as the project of Father Varela envisioned, and would at the same time have redistributed the national wealth of Cuba and avoided its concentration in a few hands. This reform, in short, by redeeming socially three hundred thousand Negro slaves and producing an equalitarian integration of the Cuban population without the addition of the half million more Africans who arrived up to 1871, would have revolutionized the Cuban economy.[11]

But the turbulence of the times kept Varela's project from reaching the floor of the Cortes. From 1827 to 1841, more than 300 cargoes of slaves came to the island's ports. By 1846, more than half of the 950,000 inhabitants were colored, with the pro-

---

[11]Herminio Portell Vilá, *Historia de Cuba, en sus relaciones con los Estados Unidos y España,* 1 ("1512-1853") : 208.

portion mounting constantly as more slave ships arrived and free white immigration diminished; and the problem of abolition became increasingly complex. Although right-thinking patriots continued to agree with Varela on the absolute necessity for abolition, it was not until 1886 that slavery was legally ended in Cuba.

* * * * *

The long confusion which the French Revolutionary armies and the legions of Napoleon had spread throughout Europe had given rise to the Holy Alliance, pledged to support the restored Bourbons on the thrones of France and Spain and Naples and to suppress any renewed agitation for republican rights. Now the Spanish monarch, Ferdinand VII, was a virtual prisoner of the Cortes which he had been forced to convene. While outwardly cooperative with the Assembly, Ferdinand was sending distress calls to his "holy allies," who had leagued together to keep Europe pacified forever under the treaties of the Vienna Congress.

Meeting at Verona, representatives of Prussia, Russia, Austria, and France agreed on the need to extirpate Spanish republicanism. Early in 1823, a crack French army descended from the north. The upper provinces of Spain welcomed the invaders as liberators from menacing infidels. Soon the French were approaching Madrid; and the members of the Cortes, deep in a clause-by-clause debate on Article 156 of Varela's *Project for Colonial Autonomy,* picked up their papers and fled to Seville, taking King Ferdinand with them. About this time they elected Tomás Gener of Matanzas to be President of the Cortes.

At the height of the excitement, with the people's delegates laboring to build by debate and decision the policies which the encircling guns of the reaction would soon destroy, Félix Varela heard read in the Cortes, on June 26, 1823, a document "which historically constitutes the first manifestation of the rebellion of Cuban youth."[12] His students from the class on the Constitution had written to the Cortes in praise of its wisdom and its enthusiasm for liberty, vowing their eternal fealty to the Constitution, their abhorrence of tyranny, and their support of those who risked

---

[12] *El padre Varela,* p. 267. The letter is there reproduced from *El revisor político y literario,* Havana, Apr. 14, 1823.

calumny and horrid persecution in their consecration to just principles. "Immortal legislators," the missive concluded, "receive now the sincere expression of gratitude and burning love from certain citizens who, although sorrowfully apart from the scene of such notable political events, desire in their hearts naught but the happiness of the nation, its independence and liberty." Appended were 43 signatures, among them the later luminaries Domingo Delmonte, Bernardo de Echavarría y O'Gavan, Fernando de Castro, José de Bulnes, Juan Francisco Rodríguez, Francisco de Sentmanat, Anacleto Bermúdez, José Duque de Heredia, and José de la Luz; also several priests and a second lieutenant of the Havana regiment. In the tenebrous days ahead, this testimonial of support from his Cuban disciples would warm the spirit of Félix Varela.

Generals were defecting from the patriot cause, earliest among them Enrique O'Donnell, brother of the nefarious Leopoldo who was to become the scourge of Cuba. Town after village admitted passively or with studied hurrahs the King's foreign relief forces. The French pushed on down the Peninsula, and Cortes and King moved again, to a showdown stand at Cádiz.

It was a cardinal principle of Catholic political philosophy, enunciated in the 17th century by the Spaniard Suárez and by the Italian, St. Robert Bellarmine (1542-1621), and restated for the nineteenth century by Félix Varela, that a monarch who did not serve his people could be removed by them. The Cortes of 1823 found King Ferdinand inept, unpatriotic, and generally unfitted to rule, and they voted to depose him and to institute a Regency until an adequate successor could be installed. Along with the majority of the deputies, three Cuban delegates put their names to this action—Varela and Gener and Santos Suárez.[13]

Hardly had this vote been registered when the armies of France, besieging Cádiz by land and attacking by sea, put to rout the forces behind the Riego government. Félix Varela has left an account of the precipitate defection of the generals and the flight of the Spanish deputies.[14] Argüelles and several companions took

---

[13] *Reforma filosófica*, p. 120.
[14] "Las Cortes," p. 125.

haven in England. Others hastened to Italy but found there no refuge.

Ferdinand VII, restored by French arms to his despotic throne, took fearful vengeance. The unfortunate Riego was hanged, and his body cut into five sections, to be displayed in five cities which had sympathized with his revolt. The King scrapped the Constitution, dissolved the Cortes, and proscribed every deputy who had voted for the Regency. Suspected liberals were rooted out and summarily executed. In Barcelona alone there were over 1,000 victims; and France and Russia, although Ferdinand's partners, protested the wanton bloodletting.

Varela escaped from Cádiz at night in a small barque under gunfire from a French man-of-war. He and Gener and Santos Suárez fled to Gibraltar. Here they assessed their position. Nowhere on the continent of Europe would they be safe from the vigilantes of reaction. Return to Cuba they could not; for that unhappy island, with a vengeful Ferdinand restored in Spain, could hope for no further leniency. Varela in particular, because he had spearheaded the battles for Cuban autonomy, for recognition of the South American republics, and for the abolition of slavery, would be a target for royal retribution wherever the Holy Alliance held sway. But in the United States of America, now in its fourth decade of life as a nation dedicated to human freedom and dignity, the Cubans who had bared their necks for those principles could expect a welcome.

It was decided. Poor, disillusioned, branded as traitors, the three deputies took ship for America. They crossed the wintry Atlantic in a freighter, the *Draper C. Thorndike,* which carried a cargo of salt and almonds.

They reached New York on December 15, 1823, in the midst of a blizzard.

While they were in passage, President James Monroe, prodded by England's Canning, had proclaimed in Congress the Monroe Doctrine, warning Spain's friendly and not-so-friendly allies to keep their hands off her one-time American empire: "We could not view an interposition for oppressing them [the Spanish-American republics] or controlling in any other manner their destiny by any European power, in any other light than as a manifestation of an unfriendly disposition toward the United States."[15] Thus Cuba and her Latin-American sisters had moved almost at a stroke from the orbit of Europe into that of their vigorous North American neighbor. The first Spanish translation of the Monroe Doctrine, made, within two weeks of its proclamation, by a Cuban, Mariano Cubí y Soler, was forwarded to President Monroe from Baltimore the very day that Varela and his companions arrived in New York.[16] In Manhattan, that December 15, the three refugees from the sunny Caribbean plowed through snow and ice to the office of Goodhue and Waters, commission merchants, on South Street near Battery Place. When Jonathan Goodhue learned their identity, he called his clerk, Cristóbal Madan, once a favorite pupil of Félix Varela at San Carlos. This lad, now seventeen, embraced his master warmly. Cristobalito conducted the wayfarers to a boardinghouse. He became interpreter and guide and sponsor to Félix Varela, who could read English but could not converse in it.

There was a considerable Spanish-speaking community in commercial New York: merchants, bankers, world travelers, political exiles. A testimonial dinner was proposed to honor the newly arrived delegates from the Spanish Cortes. Varela and his colleagues were touched, but they declined the honor. This was not, to their way of thinking, a time for celebration.

* * * *

Félix Varela was thirty-five years old. Priest, philosopher, teacher, orator, jurist—he had proven himself in every capacity. He had been Fortune's favorite—blessed in his fatherland, in his family, his friends, his rich talent, in success, in opportunity for service, and in the esteem and love of those whose lives he touched. Now, when he should be most productive, all had been snatched from him. He was a stranger in a foreign land, banned from the lush warm island which nature had endowed to be happy; and his shabby clerical robe could not protect his nervous, asthmatic frame from the unaccustomed icy blasts.

He faced an indefinite sojourn in a country whose language he

---

[15]Annual message to Congress, Dec. 2, 1823; *U.S. Congress, Debates and proceedings, 18 Cong., Sess. 1, Dec. 1, 1823-May 27, 1824,* 1: 11-19.
[16]Portell Vilá, *Historia,* 1: 240-41.

did not speak, whose climate chilled his marrow, whose people looked askance at swarthy, non-English-speaking foreigners. He must learn the prevailing tongue. He must find a source of physical sustenance and an outlet for his intellectual energy.

His stay in Madrid had matured his understanding and angered his spirit. He had gone to Spain with affectionate respect for the land which had produced his dashing father, his Morales grandfather, and his predecessors in thought—Suárez and Vitoria and Martínez and Feijóo; the land which had harbored the persecuted O'Reillys and the O'Donnells, which had effected the Constitution of 1812 and had sent Las Casas to govern Cuba and Espada to be its Bishop. One year in the Cortes had disabused him of youthful sentimentality. He saw Spain now as a nation disintegrated, unfit for empire—its King a treacherous weakling, its vaunted liberals pusillanimous and small, its men of intellect receding into legend. The judgment of Joseph-Miguel Guardia, writing in the *Revue philosophique de la France et de L'Étranger* near the close of the century, is that Spain after the death of Jovellanos in 1811 had but two great thinkers, the Cubans Varela and Luz y Caballero. Philosophy, he said, had taken root in Cuba but it could not acclimate itself in Spain. The two great Cubans owed nothing either to the Mother Country or to Latin America. *"Les sociétés qui produisent de tels hommes ne sauraient périr,"* he concluded.[17]

"Spain," wrote the trenchant Varela, "is a cadaver."[18]

The expatriate had two essential interests—his Faith and his fatherland. He was a priest in a universal Church. The Catholic Diocese of New York, then under its first resident bishop, Irish-born John Connolly, was a mission endeavor. In the metropolis it could boast of but two small churches, old St. Patrick's Cathedral in Mott Street and the pioneer chapel of St. Peter's in Barclay Street, measuring 48 feet by 80. Its 25,000 believers, struggling for survival in an Anglo-Protestant milieu, were served by a shifting

---

[17] J.-M. Guardia, "Philosophes Espagnols de Cuba: Félix Varela—José de la Luz," p. 183. Gaspar Melchior de Jovellanos, born Asturias 1744, author, jurist, cabinet minister under Godoy; died a fugitive from the invading French.
[18] Varela to Joel R. Poinsett, from New York, January 27, 1825, "Joel R. Poinsett Papers," Hist. Soc. of Pa. Also quoted by Portell Vilá, "Sobre el Ideario Político del Padre Varela," p. 256. ("Ideario Político").

handful of priests, missionaries from foreign lands, uprooted, restless, outspoken men, their unmitred leader the doughty John Power, alumnus of Maynooth and darling of his Irish flock at St. Peter's. Bishop Connolly needed consecrated and loyal hands; but he mistrusted Varela's progressive ideas and his political involvements. Before inviting him to perform sacerdotal functions in New York, Bishop Connolly asked that El Padre produce credentials.

In Cuba, Bishop Espada was fighting a battle of his own. The social reformer had fallen afoul of Ferdinand's reactionary viceroys. The Church was at his heels for his intense espousal of the new thought at San Carlos. Pleading age and illness, he begged to be relieved of his charge—let O'Gavan, his good right hand, assume the reins. But Madrid remembered O'Gavan as a deputy in the Cortes of 1812, as a protagonist of Locke and Condillac and Pestalozzi, as a foe of the Holy Office of the Inquisition. So the Coadjutor of Havana was summoned to Spain. He was offered a bishopric there—where he could be watched and checkmated, or an archiepiscopal seat in the Antilles, where he could be called to account for Espada. O'Gavan, from prudence rather than humility, declined these equivocal honors, while Bishop Espada toiled under problems more urgent than the certification of his protégé Varela.

Félix Varela, meanwhile, did not wait in idleness. Madan and fellow-Cubans in New York had a story to quicken his pulse. Commercially, their native island was prosperous—thanks to trade concessions which Arango had won from Ferdinand. Ideologically, she was facing desolation. Two weak administrators, Nicolás Mahy and Sebastian Kindelán, had been succeeded in 1823 by General Francisco Dionisio Vives, capable, suave, commissioned to render the Queen of the Antilles a fortress against attack from without and insurrection from within. Vives had served as Spanish ambassador to Washington, and Monroe's puritanical Secretary of State, John Quincy Adams, described him as "one of the most upright and honorable men with whom it has ever been my fortune to hold political relation." Many Cuban nationalists, knowing him at closer range, declared him "a military man, vicious, unmoral, and cynical."[19]

---

[19]Portell Vilá, *Historia*, p. 231. The Adams quotation is taken by Portell

HE CHARTS THE WAY TO FREEDOM

The new governor uncovered in Cuba the scheme of a Masonic club, the *Rayos y Soles de Bolívar,* for inviting Simón Bolívar to invade the island and annex it to his tri-partite Gran Columbia. This conspiracy gave Vives the excuse he needed for ridding Cuba of the remnants of freedom. The constitutional law course at the Seminary was abandoned. José Antonio Saco, propounding the views of his master in the chair of philosophy at San Carlos, was forced to flee, leaving his post to another Varela disciple, more profound than Saco but less politically militant—José de la Luz y Caballero. The poet, José María de Heredia y Campazano, also chose exile: Cuba's most vibrant lyrical voice was that of this young revolutionary. The island's zealous young intellectuals, her hope for growth and glory, had to leave her cities or perish.

Already in New York as fugitives were Varela's friends and disciples, Francisco García, Gaspar Betancourt Cisneros and the poets Heredia and José Tolón, also Francisco Sentmanat, a poet who had signed the letter to the Cortes and was plotting to help Mexico annex Cuba. José Antonio Saco arrived soon after.

Varela saw that, interpreting each the master's message in his own way, his disciples were fragmenting their efforts and traveling, in some instances, the road to destruction. His moral authority remained paramount among them. Havana might not hear his voice, but it could read his words. Pending the settlement of his clerical status in New York, he addressed himself wholly to the problems of Cuba.

Philadelphia was at this time the "Athens of America"—the center of literary, scientific, and liberal political life. It was also headquarters of an active secret organization of Freemasons whose agents were fomenting republican, anti-Spanish, and often anti-Catholic agitation in Mexico, Central America, the Antilles, and South America. The Quaker City's Masons directed much of their attention to Cuba; succeeding, so Havana's conservatives charged, even to the point of influencing Bishop Espada. Varela, who had been stricken with asthma and tubercular coughing in his first frigid months in New York, transferred his residence to Phila-

---

Vilá from a letter of Adams to Channing from Quincy, Aug. 11, 1837, publ. in *N. Y. Herald-Tribune,* Aug. 22, 1933.

delphia, either for health or in pursuit of a more congenial intellectual climate.

From Philadelphia he published an enlargement of the *Lecciones de filosofía*—the second edition under his signature, although an unsupervised second version had been issued in Havana while he was abroad. The Quaker City edition, 1824, contained for the benefit of Spanish-language readers a compendium of recent scientific advances made in Europe and America.

More immediate and more dramatic in its impact on Cuban life and on the career of its author was the Spanish magazine which he inaugurated in 1824—*El habanero, papel político, científico y literario*. Its first three numbers were issued from Philadelphia and the next four from New York. José Antonio Saco, fresh from the political byways of Cuba, probably collaborated with him in this venture, and most certainly brought him up to date on the island's internal agitation.

"Literary" *El Habanero* was not, except in the lucid style of its author-editor. "Scientific" it was to a degree, especially in the early numbers. It informed Cuban youth of recent efforts to gauge the temperature of sea water at great depths; of Professor William Wollaston's report to the Royal Society of London, June 1823, on the action of magnetism on titanium; of varying conclusions among scientists on the velocity of sound; of the experiences of Professor Benjamin Silliman of Yale with Wollaston's cryoforus, an apparatus for illustrating the freezing of water by its own evaporation; and of a new device for measuring the speed of a vessel. Saco was studying chemistry, and Varela was a man who believed one must keep abreast of all that was new in science.

From the beginning, however, *El Habanero* was essentially political, and with succeeding numbers it became almost exclusively so. It represented the effort of Cuba's ex-deputy to analyze contemporary developments for his followers and advise them on a course of action, to mold "a public opinion among the Cubans concerning the best form of Government for the people."[20]

The article titles of *El Habanero* show how Varela's thought ran: Political Subterfuges; Considerations on the Actual State of

---

[20] Paul J. Foik, *Pioneer Catholic journalism*, p. 58. (Foik).

the Island of Cuba; Conspiracies in the Island of Cuba; Secret Societies in the Island of Cuba; Tranquillity of the Island of Cuba; Ecclesiastical State of the Island of Cuba; Scare Reports in Havana; Love of Americans for Independence; Letter to a Friend Replying to Certain Ideological Doubts; Comparison of a Revolution by the Inhabitants of Cuba and One Brought About by an Invasion of Foreign Troops; French Policy in Relation to America; Dialogue in This City between a Partisan of Cuban Independence (himself) and One Opposed to It; Reflections on the Situation in Spain; Persecution of This Paper in the Island of Cuba; Military Commission in Havana; Run Run; Must Cuba Unite Itself to One of the Governments of the American Continent to Free Itself from Spain? Is it Necessary, for a Political Change in the Island of Cuba, to Hope for Troops from Colombia or Mexico? What Must One Do in Case of an Invasion? Is Invasion Likely? Is There Unity in the Island of Cuba? Two Words to the Enemies of *El Habanero;* Royal Order of Ferdinand VII Prohibiting *El Habanero;* Thoughts on the Royal Decree; Frustrated Hopes.[21]

Varela had left his island a loyal Spaniard, believing with a fervor both religious and patriotic in the power of constitutionalism to reform the monarchy. He had come to know Spain's political machine at first hand; had seen the sophisticated shallowness of its so-called liberals and the vicious duplicity of its king:—turncoats, all of them, not only suiting their policies to the vicissitudes of the hour, but denying the thoughts they had expressed a moment before. Facing reality in Cádiz, he had lost the easy illusions of youth. He could tell his *habaneros* now that they had nothing but despoliation to hope for from Madrid. Only their own resolve could make them free. They must unite on a single policy, and follow it through, at whatever cost, to the goal of independence.

But first he must convince them that they should and ultimately would be free.

The patriots of Cuba were desperately disunited.

There were those among Varela's friends and disciples who hoped for the restoration of constitutional government in Spain and

---

[21]Translated from Spanish original of 1945 ed. of *El habanero.*

her colonies—Saco would later be their spokesman. Others, like Cristóbal Madan and Gaspar Betancourt Cisneros, preferred annexation of the island by the United States. Arango y Parreña, remembering the favors he had extracted for Cuba from Ferdinand VII, wanted to ride along with the monarchy. Some sought liberation for the slaves, others would deny colored freemen the rights of citizens. The *Soles de Bolívar* advocated an invasion from Colombia; failing that, they joined Cubans in Mexico who wanted that untried but ambitious republic to free their homeland.

Félix Varela attempted to sift wisdom from the shifting sands and treacherous cross-currents of Cuban agitation. Let his people beware of political fakirs who traffic on their faith and their patriotism. Let them avoid secret societies which divide the people with ineffectual conspiracies. Let them not antagonize the clergy against their cause. Let them realize that their fatherland owed its sons nothing, but they owed it their fealty unto imprisonment and death. "One prisoner is worth a thousand proclamations."

Moral strength, he proclaimed, was more effective than intrigue. "I never have believed in the patriotism of a rogue."

The need of Cuba was for independence; of that he was certain. His political understanding had caught up with his philosophy; he who had once eulogized Ferdinand VII, who had viewed the Cortes with awe, now knew that in government, as in education, his people must take the broom and sweep away all that was not useful. He spoke, says Manuel Bisbé, with an accent heard nowhere else in Cuba until Martí.[22] "The independence of Cuba is not an object of choice but of necessity." Americans are born with freedom in their blood.

How best to separate from Spain without forging new shackles was not so simple. Was foreign help necessary or desirable? He did not think so, but many of his compatriots did. He preferred the long, slow process of self-liberation. Let Cubans not invite invasion and conquest when the goal was independence. If, however, the counsels of others were followed, and outsiders helped in driving out Spain, let those auxiliaries be paid off at once to

---

[22]Manuel Bisbé, "Los Grandes Movimientos Políticos Cubanos en la Colonia; 2: Independentismo: I. Movimientos Anteriores a 1868," in *Cuadernos de historia habanera,* no. 24 (1943) : 9. ("Independentismo").

leave Cubans alone in the enjoyment of their much-desired freedom. His warning against supposed friends from without who might use the island's internal crises to establish an alien tyranny today rings prophetic.

He envisioned the Western Hemisphere as spiritually united by the "American principle" of government deriving authority not from "legitimacy" but from the will of the people; in America, he said, there are no *conquistadores,* and any nation seeking dominion must expect reaction from the entire continent. Here, says a twentieth-century Cuban sociologist, lies the germ of pan-Americanism, of an idealist's dream which, for Cuba at least, could not be realized until the island was a free and independent member of the American family of nations.[23]

El Habanero was smuggled into Cuba from Philadelphia through Yucatan and New Orleans and distributed clandestinely. It contained up to 40 pages per issue; but its dimensions were small enough to permit folding it into a letter. The magazine caused violent repercussions. Varela's adherents circulated it avidly, although the royal government, when apprised of its existence, found it almost impossible to obtain.

One cannot pinpoint the influence of such a publication; however, the Cuban struggle throughout the nineteenth century did follow the guidelines laid down by the patriot priest. The island did not in its pursuit of freedom risk invasion from South or Central America or annexation by the United States. Rather, the self-determination to sever the Spanish ties from within grew steadily, fostered by such inheritors of the torch as Luz y Caballero, Rafael María de Mendive, and José Martí. Spain, having failed both in conciliation and in repression, knew her authority untenable when, at the close of the century, the American Rough-Riders assisted the final push toward independence.

As immediate evidence of their support, Félix Varela's followers in Havana collected 4,000 *duros* ("hard" dollars) to further the efforts of their penniless master in the States.

The government in Cuba meanwhile was planning counter-actions. Early in 1825, a pamphlet appeared in Spanish, whose

---

[23]Cf. Rosario Rexach, *El pensamiento de Félix Varela y la formación de la conciencia cubana,* pp. 117f.

title may be translated: "Notes on *El Habanero,* a Periodical Which the Priest Félix Varela Publishes in Philadelphia, Written by a Pupil of This Same Varela." It was published in Puerto Principe and financed by an aggregation of royalists—mayors, aldermen, and an attorney-general.[24] Its aim was to discredit the author of *El Habanero.*

The Varela *discípulo* who authorized this attack is identified by Dr. Hernández Travieso as Juan Agustín de Ferrety, the man who had betrayed the conspiracy of the *Rayos y Soles de Bolívar,* selling their plans to Governor Vives.[25] Of this informer, Varela had, without naming him, used hard words in the very first number of *El Habanero.* The article headed "Conspiracies in the Island of Cuba," carried a condemnation aimed at "the infamous system of spies" and at Ferrety in particular.

> The majority of informers become such to place themselves under cover; but they were accomplices of those they denounce, and I do not know if the Government is ignorant that the prisoners, or at least the majority of them, are not those who were at the bottom of, or were most prominent in the conspiracy, and that if these matters were prosecuted with rigor, it would be necessary to turn whole cities into jails.[26]

Ferrety's pamphlet, printed "with permission of the government," declared in its foreword that Cuba required the protection of a European power, which could be none other than Spain. "Independence would be her ruin, because it would deprive her of her tranquillity and also of many benefits without useful return."[27] The author, professing to weep for the lost reputation of his master, declared that Varela, who had once eulogized Ferdinand VII, was now motivated by hatred and a desire for revenge, which he concealed in a pretense of patriotism. Cuba, said Ferrety, could not become independent, for she had not the force to oust Spanish arms, nor did her inhabitants desire to trade their present prosperity for an untenable freedom. As to the prisoners from the *Soles de Bolívar* plot, Ferrety inquired with seeming innocence:

---

[24]Reprinted in *El habanero,* pp. 222-45.
[25]*El padre Varela,* pp. 295, 332.
[26]*El habanero,* no. 1, "Conspiraciones en la Isla de Cuba," p. 22.
[27]*Ibid.,* "Apuntaciones Sobre *El Habanero,*" p. 224.

"He who conspires to change the form of government under which he lives, is he not a criminal in all parts of the world?"[28]

For an assault like Ferrety's, Varela had ready response. *El Habanero* continued to hammer at the ultimate, historic necessity of independence for Cuba. He was trying to prepare the minds of Cubans for a peaceful change, under which they should be in position to give law to themselves, not receive it from anyone. If he spoke for only a crazy handful, and the masses wished to remain Spanish, why the sacrifices and sufferings now demanded of the populace by the authorities in the name of "security"? Those who find it necessary to be or to pretend to be enemies of *El Habanero* ought to note that they are on the wrong track, for this paper only expresses that which all the world is feeling and cannot be diverted from feeling.[29]

To Francisco Vives, Governor of Cuba, the outspoken Félix Varela seemed a living menace. Vives wanted the *independente* liquidated, unostentatiously if possible; and his sycophants knew it. They raised the sum of 30,000 pesos to hire an assassin. The agent left Cuba, his passage paid. He arrived in the United States in March 1825. A letter from a friend in Havana advised Varela of the man's purpose; but the priest did not let it interfere with his activities.

Word of the plot was flashed by the underground among the expatriates in New York and Philadelphia. They were warned to watch out for the would-be murderer, whose infamous name they would not speak publicly. A half century later, Varela's biographer stated darkly, "His identity is known to us, but we do not wish it enshrined in history, at least by any fault of ours."[30]

When Varela's friends urged him to go into hiding, he smiled at their solicitude and continued producing *El Habanero,* saying that a good priest has no fear of death. They notified the mayor and the chief of police, who, whatever protective measures they may have taken, did not arrest their man. As events turned out, interference by the public authorities proved unnecessary.

---

[28] *Ibid.,* p. 237.
[29] *Ibid.,* no. 5, "Dos Palabras a Los Enemigos de *El Habanero,*" p. 198.
[30] *Vida,* p. 147. *El padre Varela,* p. 329, says the man was One-Eyed Morejón, one of Vives' bullies, and that Irish Catholic immigrants whom Varela served as priest intimidated the hired assassin into leaving New York.

The would-be killer soon reëmbarked for Havana. Twenty years later, in *Verdad,* a Spanish paper published by Saco in New York City, Varela told how he had come face to face with the hired assassin and talked him out of his evil errand. Weapons and the lure of money were no match for the intense patriotism of the outlawed priest.

For the wretched man who had been sent to slay him, Varela could feel compassion. But for those who hatched the plot he showed massive scorn:

> Do you think you can destroy Truth by assassinating him who speaks it? Ah, She is superior to all human efforts, and a recourse such as you have taken only serves to weaken your cause. Nothing proves more the soundness of what I have said than the method of attack which you have adopted. I could die at the hands of an assassin, but assuredly you would not gain.
>
> I have done nothing but help men to know one another better, and know their situation, so that in an event which is by nature inevitable they will calm the passions and prevent disaster. . . . If this is a crime, here is a crime protective of humanity and conducive to justice, and here is a criminal who glories to be one.[31]

* * * * *

Although the attempt on Varela's life stemmed from Cuba, its origins traced to events in Spain. The mother country was determined to retain what hold it could on its fractious colonies, and particularly to keep in hand the Pearl of the Antilles. Orders went out to His Majesty's ministers in all foreign parts to watch out for aid channeled to Spanish-American rebels.

El Habanero was already half a year and three issues old, and had just moved from Philadelphia to New York, when Hilario de Rivas y Salmón, Spanish minister in the Quaker City, became sharply concerned over its existence. Aware, perhaps, that he had been less than duly vigilant, he tried to shift the blame to Don Tomás Stoughton, the consul in New York, writing curtly to that official on January 2, 1825:

I know for certain that Dr. Varela, ex-deputy to the Cortes,

---

[31] *El habanero,* "Suplemento al No. 3 de *El Habanero,*" pp. 152-53.

is giving to light a paper which excites the inhabitants of the Island of Cuba to independence, of which two or three numbers have already appeared. I have marveled greatly that you have not written me anything about it, when His Majesty has charged his consuls with the greatest vigilance in all that relates to the Americas.

See to it that you obtain and send to me three copies of each number.[32]

If this letter was intended to intimidate its recipient, it failed in its purpose. Stoughton, partner in the importing firm of a staunch Irish rebel, Dominick Lynch, was a founding father of St. Peter's Parish and a personal acquaintance of Father Varela. He had lived and prospered in New York long enough—albeit as His Spanish Majesty's minister—to appreciate the advantages of liberty, American style, and the disabilities suffered by Cuban colonials. He had a ready answer (January 5) for his colleague in Philadelphia:

I have the honor to tell you that the individual you mention has recently come here from Philadelphia, where he had resided three months, busy with the publication of two works, one on Philosophy, the other on Politics. . . . I was able very easily to borrow the volume on Philosophy, but the other no one had seen or was able to give an account of it; but after I had inquired very diligently, a Spaniard named Picard lent me for a quarter of an hour, before embarking for Havana, a single sample, which he said he had obtained in New York; it was a pamphlet of about forty pages, octavo, labeled with the number 1, and entitled 'political and literary paper, by Rev. Félix Varela, printed in Philadelphia in the year 1824.' I was only able to glance at it. . . . I am now told that the second number has appeared in Philadelphia, in the same style as the first, but it has not been possible for me to see a copy!

Rivas did not enjoy being reminded by Stoughton that Varela's pleas for Cuban independence had originated in Philadelphia, and he wished to clear himself with the royal government. On January 7, he forwarded to His Majesty's Secretary of State a copy of the second number of *El Habanero*, with a promise of others when he could obtain them. The publication, he warned, "has as its object to cause revolt in the Island of Cuba," and it "speaks of arms in

---

[32]Varela, *Observaciones*, pp. 189-92, gives the Rivas and Stoughton letters in full.

this place for the insurgents, more considerable than those of which I have had information." The Consul in New York, added Rivas, had been remiss in not reporting the existence of this seditious publication and in pretending he could not find copies of it.

In Cuba, simultaneously, Governor Vives, not counting on the success of the assassination plot, was taking stringent measures to prevent the circulation of *El Habanero*. The attacks on his publication pained Father Varela more than those against his life, and he lamented:

> All the letters which I have received from that island convince me that my poor *Habanero* is suffering the most cruel persecution. But why it, in particular? *El Habanero* is persecuted at the same time that all confess that it tells the truth, and when the government itself gives irrefutable proofs that it is fully convinced of this. Even the most bloodthirsty enemies of independence write that it will be inevitable if the Colombians make a landing, and that such a landing is almost inevitable; they confess that the fate of the Island will be infinitely less happy if it owes its freedom to a foreign army than if it obtains it by its own efforts; and yet the author of *El Habanero* is called a perverse man, an enemy of his fatherland, because he has had the courage to say publicly that which no one denies in private, when silence serves no other purpose than to give time to an incurable evil.[33]

For himself, Varela maintained that, having withstood the attempts which certain persons had made to rid themselves of him forever, he was now *"perfectamente curado del mal de espanto"*—"entirely immune to fear."[34]

Realizing that *El Habanero* spoke the truth about the dangers to Cuba, and finding it impossible to keep up personally with the schemes for rebellion and the threats of invasion from North and South and West, Ferdinand VII decided to shift the burden to Governor Vives. On May 28, 1825, the monarch issued a Royal Order declaring the island in a state of virtual siege, placing it under martial law, and giving extraordinary emergency powers to the governor-general:

---

[33] *El habanero,* no. 4, "Persecución de Este Papel en la Isla de Cuba," p. 157.
[34] *Ibid.,* no. 4, "Carta del Editor de Este Papel a Un Amigo," p. 176.

Desirous of preventing the embarrassments which under extraordinary circumstances might arise from a division in the command, it has pleased H. M., in conformity with the advice of his council of ministers, to authorize your excellency, fully investing you with the whole extent of power which by the royal ordinances is granted to the governors of besieged towns. . . .

H. M. expects that . . . Y. E. will use the most wakeful prudence and reserve, joined to an indefatigable activity and unyielding firmness, in the exercise of your excellency's authority, and trusts that as your excellency shall by this very pleasure and graciousness of H. M. be held to a more strict responsibility, Y. E. will redouble his vigilance that the laws be observed, that justice be administered, that H. M. faithful vassals be protected and rewarded, and punishment without partiality or indulgence inflicted on those who, forgetful of their duty and their obligations to the best and most benevolent of monarchs, shall oppose those laws, decidedly abetting sinister plots.[35]

The blackout of civil rights and privileges and the tyrannical "emergency" measures thus decreed for the people of Cuba persisted through much of the nineteenth century, under a succession of governors, less urbane than Vives, who were nefarious for cupidity, cruelty, and unabashed despotism.

Concurrent acts of His Majesty's government indicate that Félix Varela was considered one of those ungrateful subjects who by "abetting sinister plots" had called down the royal ire on Cuba. On May 11, 1825, the High Court of Seville affirmed sentences of death, with confiscation of all their goods, against Varela and 65 other surviving deputies to the Cortes of 1822-23. As it concerned Varela, so long as he remained in the Land of Liberty the sentence was a futile threat.

Against Varela's publication, however, Ferdinand instituted more effective action. On June 27, 1825, he issued another Royal Order, banning *El Habanero* from Spain and adjacent islands and enjoining his officials to take all necessary measures to secure compliance:

Don Félix Varela, ex-deputy of the so-called Cortes, now actually a refugee in the United States of America, is publish-

---

[35] [Kimball], *Cuba and the Cubans,* pp. 55-56.

ing there, a tract called *El Habanero,* in which, not content with inciting the loyal vassals of His Majesty to rebellion, he carries his audacity to the point of seeking to injure the sacred character of his lawful Sovereign.[36]

Varela, learning of the edict against his periodical from a Havana newspaper, boldly headlined it in his next number. He had long since proclaimed his indifference to the monarch's opinions: "Whether or not Ferdinand wishes it, be what may the sentiment of his vassals in the Island of Cuba, the revolution in that place is inevitable. The difference will be only one of time and manner."[37] Now he declared that he who issued the order either had not read *El Habanero,* or had read it seeking to find in it that which best fitted his intentions.

> The author of *El Habanero* has not injured, nor does he hope to injure, the character of anyone; and he is far, far from considering Ferdinand VII as his lawful sovereign. . . . The rebellion to which I have incited the vassals of Ferdinand VII in the Island of Cuba has been nothing other than a necessary escape in unavoidable danger. . . . All the world knows that I am in favor of independence, but with great caution I have always directed my reflections to a point on which all parties agree, and that is: on the necessity to save our Island, and with her the fortunes and even the lives of her present inhabitants. And is rebellion a recourse mandated by nature, and sanctioned by the sacred laws of self-preservation? Yes, I say; and I say so even to the defenders of the unlimited rights of kings.

Having reaffirmed the rightness of his crusade for Cuban independence, Varela challenged the King to gainsay him. "Whatever anyone says—all the royal mandates in the world would not avail to cloud the palpable truths which *El Habanero* has spoken and will continue to speak."[38]

Varela continued his magazine almost a year after the edict against it, defying both royal wrath and threats of death. The seventh and probably final number was issued from New York in the spring of 1826. It told of the efforts of Henry Clay, Secretary

---

[36]Quoted in *El habanero,* no. 6, "Real Orden de Fernando VII Prohibiendo 'El Habanero,'" p. 201.
[37]*Ibid.,* no. 2, "Tranquilidad de la Isla de Cuba," p. 60.
[38]*Ibid.,* no. 6, "Reflexiones Sobre La Real Orden Anterior," pp. 203-06.

of State, to enlist Russia on the side of the United States in mediation between Spain and her self-liberated American colonies. It pointed out that the United States' naval force stationed in the Pacific was now apparently on its way to the Caribbean. It discussed the economic condition of Cuba and the false sense of political security achieved there by the royal regime.[39] Censorship of incoming mail, however, gave the paper little chance of reaching its intended readers in Cuba. José Ignacio Rodríguez saw Number 7 in New York about 1876; but the Cuban scholars who republished *El Habanero* in 1945 could not locate a single copy of this final number.

Many causes contributed to the demise of *El Habanero*, of which the Cuban embargo was but one. There was the difficulty of getting it published—its seven numbers had been issued from the nation's two principal cities on the presses of four different printers. The mortal hazards to any who cooperated in smuggling it into "besieged" Cuba may have sobered the ardent editor. Also, he must have felt that his aim had been accomplished. He had analyzed the situation for his Cubans—he had laid guide lines to their eventual independence. More than that he could not, for he was essentially a man of peace. Immediate revolt within Fortress Cuba would have scant hope of success. Invasion from without could not assure liberty. Better to sow the seeds of freedom, and let time and the growing national awareness reap the fruits. Meanwhile, he had been accepted as priest into the New York diocese, and he must be busy in the vineyards of the Lord.

Today, more than a century after his death, his countrymen revere Varela as the prime apostle of a Cuba independent without obligation to any other nation.

* * * * *

During his editorship of *El Habanero*, his repeated pronouncements of the desirability and the inevitability of independence caused representatives of at least two nations with an interest other than altruistic in his Island to seek alliance with him.

One such person was the controversial American diplomat, Joel Roberts Poinsett, who, after years of undercover maneuvering in

---

[39] *Vida*, p. 146.

Latin America, would be remembered chiefly as the man who shipped to the United States from Mexico the first specimens of the plant that bears his name—the Christmas poinsettia.

American presidents, from Thomas Jefferson on, had dreamed of annexing Cuba, if they could do so under circumstances justifiable in the eyes of the world. Jefferson and Madison considered the acquisition of the island a strategic necessity. Under Monroe and John Quincy Adams, expansionism had assumed the aura of manifest destiny; and, with Florida safely incorporated, Cuba seemed the next logical move. "America for the Americans," the slogan that bolstered the Monroe Doctrine, was to many a euphemism for "America for the United States." President James Monroe was a personal friend of General Francisco Vives, "the great corruptor of the national life of Cuba;"[40] and his intervention in Cuban affairs would not be likely to help the oppressed. None the less, many Cubans, thinking rather of the idealism behind American institutions than the imperialism of American economics, looked to the United States for help in their internal problems. A fellow-countryman of Varela, Mariano Cubí y Soler, prepared the first Spanish translation of the Monroe Doctrine and presented it to the American President; he was a founder of *Revista bimestre cubana,* a periodical esteemed not only in Cuba but in the United States and abroad.[41] Another Cuban, using the name of Bernabé Sánchez, had submitted a plan for annexation which Monroe's cabinet studied in a special secret session.[42]

Joel Roberts Poinsett was an active partisan of annexation. He was also a dedicated liberal, propagandist for the ideals of the American Revolution in an era when "liberalism" demanded maximum attainable liberty for every individual. A member of Congress for South Carolina, he had gone in 1822 on a presidential mission to Mexico (recently declared independent by General Iturbide) and had returned by way of Cuba. In addition to the American foreign service, Poinsett was involved with the Yorkist Rite of the Freemasons, which had been conscientiously promoting

---

[40]Enrique Gay Calbó, "Colonialismo," *Cuadernos de historia habanera,* no. 23 (1943) : 44.
[41]Portell Vilá, *Historia,* 1 : 240.
[42]"Independentismo," pp. 10ff.

education and Bible-reading and instigating antagonism to Spain and Catholicism in Latin America. Philadelphia, as we have noted, was a fountainhead of Masonic influence; and it was there that Poinsett became acquainted in 1824 with Félix Varela, who was by no means a Mason.

José María Salazar, minister for Colombia to the United States, introduced the diplomat and the Cuban priest. Poinsett saw in Varela a leader revered by his fellow-countrymen both at home and in exile, and a Catholic clergyman disaffected with Spanish rule. Their conversation has not been recorded; but it is known that Poinsett pursued the acquaintance, sounding out Varela on various facets of American designs toward Cuba.

The depredations of pirates based in the Caribbean offered a pretext for American intervention; and the United States, from 1823 to 1825, employed David Porter, Commander-in-Chief of its West Indies squadron, to clear the infested waters. Varela, approached by Poinsett on this subject, crusaded against the pirates in *El Habanero* and blamed the Spanish government in Cuba for allowing them harbor. But he did not succumb to the suggestion that the United States should penetrate further into the island than Porter's mission required.

The patriot-priest may have toyed briefly with the idea of a protective and commercial alliance for his country with its powerful northern neighbor—at least one prominent Cuban writer suggests that he did.[43] But he knew that any form of political union would mean absorption; and Varela wanted no relationship that would jeopardize the ardently desired freedom of Cuba. His answers to Poinsett's overtures, written from New York early in 1825, after he had removed there from Philadelphia to resume the functions of priest, show clearly where he stood.

The pirates, said Varela, would never be wiped out unless United States forces were helped by an energetic interior course of action. But Spain was a corpse, and could not give out anything but corruption and the principles of death. "On the other hand, a new State (Ah, if we could but see it in the Island of Cuba!) has all the warmth of nature in its youth; it nourishes the seeds of honor

---

[43]"Ideario Político," p. 247.

and virtue; and by an irresistible impulse it tends toward good and destroys all poisonous shoots." The most powerful segment of those who loved independence in his island, Varela told Poinsett, inclined toward an alliance with the United States advantageous to both parties, but not toward becoming one of the States. Let not Poinsett's government go so far in hunting the pirates as to outrage the inhabitants.[44]

Félix Varela never doubted that, however desperate the present plight of his people, their ultimate destiny was unequivocal independence. Suspecting the purposes of Joel Roberts Poinsett, he side-stepped them with a prayer: "May the government of the United States be the free government *par excellence,* the guardian angel of a people who, without having less love for liberty, are not so fortunate in possessing it." The Washington diplomat had to look elsewhere for help in extending the power of the United States.

Poinsett had meanwhile returned to Mexico as its first accredited minister from its northern neighbor. For almost four years, he propounded his liberal doctrines there and jockeyed for advantage over the British *chargé-d'affaires,* Henry George Ward, until in 1828 the Mexican government requested the provocative American's recall. For Varela, ecclesiastical credentials from Bishop Espada of Havana had arrived in New York in 1825, and the priest was again able to practice his calling.

Later in 1825, another overture to foreign entanglement was made to the Cuban patriot through Pablo Obregón, Mexican minister to the United States. Several rebel priests had led Mexico in the upheaval against Spain and been shot for their boldness—Hidalgo, José María Morelos, Mariano Matamoras. The infant republic revered these martyr clerics; and the government saw in El Padre Varela a potentially similar hero in its liberation of Cuba.

Coteries of Cuban expatriates had formed in Mexico City the "Junta to Promote the Liberty of Cuba," with 19 deputies representing the geographical areas of Cuba, and with Juan Antonio de

---

[44]Varela's letters to Poinsett, from New York, January 27 and 28, 1825, "Joel R. Poinsett Papers." For a Masonic view of various movements against Spanish rule in Cuba during this era, see Francisco J. Ponte Domínguez, *La masonería en la independencia de Cuba.*

Unzueto as president-in-exile. With the approval of the Mexican president, an invasion was to be launched against Cuba through Yucatan from Vera Cruz. Mexico had as great a strategic interest in Cuba as did the United States; moreover, she considered herself the rightful heir to the Spanish domains in the Northern Hemisphere.

Pablo Obregón, like Poinsett, wanted the support of Cuba's ideological leader, who was widely known in Mexico through his works on philosophy and education. To Varela, then, he transmitted an invitation from President Guadalupe Victoria to transfer his abode to Mexico. The President's letter contained a passport; and orders had been given to a man-of-war stationed in New York harbor, the *Mexican Congress*—lately captured, with its 70 cannon, from the Spanish—to convey the priest with all honor, expense-free, to Vera Cruz.

Varela understood that the invitation involved more than a tribute to a Cuban patriot by a sister nation. He had known since his arrival in New York in 1823—from his disciple, Sentmanat, among others—of the Mexican invasion plans. Much as he wanted the expulsion of Spain, he desired the freedom of Cuba more. The revolutionary Cuban poet, José María de Heredia, went in 1826 to Mexico, where, when plans for the relief of Cuba fizzled, he became a civic magistrate and died at the age of 35. The United States naval commander, David Porter, also transferred to the employ of Mexico, lured by promises of a huge salary and substantial land grant; he returned after three years broken and hungering for vengeance. But El Padre Varela did not succumb to Obregón's blandishments; he thanked President Guadalupe Victoria and remained at his sacerdotal post in New York. If he could not return to Havana, he would make his home in the Land of Liberty.

He did not, however, abandon his efforts for Cuba, of which he had vowed to remain a citizen all his life. He continued to counsel her expatriates and to write for her young men at home, enlightening them against the long darkness which, he now realized, must intervene before the day of their liberation.

To help Cuba's predominantly rural economy keep pace in soil conservation, he translated into Spanish the *Elements of chemistry applied to agriculture,* by Humphrey Davy.[45] He put into his native tongue Thomas Jefferson's *Manual of parliamentary procedure,* with notes personal and explanatory.[46] Let Cubans know how the Senate of a free country operated! He collected and printed the poems of Manuel de Zequeira y Arango, the first poet to emphasize the Cuban national theme. "I wish," he said, "to conserve to usefulness the flame that enkindled his soul."[47] He continued to revise and up-date his popular *Lecciones de filosofía,* issuing the third, fourth, and fifth editions in 1828, 1832, and 1841, for this work was now the textbook in many Latin-American universities.

For over two years, 1829-31, Varela collaborated with his disciple and fellow-exile in New York, José Antonio Saco, on *El mensagero semanal (The weekly messenger),* a world news bulletin which they published from 7 Nassau Street. We have the word of Saco himself that the priest was his active partner in this venture.[48] Although somewhat more moderate than *El Habanero,* it aimed to pierce the Cuban blackout and was, like its predecessor, banned by the Spanish authorities. Saco, returning to Havana in 1832, became editor of the *Revista bimestre cubana* founded by Cubí y Soler, and he made of it the outstanding publication in the island. Varela contributed articles to the *Revista* on Spanish grammar—he persisted in promoting the dignity of the vernacular—and on the education of women. From his post in New York, he counseled the editors of *Revista Bimestre,* exhorting in a letter to Luz that they refrain from answering attacks lest they endanger their publication and thus give solace to their enemies. "It would be a pity if the editors replied, for then I would foresee doom for the *Revista.* It has one great fault, for which its enemies call the atten-

---

[45]*Elementos de química aplicada a la agricultura, en un curso de lecciones en el Instituto de Agricultura.*
[46]*Manual de práctica parlamenteria para el uso del Senado de los Estados Unidos.*
[47]Cf. "Advertencia" in Varela's *Poesías del coronel Don Manuel de Zequeira y Arango, natural de La Habana.*
[48]Foik, p. 60; cf. Saco's *Colección de papeles . . . sobre la isla de Cuba,* 1960, 1: 231. The total extent of Varela's collaboration on this weekly has not been determined. During a violent war-of-words between Saco and Ramón la Sagra over Heredia's poetry and Sagra's botanical status, Saco asked Varela for a testimonial letter. Varela complied, but in so guarded and concise a fashion as to be almost abrupt: *Colección,* pp. 330f. Perhaps the priest did not like to see Cuban demolishing Cuban.

HE CHARTS THE WAY TO FREEDOM

tion of the government to it: . . . it is the best publication in the entire Monarchy."[49]

During the 40's, Varela wrote occasionally for *La Verdad,* New York, "a journal supported by the patriots of Cuba, for the dissemination of republican principles and intelligence." In March, 1841, the *Repertorio médico habanero* reported on an apparatus whose specifications Varela had sent to Havana, designed "to lower the temperature, purify and renew the air," in hospitals—an air-conditioning device anticipatory of those developed a century later.[50]

In 1835, the exiled priest began the publication of his tribute to hope, *Cartas a Elpidio (Letters to Elpidio),* in which he continued to advise the young men of his fatherland against ignorance, prejudice, and fanaticism. He was now Vicar-General of the Diocese of New York; but in the solitary hours when he wrote his heart out, he was again the professor of philosophy and constitutional law at San Carlos, exhorting his *habaneros* to be wise, self-controlled, and free.

---

[49] Rodríguez, *Vida de Don José de la Luz y Caballero,* pp. 44-45, quotes from Varela to Luz, N.Y., Mar. 7, 1832.
[50] González del Valle, "Cartas Inéditas del Padre Varela," gives letter, Varela to Luz, "Nueva York 5 de junio de 1839," pp. 67-68; also González del Valle's comment, p. 63. ("Cartas Inéditas").

CHAPTER III

HE SERVES AS PRIEST IN NEW YORK

The United States was mission territory for the Church of Rome during the nineteenth century. New York until the Revolution had proscribed Catholic priests and those who harbored them, on pain of fine, imprisonment, or death. Old St. Peter's in Barclay Street, pioneer church in the diocese, stood near the site where, in 1741, an English clergyman had been hanged by fanatics who believed him a papist in disguise. Although the Constitution guaranteed religious liberty, known Catholics in New York City in 1825 formed but a small percentage of the population and, with a few notable exceptions, occupied the lowest economic and social position. Distrust and misunderstanding choked off communication between the two major segments of Christianity, and uneasiness prevailed.

The Catholics in the city had only two churches and five or six priests, and their pastors depended for financial help on Paris, Vienna, Rome, and Madrid.

The Church in New York, already predominantly (but not yet preponderantly) Irish, owed much to Hispanic Catholics. Don Diego de Gardoqui, His Most Catholic Majesty's minister to the United States, had laid the cornerstone of St. Peter's on October 5, 1785, enclosing in it specimens of the coinage of Spain; and in response to a petition from the trustees, King Charles III of Spain sent a contribution of $1,000. At the Spanish Embassy, the chaplain, John O'Connell, a missionary from Bilbao, said Mass for the city's Catholics until, on November 4, 1786, the feastday of St. Charles Borromeo—a date chosen in honor of Charles III—the first High Mass was solemnized in the partly completed edifice on Barclay Street. Andrew Nugent, private chaplain of the wealthy Portuguese merchant, José Roiz Silva, officiated. Priests from the French and Spanish embassies assisted; language was not a problem, because in those days the Mass was said in all countries of the West in Latin, without the complication of passages spoken in the vernacular. After the service, Gardoqui held a dedication dinner at his residence in the Kennedy Mansion at No. 1 Broadway—a gala affair attended by high civil functionaries.

Roiz Silva was one of the four original trustees of St. Peter's. Don Tomás Stoughton, long-term Spanish consul in New York and church trustee, held the property deed for many years in his place of business on Little Dock (Water) Street. When the Reverend William O'Brien, pastor, needed funds to complete the church, he made a tortuous journey to Mexico, returning with $6,000 and several paintings, among them "The Crucifixion," by the Mexican, José María Vallejo, which hangs to this day behind the main altar of St. Peter's.

In a very real sense, therefore, Catholicism had been officially launched in New York under Hispanic sponsorship.

Stoughton, forthright believer and successful man of business, was serving Ferdinand VII as consul in New York when Varela and his *Habanero* came to town. Descendant of an Irishman who had fled to Spain from British oppression, he could wink at the priest's political views; for others in the Spanish-speaking community, among them the lexicographer, Mariano Velázquez de la Cadena, whose *Elements of Spanish grammar* the priest had reviewed for the Royal Economic Society, could assure him that Varela was educator and idealist rather than conspirator.[1]

Dedicating himself to mission work in New York, the scholarly Cuban would find that, however, the city's Anglophile majority might condemn his Spanish and *criollo* antecedents, Catholics were conditioned to accept with gratitude his efforts in their behalf.

Bishop John Connolly, from whom he is said to have received his diocesan faculties,[2] died early in February 1825. The Reverend John Power, pastor of St. Peter's, became Vicar General of the diocese, with powers of administration. The trustees of St. Peter's and of the Cathedral sought to have Power as their next bishop; and the trustees of St. Patrick's, voting unanimously on February 26, 1825, transmitted a memorial urging his appointment to the

---

[1]Velázquez later became professor of Spanish at Columbia University. His *Pronouncing dictionary of the Spanish and English languages* continues, in updated form, to serve as standard; N.Y., Appleton-Century-Crofts, 1962.
[2]*Ceremonies at the laying of the corner stone of a chapel*, p. 9. Leo Raymond Ryan, however, says Varela was received into the diocese by Vicar General Power: *Old St. Peter's*, p. 164. Don Tomás Stoughton, the Spanish consul who befriended Varela, was one of the church trustees unfriendly to the Irish-born Bishop Connolly.

Prefect of the Propaganda in Rome.[3] Varela, serving in Barclay Street with the able young cleric, established himself quickly as an invaluable aide—saying Mass, baptizing, hearing confessions, visiting the sick, instructing the young and counseling the mature. His first baptism appears on St. Peter's register on February 24, 1825. He was competent now in English, not only for ordinary parish duties but for participation in the beginnings of American Catholic journalism. Undoubtedly the *Elementos de la lengua inglesa para uso de los españoles* (New York, Long, 1810) prepared by his compatriot Velázquez helped him to become at home in his adopted tongue.

America must have seemed to the learned Cuban a far cry from Havana. In his native land, all of life and love and toil and play was pervaded by religion; as he himself put it, without Catholicism, Hispanic culture would be an empty shell. The Church was dominant not only in its own special religious sphere but also in art, education, and social progress. In New York City, on the other hand, the so-styled Public School Society was Quaker- and Presbyterian-oriented, and its institutions, although professedly non-denominational, were steeped in the Protestant tradition. The public aid formerly given to all free schools, regardless of religious affiliation, was abrogated in 1825; and while the state subsidized the New York Orphan Society (which practised Dutch Reformed ritual), the Roman Catholic Orphan Asylum faced a long, bitter fight to obtain similar aid. Moreover, by state law the laity, in both Protestant and Catholic churches, had control of the purse strings, and of the hiring and firing of teachers and pastors. Father Power had come to St. Peter's from Ireland on the invitation of the lay trustees. The Bishop of New York received his salary and expense allowance for himself and two assistants—$1,200 in all—from the trustees of St. Patrick's Cathedral; and they threatened to withhold that pittance when he failed to consult their pleasure. The Latin American Padre Varela, who had unhesitatingly sacrificed his own inclinations in obeying Bishop Espada, found the leading of the shepherd by the sheep a peculiar inversion of normal controls.

---

[3] Typewritten copy of appeal sent by vessel for Havre to His Eminence, Cardinal de la Somaglia, Archives of the Archdiocese of New York, (AANY), E-12. Benedict Joseph Fenwick, a Jesuit who was the trustees' second choice, was chosen bishop of New England (Boston) later that year.

But he was happy in his relations with John Power. The two young priests had much in common. Both men were completely devoted to their calling. Both were scholarly, well trained in theology. Each had fled a beloved homeland that was victimized by political tyranny: Power was a pioneer alumnus of Maynooth, the first Catholic seminary in modern Ireland, tolerated by the British to keep the local papist clergy from the revolutionary contamination of continental universities.

Both priests, while retaining a deep fealty to their native isles, appreciated the unprecedented freedom from harassment of the individual in the United States. Both were eloquent, both highly literate, turning easily from pulpit to press. Like Varela, Power supplemented his teaching with books of his own authorship—a prayer-book entitled *True Piety*, a translation of the Bible of de Royaumont, and the *Laity's Directory*. Both drew people to them by their sincerity, their intelligence, their warm personal magnetism. Their one significant difference would help them to work together. To John Power, a position of authority mattered more: he took steps to attain the episcopacy, while Félix Varela, content with accomplishment, readily left superiority of status to others.

With the death of Bishop Connolly and the temporary assumption of the reins by Vicar General Power, the Catholic Church in the city surged forward. A third church was opened, and a permanent structure was erected for the Catholic Orphan Asylum in Prince Street. John Power and Bishop John England of Charleston, South Carolina, preached fund-raising sermons for the orphanage; and the Garcia Italian opera troupe, with Madame Malibran participating, sang a benefit Oratorio in St. Patrick's Cathedral. Two laymen, George Pardow and William Denman, undertook to publish the *Truth Teller* (begun April 2, 1825), a quasi-diocesan weekly sponsored by Power.[4] Don Félix Varela advertised in *Truth Teller,* announcing his availability to teach Spanish and presenting the prospectus of *The Youth's Friend* (*El amigo de la juventud*), a bilingual periodical which aimed, like the *Dictionary* of Velázquez, to "contribute to a mutual good understanding between the peoples

---
[4] The first six issues of *Truth Teller* list as publisher William E. Andrews, who edited the London magazine of the same name. Cf. Foik, pp. 24ff.

who speak the two languages most widely spread over the earth."
In May 1825, in the *Truth Teller,* Power endorsed the editor of
The Youth's Friend as a "gentleman well known in the literary
world" and as "the author of an invaluable treatise on philosophy."
This pioneer children's magazine in the Diocese of New York
represented the first of the Cuban priest's many English-language
periodicals. Varela also wrote articles for the *Truth Teller,* most
of which his modesty kept anonymous.

The Catholics of New York, short of everything, particularly
lacked places of worship. St. Peter's was so inadequate that crowds
of the faithful stood outside in the street to hear Mass. The new
parish, St. Mary's, organized in 1826, worshipped in a little brick-
fronted wooden building, 45' by 60', in Sheriff Street. It had been
purchased, under Power, from the Seventh Presbyterian congregation. Its distinguishing feature was a steeple with a large bell dear
to Irish Catholics, who had been denied church bells in their native
land. These two tiny structures, together with St. Patrick's in
Mulberry Street, served some 30,000 known Catholic individuals
in New York when Jean Dubois was consecrated on October 1826
as the third Bishop of New York.[5]

The elderly Dubois faced a difficult assignment.

A Frenchman who in 1791 had fled in disguise from the fana-
tically anti-religious Reign of Terror, the new prelate was scholarly, studious, and devout. He had founded and presided over Mt.
St. Mary's College and Seminary in Emmitsburg, Maryland; he
had aided Mother Elizabeth Seton in organizing the American
community of Sisters of Charity at nearby St. Joseph's. In New
York, if at first he mistrusted El Padre Varela's agitation for
Cuban independence, he soon came to appreciate the cultured
refugee who, almost alone among the priests, had an ingrained
respect for his episcopal position. Dubois' path was beset with
nettles: some of his Irish immigrant flock derided his heavy French
accent, the unmanageable trustees bullied him and flouted his decisions, and Power regarded him as a well-meaning incompetent.
The historian of the Catholic Church in the metropolis, the Reverend John Talbot Smith, says that Félix Varela's gentle ways did

---

[5]For a life of Dubois, see Charles G. Herbermann, *The Right Reverend John Dubois, D. D., third bishop of New York.*

much to smooth relations between Bishop Dubois and the Vicar-General.[6]

Early in Dubois' *regnum*, the Cuban bought a church for him.

While serving as assistant pastor at St. Peter's, Varela learned from a servant girl in his flock that the Episcopalian trustees of Christ Church in Ann Street wished to sell. The building was of stone, 61 by 80 feet, 32 years old, and located in an area convenient to the overflow from Barclay Street. It had been built by a wealthy Londoner for his son, a minister now deceased, and most of the congregation had moved to a more elegant structure in Anthony Street. A group of horseriders was offering a generous sum to obtain it as a clubhouse, but the elders would let it go for much less to keep it a house of worship. With funds provided by John Baptist Lasala (Juan Bautista La Sala). Silvester Alfonso, Francisco de la O. García, and others, Varela, in March 1827, bought for $19,000 the building, its organ and other furnishings (a Bible excluded), and the vaults, sepulchers, headstones, and remains of departed Episcopalians. Varela, we are told by Lasala, shed tears when he found he could buy the church, and retired to a corner to recite a *Te Deum*.[7]

Christ Church, solemnly dedicated in August 1827, became the second in a series of outgrown Protestant edifices converted to Catholic use in New York. Dubois named the Cuban priest as pastor; and he, on his part, to avoid dictation by high-handed laymen, registered the deed in the Bishop's name. Varela thus established a plan of church ownership which later became the rule among American Catholics; but at the time it elicited an outcry from the cathedral trustees, who publicly termed their Bishop a violator of state law and a virtual thief.

El Padre Varela, Cuban philosopher and revolutionary, was now almost completely absorbed in Father Varela, the zealous American pastor. Almost, but not quite. He continued to welcome Cuban disciples who fled to New York, to collaborate with Saco on *El Mensagero*, to write for *Revista Bimestre*, to prepare new editions of his three-volume *Lecciones de filosofía* (1828, 1832, 1841).

---

[6] John Talbot Smith, *The Catholic Church in New York*, 1: 78.
[7] John B. Lasala, memorandum for Hughes, dated "N. York March 7th 1853," detailing the life of Varela; AANY, Archbishop John J. Hughes Papers (AHP), A-13. Lasala cites $18,000 as the purchase price.

But for the most part, his pen was producing articles for the *Truth Teller* and other New York publications. He wrote a Catechism of Christian doctrine for classes in religion. He opened day schools for both boys and girls adjacent to the church in Ann Street—supplementing the free Catholic schools already in operation at St. Peter's and St. Patrick's. He hired teachers for these schools, but much of the instruction, in them and in his free Sunday School, he imparted in person. With his assistant, Father Joseph A. Schneller, an Austrian ex-Jesuit, he published the *New York weekly register and Catholic diary,* which catered particularly to Irish-Americans. The irascible Schneller was titular editor, with special concern for the religious section; but the influence of the temperate, intellectual pastor, who wrote copiously for the newspaper, was paramount. The secular department was edited by the Irish educator and patriot, Patrick S. Casserly.[8] During its nearly four years of life, this periodical, which supported Dubois against the fractious lay trustees of St. Patrick's Cathedral and defended Catholicism against the calumnies of its enemies, supplanted the *Truth Teller* as the outstanding Catholic voice in New York.[9] After Schneller left it, Varela started the *Catholic Observer,* of which at present little is known.[10]

Money for the support of Christ Church—for its poor immigrant flock had starving relatives in Ireland to succor—came chiefly from New York well-wishers and from Father Varela's private resources. His half-brother Manuel was doing well in tobacco, the Morales cousins were flourishing, and the disciples in Havana did not forget their master. The priest's *Lecciones de filosofía,* widely used as a textbook in Latin America, also provided an income which he invested in spiritual and charitable works in New York.

Bishop Dubois sailed to Europe in September 1829, in quest of priests and funds for his mission diocese. He named John Power and Félix Varela as Vicars General, and designated the former to represent him at the First Provincial Council in Baltimore, scheduled to open October 1, 1829.

The tactful and cooperative Varela ceded primacy to his Irish-

---
[8]Foik, p. 121.
[9]*Souvenir of the blessing of the cornerstone of the new seminary of St. Joseph,* p. 164.
[10]Foik, p. 61.

born colleague. Power signed himself officially as "Vicar General of New York," with the name of Félix Varela subjoined as "Vicar General." Despite rumors which reached Spain to the contrary, they "got along together quite amicably."[11] Supported by enthusiastic and cooperative laymen, the two Vicars accomplished much. Outside of the city, six new churches were dedicated in the diocese during the Bishop's absence, and a seventh had its cornerstone-laying. The Sisters of Charity opened schools for girls in Mulberry Street, in Barclay Street, and at Albany. Varela's schools in Ann Street and John Street offered, beside the three R's, instruction in grammar, orthography, needlework, music with use of pianoforte, and, from 5 to 6 P. M., lessons in French and Spanish.[12]

A pious lady presented $800 to Father Varela, which he invested in a day nursery and half-orphan asylum for the children of poor widows and widowers. This institution, originally at Sixth Avenue but later at Fifth Avenue and 15th Street in the village of Greenwich, was managed by the Sisters of Charity. Funds were raised for it by special sermons in Christ Church and by benefit socials: on St. Patrick's Day, 1834, the Hibernian Universal Benevolent Society of the City of New York produced a handsome collection, and Varela toasted "St. Patrick's Charity kept by his children."[13] The philanthropic Cornelius Heeney, one-time partner of John Jacob Astor, also contributed money and a building site to Varela's crèches for fatherless children.[14] The Half-Orphan Asylum was incorporated shortly before Varela's death into the Roman Catholic Orphan Asylum, and its buildings eventually became part of St. Vincent's Hospital.

There was a tragedy under the administration of the Vicars General. Fanatics looted St. Mary's Church in Sheriff Street, bound up the precious bell and set the structure afire. It was a total loss, and the stricken pastor, the Reverend Luke Berry, first priest ordained by Bishop Dubois, died a month later. Now the Catholics of the area were again reduced to three churches.

But these setbacks did not quench the determination of New

---

[11] Smith, 1: 78.
[12] Herbermann, pp. 320-31, quoting from *Truth Teller*, Jan. 12, 1830.
[13] *N. Y. weekly register and Catholic diary*, Mar. 23, 1834.
[14] Pamphlet, n. auth., *Cornelius Heeney, 1754-1848*, commemorating centenary of his death in his 94th year.

York's Catholics. Plans for a new St. Mary's were set afoot, and when the building was dedicated, on June 9, 1833, the music—Hayden's First Mass—was notable, John Power's sermon rang with eloquence, and many high-ranking Protestants lent their presence to the impressive ceremony.

Bishop Dubois lingered in Europe some two years, paying visits of state in Rome and refreshing his battered spirit in his native France. The Congregation of the Propaganda in Rome granted him funds for a diocesan seminary and the French Society of the Propagation of the Faith appropriated, from 1829 to 1838, upward of 120,000 francs. He also obtained books for a diocesan library; but he could not persuade any young priest to return with him to the missionary life in America.

During the Bishop's prolonged absence (September 1829-November 1831), whispers began to circulate that he would not return—that he wished to retire to France. He was now over 65. His vigor had been sapped by arduous visitations across a sparsely settled diocese that encompassed all of New York State and part of New Jersey. His serenity was undermined by the tug-of-war with overbearing trustees and disaffected clergy. The same rumormongers who, perhaps from wishful thinking, declared that he was finished with New York, added the supposition that, to spite John Power, he would have Varela appointed to his see.

These speculations gained sufficient currency to reach the royal ears in Madrid. On March 14, 1830, Francisco Tacón, minister of Spain in the United States, wrote from Philadelphia to His Excellency, Don Manuel González Salmón, His Majesty's Minister of State:

> The emigré priest Varela, resident in New York, and of whom I informed Your Excellency in dispatches No. 698 and 860, is at present intriguing to assemble evidence of his apostolic zeal to send to Rome, accompanied by the most powerful endorsement by many citizens of that place who profess our Holy Faith, in order to obtain from the Holy See the post of Bishop in case the Illustrious Dubois of New York, now in Europe, obtains a transfer to one of the churches in France, or if another see becomes vacant in the United States; and as the election of such a wicked Spaniard to the honor which he seeks would be very prejudicial to the interests of the King

Our Master in . . . the Island of Cuba, I hasten to communicate this to Your Excellency for the necessary information of His Majesty.

Tacón went on to remind the Minister of State that this Varela, whom New York's merchants were now nominating for its mitre, had published an incendiary periodical inciting the faithful inhabitants of Cuba and Puerto Rico to rebellion. The late John Connolly, first resident Bishop of New York, had been recommended for his post by the Queen of Etruria; Bishop Dubois had been selected by the government of France—so wrote Tacón. "By the nature of the government of this Union, there are not and cannot be Concordats with the Holy See; and consequently, the Catholic establishments here are missions proceeding directly from the Court of Rome." Let Spain now intercede against further honors for this worthless Spanish priest, who had already been designated a Vicar General. His misdeeds "should have sufficed to have him barred, or at least suspended, from the exercise of ecclesiastical functions; but in this Republic they have produced for him friends and popularity."[15]

The alarm thus sounded triggered a fusillade of letters between Madrid and Rome. His Majesty's Minister of State wrote to the Spanish ambassador in Rome that Varela, the "bad Spaniard and worse priest, has maintained intimate and criminal relations with some of the leading agitators behind the revolts and disturbances which afflict His Majesty's dominions in America," and that, "begrudging the tranquillity which those regions enjoy which have remained faithful to our King, he has excited with his writings the inhabitants of the Islands of Cuba and Puerto Rico to separate themselves from His Majesty's empire." This hypocritical cleric, the message read, had insinuated himself into the good graces of Bishop Dubois and was now seeking promotion to the episcopacy.

The Ambassador, in turn, wrote to Giuseppe Cardinal Albani, Secretary of State of His Holiness, urging that the proposed advancement of Félix Varela must never take place, as it would be dangerous both to Spanish colonialism and to the Holy Faith.[16]

---

[15]This and the succeeding letters are given in *Vida,* App., pp. 293-97.

[16]Cf. typescript, "Eminmo. Signor Cardinal Albani, Segretario di Stati di Sua Santitá. Ritorni . . . la confidenziale del Signor Ambasciatore di Spagna sul sacerdote D. Felici Valera [Varela]," 1830. Giuseppe Cardinal Albani, 1750-1834, native of Rome, was administrator in the Vatican from

The reply of Cardinal Albani sought to allay the apprenhensions of Ambassador González Salvador. No proposal to elevate the Cuban philosopher had reached his office.

The name of the Spanish priest, Varela, to which your confidential message refers, is unknown here except through his correspondence with the Bishop of New York during that Prelate's recent stay in Rome. It would have been desirable to have received Your Excellency's packet before the Bishop of New York left here; it would then have been possible to call his attention to this priest much better than can now be done by writing at such a distance.

With the present critical situation in France, Albani explained, there was scant possibility that Bishop Dubois would be transferred there from New York.

Moreover, if by chance it should happen that some day Varela should actually be proposed to the Holy See to be named a Bishop, Your Excellency may rest assured that the Papal Minister will not forget the memoranda in regard to him which have been transmitted by Your Excellency.

The Ambassador now informed the Spanish Secretary of State that the Cardinal deemed it improbable that Varela's name would come up for consideration in the selection of bishops. There the matter rested.

Actually the concern of the Spanish authorities as to Varela's ambition was unfounded. He was not seeking the episcopal throne in New York or elsewhere; any representations in his behalf by influential friends must be spontaneous, without authorization from him—and the evidence is that none such had reached the ears of Rome.[17]

Whence, then, arose the rumors that troubled the ministers of Spain? The correspondence between Madrid and Rome provides a clue: it mentions repeatedly that the two Vicars General of New York were not in accord. Yet Varela and Power, of differing cultures and nationalities, worked nevertheless well together on a

---

1814 on, serving under Popes Pius VII, Leo XII, Pius VIII, and Gregory XVI.

[17] Some six years later, when there was talk of advancement for Varela at the Provincial Council in Baltimore, the strongest opposition came from Varela himself.

variety of projects, and the Cuban always deferred publicly to his colleague. There was one signal point of difference, however: Power was restive under Bishop Dubois, and he was prone to complain about him in letters to friends in Rome.[18]

The devoted followers of Power, those who had promoted him to succeed Bishop Connolly and who now hoped he would supplant Dubois, may have feared lest yet another "foreigner" elbow out their hero.[19] Of such feelings are rumors born.

That these fears, so far as concerned competition from Varela, were groundless, is borne out by the fact that the young Father John McCloskey, sailing for Europe in November 1834, carried two packets addressed to Rome. One, from Dubois, asked for the appointment of a Coadjutor, and recommended Dr. Charles Constantine Pise or Father Thomas F. Mulledy, S.J. The other, directed to Thomas Cardinal Weld, was "from Very Rev. Dr. Power, V. G., whose friends thought that the best interests of religion called for his appointment to the position."[20] Power also wrote on this subject to Father Anthony Kohlmann, S.J., a pioneer administrator of the New York diocese, who used his influence in the Propaganda, as did Bishop Simon Bruté. But Rome knew of Power's antagonism to Dubois and hesitated to appoint the Vicar General as Coadjutor.

A matter of grave concern was claiming the attention of the Vicars General in New York.

Anti-Catholicism, which had been in eclipse during the liberal early years of the Republic, was now swinging back onto the American scene with rampaging force. The Reverend Charles G. Finney was leading a revival of fundamentalist Protestantism. Dozens of "Christian" periodicals had sprung into being, their main purpose to attack and vilify "Popery." The American Bible Society was flooding the land with Protestant-prepared Scriptures

---

[18]*E.g.*, in 1833 Power proposed that the Sacred Congregation of the Propaganda transfer to him for completion the Seminary property at Nyack which Dubois was financing with Propaganda funds. "The Bishop," he alleged, "will never get any help from the people, because they have no opinion of his prudence." See copy of letter, Power to Dr. Cullen in Rome, from New York, Sept. 15, 1833, in AANY, AHP, A-35.
[19]Power was himself born outside the United States, and was an immigrant equally with Connolly, Dubois, Varela, and John J. Hughes.
[20]John Cardinal Farley, *The life of John Cardinal McCloskey*, p. 95.

and with denunciations of alleged papist foes of the Sacred Word. The economically and socially unsettling influx of Irish pauper hordes was feeding the flames of prejudice, and the passage in England, in 1829, of the long-denied Catholic Emancipation Act caused Anglo-Saxon-Protestant supremacists in America to shudder.

The Second Provincial Council of the American Catholic bishops in Baltimore, 1833, took note of the danger, but advised silence and forbearance:

> Not only do they assail us and our institutions in a style of vituperation and offense, misrepresent our tenets, vilify our practices, repeat the hundred times refuted calumnies of days of angry and bitter contention in other lands, but they have even denounced you and us as enemies to the liberties of the republic, and have openly proclaimed the fancied necessity of not only obstructing our progress, but of using their best efforts to extirpate our religion. . . . It is neither our principle nor our practice to render evil for evil, nor railing for railing: and we exhort you rather to the contrary, to render blessing.[21]

On January 2, 1830, the anti-Catholic campaign was unified with the inauguration in New York of *The Protestant,* a periodical whose prospectus announced:

> The sole objects of this publication are, to inculcate Gospel doctrines against Romish corruptions—to maintain the purity and sufficiency of the Holy Scriptures against Monkish traditions—to exemplify the watchful care of Immanuel over the 'Church of God which he hath purchased with his own blood,' and to defend that revealed truth . . . against the creed of Pope Pius IV and the cannons [*sic*] of the Council of Trent.[22]

The helm of this enterprise was taken over within a year by the Reverend William Craig Brownlee, who also organized the militant New York Protestant Association and soon emerged as the outstanding ministerial hatemonger in what Ray Allen Billington critically terms "The Protestant Crusade."

Power and Varela did not let the challenge of *The Protestant* go unanswered. They were both trained theologians and skilled polemicists, adept with the pen and the spoken word, able to counter

---
[21] Peter Guilday, *The national pastorals,* p. 78.
[22] Ray Allen Billington, *The Protestant crusade,* pp. 53f.

exaggerations with fact, name-calling with dialectic. They and other diocesan priests met with Dr. Brownlee on lecture platforms—the public forum before radio and TV took over—in Broadway Hall, Clinton Hall, and in the Reverend Dr. Archibald Maclay's church in Mulberry Street. The debated topics, as proposed by the Protestants, showed how current majority thinking was loaded: "Is the Roman hierarchy the man of sin, the son of perdition, which Paul predicted in his Epistle to the Thessalonians?"—"Are the Catholic clergy justified in alienating the people from the Scriptures?"—"Is the Pope the wicked son of perdition?" —and similar propositions.

Dr. Hernández Travieso tells us that, in one discussion, the angry John Power declared that his Church did not deem it wise to place the Holy Book in the hands of all. When the opposition seized on this admission by the pastor of St. Peter's as proof that the Church forbade Bible-reading, as they had been charging all along, Varela saved the day by producing an English-language Bible approved by the Pope in 1609—37 years after the Council of Trent—and an authorized French version published in 1764. Then he presented a long list of popes and bishops, in various epochs, who had sanctioned the reading of the Holy Book. "Thus like a magician he had snatched Power from the fire and at the same time closed the mouths of the opposition."[23]

The *Truth Teller* and some of the Protestant journals opened their columns to these debates; by agreement, each paper was to publish the expositions of both sides. The *New York Observer,* a rabid nativist mouthpiece of the brothers of Samuel B. Morse (of telegraph fame) entered the lists eagerly, but less as news purveyor than as controversialist. After a few months, this particular war of words was terminated because, says Billington, Dr. Brownlee had become so abusive that the *Truth Teller's* readership declaimed against its inclusion of his articles. "Your substitute for arguments," Brownlee was told, "are falsehood, ribald words, gross invective, disgusting calumny, and the recommendation of an obscene tale."[24]

Of the principal Catholic protagonists—Fathers Power, Varela,

---

[23] *El padre Varela,* pp. 379f.
[24] Quoted by Billington, p. 64.

Joseph A. Schneller, and Thomas C. Levins, the intellectual Cuban was the most restrained and scholarly. Avoiding rhetoric and invective, he cited chapter and verse and historical fact to correct his adversaries and, concurrently, to enlighten the over-credulous and the ignorant among his own people. We are told that he shunned the *Truth Teller—Observer* controversy;[25] its temper was too rancorous on both sides for his equable judgment. But he organized a series of weekly conferences on Christian doctrine, in which all the priests of the city participated, so that Catholics might the better know their Faith before they sought to defend it.[26] He published a pamphlet on the diverse Scriptures being disseminated by the New York Bible Society, showing that, since they varied greatly in text, they could not all pass for Divine Revelation. He was a few years later to return to this theme with a broader coverage, in his *Expositor*. With Schneller, his curate at Christ Church, he also expounded misunderstood doctrines of Catholicism in his parish organ, the *New York weekly register and Catholic diary*. The motto of this journal was: "All things whatsoever you would that men should do to you, do you also to them."[27] Its opening editorial promised that it would be "purely republican, inflexibly impartial, and thoroughly Irish." There were then an estimated 40,000 Irish in New York City alone.

The *Register* carried in its early numbers a clear, factually authenticated "Dissertation on the Antiquity of the Catholic Doctrine. By the Rev. Felix Varela." It printed excerpts in support of Dr. Brownlee by the *Journal of Commerce* and dissents by the *Evening Post* and the *National Gazette*. But it refused to publish a letter from "F. H." as being too harsh against a certain Protestant clergyman of New York, reminding the former that men must embrace one another with "the arms of tenderness and brotherly affection."[28]

A notable achievement of the *Weekly register and Catholic diary* was its exposure of the fraudulence of the *Awful disclosures of Maria Monk,* the best-seller which was then inflaming Americans against Catholics in general and against their houses of

---
[25]Blakeslee, p. 39.
[26]*El padre Varela*, p. 380.
[27]*Op. cit.,* vol. 1, no. 1, Oct. 5, 1833.
[28]*Ibid.,* Oct. 12, 1833.

religion in particular. The publication in the *Register* of sworn affidavits and other evidence from Canada prompted William L. Stone of the *Commercial Advertiser* to a journey of investigation in Montreal. Although himself anti-Catholic, Stone was impelled in fair-mindedness to publish conclusive evidence that the *Disclosures* constituted a vicious hoax.[29]

In an era of blinding religious animosities, Varela was the pioneer ecumenist, able to conduct dialogue without violence, astonishing his opponents by his learning, his patient exposition, his liberalism. Father John Hughes of Philadelphia, later to become Bishop and then Archbishop of New York, played a humiliating trick on the editors of *The Protestant:* under the pseudonym of "Cranmer," he submitted a series of wildly exaggerated but supposedly factual accounts of Catholic misdoings which the editors gullibly printed until the author revealed them as a hoax. John Power traded blow for blow. But Varela exemplified a type of Catholic—secure in his own Faith, broad in his understanding and apt in his expounding of it, yet respectful of honest question—who is coming into his own in the world today.

Catholics during the 1830's were seething over the deliberate, unpunished burning by a mob of the Ursuline convent and library at Charlestown, Massachusetts, and in New York they hinted darkly of arson in the destruction of St. Mary's Church in Sheriff Street, of Bishop Dubois' seminary at Nyack, and of the Sisters of Charity School in Mulberry Street. Yet the ecumenical Félix Varela, writing to his Cuban friends from New York, spoke of the universal church and urged forbearance:

> When they speak to me of the Catholic congregation of this country, I am wont to say that it consists of many who come to our churches and of many who go to 'heretical' churches without knowing where they go or why. But who are they? Who are those truly innocent, who in spite of believing heresies are not heretics? This is a point we leave to Divine Justice, following the counsel of the Apostle: 'You who would judge another's servant, go on foot or bow down before his master.' This is the true tolerance. We condemn none, but suppose all innocent until they give proof of not being so. Some say that heretics do not partake of Christ and that, in

---

[29] Foik, p. 120.

so believing they merely uphold the evangelical doctrine; but these people have not ascertained who are the heretics—as if they said that they condemned a robbery without verifying who are the thieves.[30]

Félix Varela's dialectical style may be instanced from a magazine of which he published some six numbers in answer to *The Protestant* during 1830 and 1831. Its title, *The Protestant's abridger and annotator,* discloses its purpose. The author's foreword, moderate, friendly, and hopeful in tone, absolves most non-Catholics from the fanaticism displayed by *The Protestant.*

> It may be imagined that the *Protestant,* a weekly paper, is the organ of an attack made by all the Christian sects on the Catholic Church; but, in reality, it is intended to be, and is conducted, by the leaders of only one of them, and has not met with the general approbation of Protestants, in as much as a great many of them consider it a slanderous, impolitic, and useless undertaking. Neither insult nor injury are spared. Catholics are called *uncircumcised Philistines,* and their Priests represented as imposters. My religion, my honour, and my office, oblige me to become the Protestant's Annotator, and to show that he is, at least, mistaken.[31]

To *The Protestant's* charge that "the increase of Popery in the United States is alarming, combined with the firmly rooted establishment of *that anti-Christian denomination in Lower Canada,* and the constant exertions of the devotees of the Man of Sin," Varela answered quietly: "And *The Protestant* will increase it, by supporting a *human cause* in a human manner, that is to say, by abusive language!"

To the statement that the Roman Church believes there is no salvation outside of its communion, Varela replied in a spirit of universality: "There is but one Church, which is the Catholic; and there is but one baptism; no matter whether it be administered by a man or woman, by a Catholic, Heretic, or heathen. Whoever

---

[30] Félix Varela y Morales, *Cartas a Elpidio,* 1944-45 ed., 2: 140.
[31] *The Protestant's abridger and annotator,* no. 1, p. 2, "Advertisement." Many Protestants had shown themselves cooperative with Catholics: the vestry of Trinity Church had made land available in Barclay Street for St. Peter's, and Episcopalian trustees of Christ Church had sold their building to Varela for a much lower price than was offered by another buyer. Bishop Dubois possessed close friends among the Anglican clergy, and there were several notable converts.

is baptized is a member of the church." A great many members of the Christian sects "belong in reality to the Roman Catholic Church." As to the heathen, who has never heard of the Church, he will be condemned only for sins "committed against the law of nature;" and if his life be just, "he would be united by charity to the same Lord. . . . he would be united to the only Church of Jesus Christ, to that church, whose head on earth is the Bishop of Rome, although he should not have any idea of such a Bishop nor of that city."[32] Concerning the fate of unbaptized children, theologians differed; but Varela declared he could not believe that they would suffer in the after life.

Although the doctrine of papal infallibility had not yet been promulgated, many Catholics subscribed to it, and Protestants assailed it as a most dangerous dogma. Said *The Protestant* magazine scornfully: "One pretended infallible Ganganelli, from *mistaken notions,* abolished the order of Jesuits; but the late Pontiff, another infallible, has restored them. Two flat contradictories prove one infallibility. Quis credat? [Who would believe that?]"

"The infallibility of the Pope," responded Varela, "is not an article of the Catholic faith; on the contrary, it is denied by a great many Catholic divines, without the least censure on the part of the see of Rome. Even those who admit the infallibility of the Pope, will never say that he is infallible but in matters of faith and morality, and not when he gives his opinion as a *private Doctor,* but when he decides as the head of the Church." Here Varela anticipated the limitations which were to be inserted in the pronouncement promulgated by Vatican Council I, 4th Session, on July 18, 1870, 40 years later[33]—a few months before the Council was dissolved because of the Franco-Prussian War.

---

[32]*Ibid.,* p. 11.
[33]Opposition to the infallibility decree, as being untimely or impolitic, was typified in England by Gladstone and Newman, and in America by seven bishops of the Church who fought the decree in Council—Domenec of Pittsburgh, Fitzgerald of Little Rock, Kenrick of St. Louis, McCloskey of Louisville, McQuaid of Rochester, Mrak of Marquette, and Verot of Savannah, Vicar of Florida.
Translations of part or all of the decree may be found in Geddes MacGregor, *The Vatican revolution;* in *Décrets et canons du Concile oecumenique et general du Vatican, en latin et en français avec les documents qui s'y rattachent;* in *Catholic encyclopedia,* 15: 308a; and Anne Fremantle, ed., *The papal encyclicals in their historical context.*

"If any one should dare to say that the infallibility of the Pope is an article of faith," continued Varela, "he would be immediately condemned as a heretic by the very Pope himself;" moreover, since the establishment of a religious order was not a matter of faith or morals, "*The Protestant* attacks a fictitious enemy."[34] Thus in a few sentences he made clear that papal infallibility in any form was not at the time a dogma at all, that if it became a dogma its applicability would be limited, and that, since the restoration of the Jesuit Order had nothing to do with faith or morals, it had no bearing on the question of papal infallibility.

So calm, so well-documented, and on many points so surprising was Varela's clarification of his faith that the Reverend Dr. Brownlee, congratulating his audience on having heard such liberal sentiments from the lips of a Roman cleric, labeled his statements "Spanish jesuitry" and accused him of misstating Catholic doctrine. "Señor Varela expresses his own ideas and not the doctrine of the Roman Church; and if they caught him in Rome, they would burn him alive. He only speaks that way because he is in America." The audience laughed at this sally, and even Varela could not suppress a chuckle.

"I am sure," added a colleague of Brownlee, "that this gentleman (Varela) will not last another 24 hours as a priest without being suspended by his Bishop."[35] Years later, Varela found himself smiling in retrospect at the vehemence of this prophecy.

Both Catholic and Protestant prognostications about Bishop Dubois proved incorrect. The venerable prelate did not surrender his post in New York and he did not censure his valiant priest. Dubois returned with the winter, late in 1831, to the unequal contest against financially omnipotent trustees—against laymen who would assign, as principal of the Cathedral school, Father Thomas C. Levins, after the Bishop had suspended him for insubordination. As his administrative woes increased and his strength diminished, the harried prelate leaned ever more on his loyal, intelligent Cuban priest.

Dubois was respected by cultured non-Catholics. He had studied English with Patrick Henry, was friendly with President James

---

[34]*The Protestant's abridger*, no. 1, p. 12.
[35]*Cartas a Elpidio*, 2: 146-47.

Madison and the Randolphs of Virginia, and was once described by President Jackson as "the most complete gentleman I have ever met."[36] Several outstanding conversions took place during his prelacy, and New York State's political leaders, DeWitt Clinton and William Henry Seward, showed themselves sympathetic to the progress of the Church. The scholarly Dubois did not favor the acrimonious religious debates which seemed only to exacerbate feelings. But he was pleased with the temperate and well-documented expositions of Varela, instructive as they were to Catholics and disarming to the Church's assailants.

An epidemic of cholera, which numbed the city in 1832, brought a ban on public meetings and closed churches and schools. Prosperous business men sent their wives and children to rural retreats —north of Canal Street—and many of them closed up shop for the duration. John Power, however, remained at his post in St. Peter's, ministering to the dying and the bereaved. Bishop Dubois, returning from an exhausting upstate visitation, was urged to shun the stricken city; but he resumed his pastoral work at St. Patrick's in Mulberry Street, preferring to share the crisis with his flock. As for the frail Varela, the writer of his obituary in the *Freeman's Journal,* two decades later, was to recall that he "virtually lived in the hospitals." He visited the immigrant ships, suspected of bringing the scourge to the city; he begged and argued his way into Quarantine to carry the consolation of the Sacraments to the afflicted. Native Americans cried out against the Irish refugees, whose unwelcome imports now included plague as well as poverty and papistry; but they had an almost envious praise for the selfless devotion of the Catholic clergy to their unfortunate brethren.

The epidemic passed, and urban life resumed its pace. Bishop Dubois dedicated a new St. Mary's at Grand and Ridge Streets, to replace the structure lost by fire. A conflagration destroyed the school of the Sisters of Charity in Mulberry Street; another, of suspicious origin, consumed the Bishop's unfinished Seminary at Nyack and, with it, the financial proceeds of his two-years' journey to Europe. Short of schools for his flock, the Catholic prelate tried

---

[36]*Archdiocese of New York,* centenary brochure, 1950, p. 5. Cf. also ALS, Varela "To the Most Revd The Arch Bishop of Baltimore [James Whitfield]," from "New York 23d September 1829," Archives Archd. Baltimore.

in 1834 to effect some sort of partnership with the privately incorporated, Quaker-oriented Public School Society of the City of New York; but, although the amenities were observed all around, the effort fell flat.

Félix Varela, constant in his pastoral duties, teaching, defending the faith, publishing a weekly newspaper, writing ceaselessly for the youth of Cuba and for young and old in New York, shared also the Bishop's burdens. "He was frequently sent to distant parts of the State," says Shea, "to settle difficulties, to examine charges brought, and represent the Right Reverend Bishop in most delicate questions."[37]

On one occasion, he went out of New York on a mission of compassion. The City of Boston, rancorous and unrepentant after the burning of the Ursuline Convent in Charlestown by Native Americans, was hanging for piracy a Spanish ship-captain, Don Pedro Gibert, and nine of his men. The intellectual capital of New England, one Catholic historian comments ruefully, could exonerate those who burned and pillaged convents, but it had no mercy for Spanish sailors.[38] Bishop Benedict J. Fenwick, wishing the convicted men to have spiritual consolation from a priest who spoke their tongue, sent for Varela. On June 11, 1835, the Cuban priest walked with the condemned men to the gallows; and as the noose was adjusted, his words rose above the multitude: "Spaniards, ascend to Heaven."[39]

Stories that had reached Rome, that Varela was dissatisfied in New York and would seek another station, proved without basis in fact. His involvement with the welfare of his co-religionists in New York was, as far as he was concerned, complete and final. When the door was opened for him to return to his beloved Cuba, he declined the opportunity.

The stringent Governor Vives gave place in 1832 to Mariano Ricafort, and there was hope for relaxation of controls. Then

---

[37] John Dawson Gilmary Shea, *The Catholic churches of New York City,* p. 689.
[38] Shea, *History of the Catholic Church,* 3: 487.
[39] Germán Arciniegas, *Caribbean, sea of the new world,* tr. by Harriet de Onís, p. 356. For details about the pirates and their sensational trial, cf. Henry K. Brooke, *Book of pirates,* pp. 171-83. Also see *Report of the trial of the Spanish pirates, by a Congressional Stenographer.*

Ferdinand VII died, leaving the Spanish throne to the infant daughter of his fourth wife, and Spain again had too many problems at home to keep a firm hand on the islands. Miguel Tacón, military governor in Havana from 1834 to 1838, began his hated regime, ironically, with an amnesty for political prisoners.

The exiles were seeping back into Cuba.

Tomás Gener, since fleeing with Varela from the ill-fated Cortes in 1823, had gone into business with Appleton's in New York, had written a book on banking and earned an honorary doctorate of laws from Columbia University.[40] Like Varela, he had harbored and aided many Hispanic-American refugees. Now he returned to Matanzas, where he died soon after, on August 15, 1835.[41]

José Antonio Saco, collaborator with Varela on *El mensagero semanal*, transferred his activities to Havana in 1832, becoming editor of the influential *Revista bimestre cubana*. But in trying to establish a progressive Academy of Literature he ran afoul of the Patriotic Society, now turned reactionary under the much-chastened Dr. O'Gavan. Within two years, Saco fled by way of Falmouth, England, to Madrid, there to agitate Cuba's need for social reform. The patriot poet José de la Heredia, whose merits Varela and Saco had defended against Cuban royalists in the pages of *Mensagero,* took advantage of Tacón's offer for a few months in 1836, then withdrew again to self-imposed expatriation in Mexico.

But Varela was not tempted. His patron, the forward-looking Bishop Espada y Landa, had recently died, and subsequent diocesan administrators feared to displease government and other vested interests. The Chair of Constitutional Law had been eliminated at San Carlos. Repressive laws initiated in the time of Vives were being put to sinister purpose. Tacón's became a name to execrate, as synonymous with greed and despotic cruelty. Saco pronounced him "servile in Spain and in Cuba a tyrant . . . a new Nero, a modern Caligula."[42] The one place, other than his parish

---

[40] Portell Vilá, *Historia,* 1: 241.
[41] Cf. Varela, letter of condolence to Gener's widow, "Nueva York septiembre 3 de 1835," in "Cartas Inéditas," p. 66. Varela's other co-delegate, José Leonardo Santos Suárez y Perez (b. Santa Clara 1795), who had studied law at San Carlos under Varela, died in Madrid in 1874. The Peraza Sarausa *Dicc. biogr. cub.* gives notices of all three.
[42] Quoted from Saco's *Memorias* in Espasa, 58: 1477.

in New York, that Félix Varela loved was Cuba; but he would not sacrifice his principles to resume life there. Better to remain in New York, where a man could speak his convictions without fear of reprisal.

In the winter nights when the ice-bound city slept, the son of the caloric Caribbean communed in solitude with his homeland. To Saco and his associates in Havana he wrote:

> I keep vigil when all sleep and toil when all repose. I enjoy life when all others leave off enjoying it, and I find myself free only when society importunes to lie down in chains. Everything is peaceful, and now I can write, but my mind finds nothing to stimulate it. In these silent moments, for it is 12 midnight, my lively imagination presents me only with skeletal trees, frozen lakes, mountains of snow, and desolate fields. But then a kindly memory snatches me from this scene of lifelessness and transports me to the garden of the Antilles, where all is vital. I see leafy trees, restless streams, thick-topped mountains, and flowering plains. . . These delights of my imagination are enhanced by their contrast with the appearance of the small chamber where I write, thanks to a good fireplace, which is not a yard away from me; and I am even closer to my couch, covered with heavy blankets. But I am really among you, I see you all, I speak with all of you.[43]

It was in such a mood, and under such circumstances, that he wrote his *Cartas a Elpidio*. Volume 1 saw the light in New York, 1835; Volume 2 in Madrid 1836 and New York 1838; and a projected Volume 3 he did not publish, or perhaps did not even write, his pen being then occupied with English prose. The *Cartas* were letters to his young friends in Havana—possibly intended for José de la Luz or José María Casal or some other disciple, but probably directed at all freedom-minded youths, for "Elpis" is the Greek word for "hope." They were philosophic, yet personal in tone, offering glimpses of his life in America and developing his mature judgments on the problems of society. They stressed the need for religion—a constructive, positive, forward-looking religion of love, cognizant of the inestimable worth of every human being,

---

[43] José Antonio Fernández de Castro gives the nostalgic letter, Varela to the editors of *Rev. bim. cub.*, dated "Nueva York, 28 de febrero de 1832," in *Medio siglo*, pp. 37-39.

as the basis for a just society. Varela warned especially against demagogues who feed on the people's lack of faith and moral purpose, or who take advantage of their superstition, ignorance, and fanaticism.

The world, says Varela in his *Cartas,* witnesses often the glorification of the evil and the persecution of the noble. This tendency is furthered by the lack, among the masses, of a vital, effective faith in goodness and truth. Absence of such faith causes social unrest; it destroys the courage of the people and serves as a springboard for despotism.

But the scoffers, continues the priest, must not be attacked with harsh words, for they, too, are God's handiwork, and their human dignity must be respected.

> How, then, ought we to handle unbelievers? According to the precepts of the Evangelist—with love and sweetness and at the same time with firmness; not—and this we must emphasize—not by means of persecutions, which, as reason and experience prove, serve only to fan the devouring fire of unbelief; but rather by a noble and valiant character on the part of believers. . . .
> Nothing is more inimical to conversion than insults, and disgracefully we see these practised by very pious men when they attack non-believers. They indulge in mockery, imitating their opponents in buffoonery, and think that by making laugh a little those who do not doubt the truth of their religion they can convince those who deny it. This is an unevangelical means which serves only to satisfy human passions, taking revenge for insults received. . . .
> These words recall to me a doctrine of St. Augustine. . . . 'Distinguish'—says this Holy Father—'in the evil-doer the work of God and the work of the Devil. The man is the work of the former, the sin of the latter.' On no occasion ought one, my Elpidio, hate any of the works of the Supreme Being.[44]

"With reason," reminded Félix Varela, "do non-believers complain of the cruelty with which they have often been treated."[45] His counsel to mutual respect, heard often in the age of ecumenism, sounded a lonely clarion in an era when Protestants, inflamed by the lies of "Maria Monk" and the fears of the misinformed, held

---

[44]*Cartas de Elpidio,* 1: 93-95.
[45]*Ibid.,* 1: 141.

massive meetings against papist infiltration, in a city where Catholics, seeking to fight back, invaded anti-Catholic rallies with rocks and bottles.

In the second volume of *Cartas,* Varela devoted his attention to *"superstición,"* which he conceived broadly as that substitute for religion which "opposes all reform and does not recognize abuses."

> Imprisoning the understanding and numbing the heart with fear, it reduces man to a state of senseless frenzy. In vain do the truly religious and intelligent clamor for the reforms needful for the good of the fatherland and of the faith. . . . A multitude of the misled, guided by a corps of determined theologians, leap to the fray—they scream, insult, torment, and persist in defending with intrepidity the cause of the Devil while representing themselves as advocates of God and as His army of faith. Neither reputation nor honor do they leave unassailed.

Félix Varela, man for our times, protested that bigots injure those whom they attack; they stand in the way of progress and they also damage the cause which they claim to support, repelling its true defenders in disgust. "Angered, the good men attack these narrow-minded fools, but not with prudence; and so they produce much scandal, which serves to stimulate persecutions and perpetuates hatred in all classes of society. This commonly results in a duel of injuries and calumnies, a flinging of odious epithets which, fixed in the memory, keeps always enkindled the flame of discord."[46]

Church leaders in Havana and Madrid did not fancy Varela's views on superstition and religious fanaticism; they wanted the faithful docile, and they mistrusted freedom of thought. The deaths of Bishop Espada and of José Agustín Caballero, who breathed his last in 1835, had closed Cuban Catholicism's liberal era. Why, Varela inquired of Luz y Caballero, was the *Cartas* not selling as well in Cuba as did his earlier works? Was his style at fault, or his views?[47] At least one *varelista* complained that the revered master-philosopher should write in a manner so light and informal.[48] However, the essential trouble lay not with the *Cartas,* but with

---

[46]*Ibid.,* 2: 11-12.
[47]Varela to Luz, "Nueva York 2 de junio de 1835," and "Nueva York 5 de junio de 1839," in "Cartas Inéditas," pp. 67-68.
[48]Félix M. Tanco to Domingo del Monte (Delmonte), 1836; del Monte's *Centón epistolario,* 7: 62.

the Cuban hierarchy, which was blanketing Varela's name in an official ecclesiastical silence that would persist for more than a century.

Unlike many thinkers of his day, Varela did not find religion inconsistent with scientific experiment and social change. Quite the opposite; eschewing religiosity and fanaticism, he saw religion as an underlying rule of life, an effort to open up God's creation to man and to bring humankind into greater fulfillment of its God-given potentials. Such religion demanded a free society. With St. Paul, he declared, "Where there is the Spirit of the Lord, there is liberty."[49]

"According to him, religion is essential to society, it is beneficial to the human race, it is the cement of the sumptuous edifice of the State." Thus does a twentieth-century Cuban assay Varela's attitude toward religion. But it must be "a religion of truth, a religion of social progress and of the full realization of the capacities of man—a religion—to use his own words—'encouraging human participation and taking glory from the progress of enlightenment.' "[50]

A note of homesickness runs through the *Cartas*. Though the breakdown of faith may have been more ominous elsewhere, the intolerance and superstition he lamented were omnipresent in America. He had found challenge enough in New York to demand full consecration of his energies. Here, where there were freedom and friends and a demanding mission, he had resolved to live out his years; yet his heart beat for Cuba:

> There is perhaps no man more devoted than I to this country [the United States], in which I have lived for so many years, in spite of having endangered my life during the earliest years because of the climate and suffered many privations from ignorance of the idiom. I have had during this time various and honorable invitations to locate in other countries, but I have accepted none. After familiarizing myself with the language of these people, I have adapted myself to them and have acquired so many good friends that without ingratitude I could never be unmindful of their attentions and favors.
> I am in effect a native of this country, although I am not a citizen nor will I ever be, because I have formed a firm res-

---

[49]*Cartas a Elpidio*, 2: 172.
[50]Agramonte, "El Padre Varela," p. 77.

olution not to be one of any place on earth since circumstances of which you know have separated me from my fatherland. I do not plan to return there, but I think I owe it the tribute of my love and respect not to unite myself with any other.[51]

Yet when his sister, María de Jesús, whom he has not seen in more than twenty years, writes a melancholy letter urging him to visit his kin, he bids her submit to the will of God. "My separation from my fatherland is inevitable, and to this my faithful friends assent. Perhaps I have committed the fault of loving it too much, but this is the one fault which I do not repent."[52]

His sister would have to content herself with his picture, in miniature, which, at her request, he would send when he could afford it.

---

[51] *Cartas a Elpidio,* 2: 100.
[52] Varela to "Mi querida hermana" from "Nueva York 30 de diciembre de 1842," in "Cartas Inéditas," pp. 70-71.

CHAPTER IV

HE CREATES THE CHURCH OF THE TRANSFIGURATION

The Cuban exile's sacerdotal activities left little time for self-pity.

Excavations for new construction were going on in Ann Street, close to the west wall of Christ Church. The wall appeared to be buckling, although inspectors declared it sound.

On Sunday, October 27, 1833, while the Reverend Joseph Schneller was administering Holy Communion, a disturbance arose in the choir-loft. A huge fissure had spread across the interior wall. When a sudden wind rattled the blinds, the cry was raised that the church was collapsing. Gripped by terror, the congregation fled the building, and several persons were hurt in the mêlée.

Christ Church was doomed. A lay committee—Dr. William Macneven, Robert McKeon, John Everard, John Doyle, and Dr. Mariano Velázquez—considered the situation. A second inspection gave the structure a brief respite, but Bishop Dubois was uneasy about holding services there. The building was 40 years old, the foundation was clearly undermined by the adjoining hole, and attempts to shore it up proved unavailing.[1] The pastor rented temporary quarters nearby—first on the second floor of 208 William Street, then at 45 Ann Street. On August 2, 1835, the second floor loft at 33 Ann Street was blessed as a chapel. It appears from Rodríguez's *Vida* and other sources that Christ Church suffered two fires, of which the second—probably the Great Fire of December 16, 1835, most disastrous to date in any American city—forced the search for another location.

From these makeshift arrangements, there emerged two parishes. The corporation of Christ Church obtained land on James Street, and a solid Romanesque edifice was erected there. This new Christ Church, which became known as St. James, cost with its site $59,000; and it was destined to outlast all other Catholic church buildings in the metropolis. Its high basement, constructed to house the school, became a meeting place of the Catholic Association, which agitated in the 1840's for public aid to education. St. James was dedicated in September 1836, and Dubois appointed as pastor

---

[1] *N.Y. weekly register*, 1, Oct. 26-Nov. 30, 1833, *et al.*

Andrew Byrne, an Irish-born priest who had served as Vicar-General of Charleston.[2]

Some of Varela's congregation transferred to St. James, but most of them—their church-going was done on foot—declared it too far uptown. Moreover, they were bound to their pastor by his energetic leadership, by his rare compassion, by the glow of his goodness. Already, his virtues were becoming legendary.

The Reformed Scotch Presbyterian Church in Chambers Street, opposite the Park, was on the auction block. John Delmonico happened to pass by while the sale was in progress. A native of Switzerland, Delmonico had captained a vessel between the United States and Cuba and had prospered as a wine merchant before settling into the restaurant business with his nephew Lorenzo. He was a devout Catholic and a warm admirer of Father Varela. Knowing that his pastor needed a church, Delmonico, almost on impulse, made the successful bid.

The purchase price was $55,000—and payments on it were raised from the Cuban priest's private fortune, from gifts by Cuban disciples, and from substantial donations by Delmonico and other parishioners. The building was of brick, 50 feet by 70. Behind it, at 23 Reade Street, was a house which Varela purchased as his pastoral residence. This became his home for his remaining years in New York, and served also as a reception center for priests from other countries and for Cubans in search of counsel.

As if to trumpet his belief in the transcendancy of the spiritual over the material, Father Varela renamed the second-hand house of worship Church of the Transfiguration of Our Lord. To the faithful it became known simply as "Father Varela's Church." It was dedicated on March 31, 1836 and, says the historian, "it soon had a large and docile congregation who, under the guidance of so excellent a priest, showed the influence of their holy faith."[3] In compliance with state law, and to shield Bishop Dubois from such assaults as had followed the purchase of Christ Church, Varela had the deed conveyed to a lay board of trustees in March 1837.

From the Church of the Transfiguration radiated the life work

---

[2]The story of Varela's three churches in New York City is told in Shea, *Catholic churches*, pp. 389-401, 686-96.
[3]*Ibid.*, p. 689.

of Félix Varela from that time on; and a potent existence it was, shedding its influence far beyond its place and moment in history. His love of humanity, emanating from his love of the Mystical Body, warmed hearts and burned through barriers. Catholic congregations, then and long after, tended to be ethnically clannish: Irish immigrants were known to leave church when Bishop Dubois addressed them; Germans and Italians and Poles demanded preachers who spoke their native tongues.[4] By contrast, Transfiguration represented an amicable league of nations. Its early trustees were men of many races: Felix O'Neil, John Delmonico, François Everard, John P. García, Michael Burke. Mariano Velázquez, the eminent Spanish-Cuban lexicographer, served as financial auditor. The assistant priests also stemmed from many lands: Joseph Schneller, Austrian; Dr. Charles Constantine Pise, whose Italian father had married a Philadelphian; John Freitas, Portuguese; Lewis Terhykowicz, Polish; Bernardo Antonio Llaneza, a Cuban trained at Rose Hill (Fordham) who later returned to Havana; William McClellan, an Irishman from Rose Hill; and, from 1842 to 1846, an Italian Carthusian, Alexander Muppietti, who, like the pastor, was venerated by the faithful. Muppietti, worn out by missionary work in Turkey, had been headed South for his health when he met Varela and cast his lot with this kindred spirit.

Father Varela and his church accounted for many "firsts" in diocesan history. It was before the era of sodalities, but Varela saw the value of lay participation. He organized a Total Abstinence Society[5] almost a decade before Ireland's Father Theobald Mathew began administering "the pledge" to American audiences. Women of the parish, in the Ladies' Aid, or Sewing Society, provided garments for hard-pressed clients of the Half-Orphan Asylum which had been officially incorporated on May 2, 1835 as "The Asylum for the Relief of the Children of Poor Widowers or Widows."[6] Varela had organized this Society at Christ Church on March 4, 1833, as the Ladies' Society of Charity.[7]

Supplementing the instruction of the Sunday School, the Cuban

---

[4]*Ibid.*, p. 493. St. Mary's on Grand Street had a German-language congregation meeting in the basement in 1835.
[5]*Freeman's jrnl. and Cath. register*, Mar. 20, 1841.
[6]Bayley, *Brief sketch*, p. 156.
[7]1st Annual Report, *N.Y. weekly reg.*, May 24, 1834.

priest used the *Children's Catholic magazine,* which, in an era when literacy was a luxury accomplishment, attained a reported circulation of 13,000.[8] This monthly, founded in March 1838 by prominent laymen, John George and Cornelius H. Gottsberger, blundered in its first issue by using the Protestant version for a versification of the Ten Commandments; and Father Varela was called upon to provide clerical supervision.[9] Small though it was and intended for children, whose prose and verses it often printed, the magazine was yet able to attract notice from eminent opposition sheets, the *Protestant Vindicator* and the *Churchman.* It also won praise from the Catholic *Truth Teller,* from the *Herald, Advocate,* and Boston *Pilot,* and from the secular *New York Gazette.* The magazine in the summer of 1838 called attention to the slanders against Catholics, and against Irish Catholics in particular, in texts and library books supplied by the New York Public School Society.[10] This disclosure prompted Catholic school trustees, early in 1840, to demand public aid for their own institutions, and led to the famous School Crisis of 1840-42 and, eventually, to the founding of the secular public school system of New York City.

The *Children's Catholic magazine* endured only two years, 1838-40, but the following January found Varela advertising its successor, *The Young Catholic's magazine,* in the *Freeman's journal.*[11]

The institution known as the parish "mission" also began with Varela. There were as yet no priest-specialists in this field; but the pastor of Transfiguration often appointed the week before a holyday for a series of edifying and instructive sermons. Knowing the Eucharist to be at the center of Catholic worship, he particularly prepared his people in this way for the Feast of Corpus Christi.

Most important as a vivifying factor in the parish of the Transfiguration was the living example of the pastor. He gave himself completely to his work; when his family in Havana asked him to shelter and educate his nephew, he refused, saying he was at home so little that the boy would be neglected.[12]

---

[8] John B. Sheerin, C.S.P., *The development of the Catholic magazine,* p. 7.
[9] Martin I. J. Griffin, "'The Children's Catholic Magazine,'" pp. 164-65.
[10] Foik, p. 161.
[11] Jan. 9, 1841, *et al.*
[12] Varela to his sister, "Nueva York, 30 de diciembre de 1842," in "Cartas Inéditas," p. 70.

The New York City Hospital was his daily beat for almost 25 years. Its management was Protestant, its patients mostly destitute Catholics. Varela's "charity which opens doors," his radiant humility, won him ingress without question to the bedsides of pain at all times and any hour. But when his own illness terminated his ministrations, a new regulation barred the Catholic priest assigned to the hospital from entering the premises unless officially summoned.[13]

Varela was the embodiment of selflessness—a prototype, as his compatriots later pointed out, of the venerable Bishop Miriel in Victor Hugo's *Les Miserables*. His income from Cuba and the gifts of prosperous friends were instantly diverted to the needs of his church and its poor. "In reading *Les Miserables*," says a recent historian, "one feels that, if Hugo had known Varela, he would not have depicted a bishop, but rather a Cuban priest—*El Padre* Varela."[14]

His acts of benevolence, much as he tried to hide them, became the talk of the town. When a distressed mother came begging as he sat at table, he told her, "Money I have none. But take this silver spoon, the last from my homeland, and sell it—it will fetch enough to feed your family." Therewith he washed the spoon he was using and gave it to her. This gracious deed almost backfired; for the silver bore its donor's initials and the police accused the woman of stealing it, and the priest had to go to the station house to confirm her innocence. After a second, similar incident, the police came to recognize Varela's freehanded way with his possessions, and the press of New York gave him unwanted publicity.

In the dead of winter, a woman clad in a threadbare shawl, with a tiny child in her arms, was walking along Chambers Street soliciting alms. The cold was intense and an icy wind blew across the park. The woman's head was bare, for her shawl scarcely sufficed to cover the infant at her breast. Both mother and child were blue with cold. Coming up from behind them, a gentleman suddenly

---

[13]This new attitude on the part of the hospital gave rise to much correspondence. Cf., for example, the copy of the Memorial of Rev. Henry O'Neill to the governors of the hospital, n. d., AANY, AHP, A-14.

[14]Francisco González del Valle, "Varela, Más Que Humano," pp. 7-25 of *Vida y pensamiento de Félix Varela;* I, vol. 25 of Cuba, Havana (City), Historian, *Cuadernos de historia habanera*.

took off his cloak, and, having glanced in all directions to be sure he was unobserved, threw it over the trembling pair. Then he darted across the street, quickening his pace to escape the mother's cries of benediction. Two merchants, who had happened to see his gesture, followed the man. They identified him as their pastor when he turned in at the Church of the Transfiguration.[15]

Father Varela's housekeeper, at his residence in Reade Street, had a constant battle to keep him supplied with essentials. Whatever was nearest to hand—his watch, his silver, the dishes from his table, the household linens and blankets, his own garments—he gave to those in need. To elude the vigilance of his faithful and worried household helper, he often supplied the receivers of alms through a side window or rear door.[16]

One time, so Cristóbal Madan relates, the solicitous woman outwitted her employer. Knowing that his wardrobe was inadequate for the approaching winter, that there were no blankets in the house, and that he had just received a gift of money, she told him a yarn about a cultured stranger, lately arrived in the city, who had not the means to purchase clothing suitable for the employment his talents merited. With his usual compassion, Varela gave her the money for the unfortunate gentleman. She thereupon spent it to stock the pastor with underwear, bed clothes, and an outer wrap. Surprised indeed he was to discover that he was the object of his own charity.

Such are the stories about the man who, following in the footsteps of his Master, was blessing his people at the Church of the Transfiguration.

The aged Bishop Dubois was finding his strength ever more unequal to the demands of his vast diocese. In 1837, being himself too infirm to travel, he chose Vicar General Varela to represent him as procurator at the Third Provincial Council, which convened

---

[15] *Ilustración americana de Frank Leslie*, N.Y., 3 (no. 56, Nov. 12, 1867): 59, "El Padre Varela: Un Episodio Para la Historia de Cuba," a fanciful account by an anonymous Cuban disciple of Varela, quoted both in *Vida* and in "Más Que Humano."

[16] "Father Felix Varela," p. 474. Adelaide O'Sullivan, who was stimulated toward her vocation in religion by Varela, told many years later about his persistence in almsgiving: Madan to Rodríguez, May 27, 1877, JIRP, Box 14.

in Baltimore on April 16.[17] Bishops Francis Patrick Kenrick, coadjutor of Philadelphia, and Simon Guillaume Gabriel Bruté de Rémur, of Vincennes, Indiana, urged that Varela be permitted to attend the private sessions, to vote, and to sign the canons of the Council in Dubois' name; but they were overruled.[18] Although he questioned this decision himself, Varela tried to gloss it over in a letter to his perturbed Bishop, whom he counselled to take no action on the slight until he presented the facts to him in person.[19]

Also present in Baltimore, as theologian to Bishop Anthony Blanc of New Orleans, was Father Augustin Verot,[20] who many years later—when both he and Varela were long interred—would unwittingly cause anguish to the fellow-countrymen of the Cuban priest.

Dubois asked the Council to appoint a coadjutor to assist him in the See of New York. The name of Varela was mentioned in this connection—it was known that the bishop and many of the faithful would be favorable to his appointment. But Spain would consider it an affront, and so would admirers of the other Vicar General, John Power, whose advancement was supported at the Council by Bishop John England but opposed by Bishop Kenrick.[21]

The greatest objection to Varela's elevation to the episcopacy came from Varela himself. His intimate friends, Juan Manuel Valerino and Cristóbal Madan, later told his biographer that Varela set himself positively against such preferment;[22] that he never exerted himself more diligently for any goal than he now did to avoid episcopal honors.

The choice fell not on Power, as many New York Catholics had wished, but on John Hughes, an Irish priest stationed in Philadelphia who was present at the Council as a consulting theologian. Hughes became Coadjutor Bishop of New York in 1838 and Administrator in 1839. Meanwhile, both Power and Varela con-

---

[17] Peter Guilday, *History of the Councils of Baltimore*, p. 112.
[18] Kenrick to Dr. Cullen in Rome, "Phil. May 22, 1837," Amer. Catholic Hist. Soc. of Phila., *Records*, 7 (1896): 294, reproduced from original in American Papers in archives of Irish College, Rome.
[19] ALS, Varela to "Right Reverend Sir," dated Baltimore, April 23, 1837, AANY, AHP, A-14.
[20] Guilday, *Hist. of the Councils*, p. 114.
[21] Kenrick to Cullen, "Phil. May 22, 1837."
[22] *Vida*, p. 222.

tinued as Vicars General, while Bishop Dubois lapsed into general debility.

Bishop Hughes was in Europe, seeking aid for his mission diocese, from late 1839 to mid-1840. Bishop Dubois, whom he had superseded, was waiting out his last weary years, preparing himself for eternity. It was during this period, while Power and Varela had management of the diocese, that the School Aid Crisis erupted.

The Public School Society, although a private organization, had obtained a virtual monopoly on public education funds. But the Society's schools scheduled sermons by Protestant ministers, which all pupils had to attend; they incorporated Protestant prayers and hymns and homilies into the curriculum; and their textbooks abounded with references derogatory to Catholicism. Meanwhile, the Catholic parish schools, crowded into unsanitary church basements or rented rooms, were underfinanced and undermanned and frequently, for want of better, had to use the same objectionable textbooks.

Bishop Dubois had made a futile gesture in 1834 against the Public School Society's anti-Catholic bias. Four years later, in July 1838, the *Children's Catholic magazine,* under Félix Varela, sounded a warning in an article on "School Books Which Have Attacks on the Catholic Religion."[23] Thus the effort to eliminate bigotry in New York's so-called public schools, for which Bishop John Hughes was later to earn both fame and notoriety, really began under Dubois, with the learned support of his Cuban-born Vicar-General.

When Governor William Henry Seward's Address to the Legislature of New York in January 1840 raised the hope that church-affiliated schools might again obtain state aid—denied to them since 1825[24]—the trustees of the Catholic schools, led by Vicar General Power, inaugurated a campaign for public assistance. In the bitter conflict which ensued, between the Protestants rallied by the Public School Society on the one side and the Catholics sparked by Power and, soon, by Bishop Hughes, on the other, Félix Varela stood out as thoughtful, sure-handed, yet conciliatory.

---

[23] Griffin, pp. 164-65.
[24] Joseph J. McCadden, "Governor Seward's Friendship With Bishop Hughes."

To investigate further complaint against the Society's textbooks, Varela requested copies; and the Society's trustees, who wished their schools to attract children of all faiths, readily complied, promising: "Any suggestion or remarks which the Rev. Mr. Varela may deem it right to make, on his own behalf and that of his associates, after said books have been examined, shall receive the most serious and respectful consideration of this board."[25]

True to its word, the Public School Society appointed a committee to examine the objectionable passages cited by Varela, and to eradicate from its class and library books any additional slurs on the religion or nationality of Catholics. Thinking to win cooperation from the other Vicar General, they also waited on John Power with a complete set of their schoolbooks. The Common Council had just ruled against the Catholic petition for a share in the school funds, and the Society, to solidify the victory, was seeking advice toward making its schools acceptable to everyone. Vicar General Power, however, was not accepting defeat. Although he received the Society's delegation cordially, he let two months elapse before acting on their request for expurgation suggestions. When he did reply, his answer took the form of an angry open letter in the *Freeman's Journal,* a diocesan organ established by him on July 4, 1840 to supplant the *Truth Teller,* whose editors saw advantage in the mingling of children of diverse creeds in American primary schools. Power's blast signaled a war to the death on the Public School Society.

Varela, whose *Weekly Register* had fallen victim to a series of fires, had founded in September 1839 another periodical, the *Catholic Register,* which followed Bishop Hughes on his European travels and kept him informed on the school issue. The new *Register,* which soon had over 2,000 subscribers, contained, besides "a simple, logical explanation of the Church's teaching," sections on the arts and sciences and a weekly epitome of events in Europe and America of interest to Catholics. Having no longer the assistance of Father Schneller, Varela did most of the writing and editing himself.[26]

[25] For the trustees' resolution, dated March 24, 1840, see William Oland Bourne, *Hist. of the Public School Soc.,* p. 325.
[26] Foik, p. 150.

In the *Register's* columns, Varela took the stand that the tax-supported "public" schools were really Protestant, and that since Catholics paid their share of taxes, they should in all fairness receive part of the education fund for their schools. He believed that religion, being at the heart of law and morality, was essential to education, particularly in a republic, where good government was contingent upon an enlightened and virtuous electorate. He chided those Catholics who beclouded the issue with political considerations—let them all unite, ideologically, on the need for equal support of schools of every faith. Hughes, writing to Varela from Dublin on June 1, 1840, thanked him for reporting events in the diocese:

> Many thanks for the constancy of your kindness in furnishing me with copies of *The Catholic Register* at so many points of my wandering in Europe. To appreciate the value of this attention, one must be, or imagine himself, in my situation, absent from the scene which claims the solicitude of his mind and the affections of his heart. His eye may be delighted with what he sees—his ear charmed with what he hears—but his memory and inward feelings are perpetually reverting to other sights, and sounds, and objects, to him more dear and interesting. Now of all these a newspaper is a kind of daguerrotype impression; and nothing can be more pleasant than to be met or pursued by such missives in distant countries.[27]

The Bishop's chief concern seemed to be the acquiring of funds and materials for a diocesan college and seminary. But he expressed himself as pleased with the efforts to obtain school aid. "Nothing could be more cruel and unjust in principle," he agreed, "than to tax the Catholic father for a fund which is to be expended in perverting his child, under the name of public education."[28]

Hughes had learned, from accounts in the *Register,* that some Catholics were opposing public aid because, as Democrats, they could not favor a measure which Seward, a Whig, seemed to support. Like the Vicars General, the Bishop deplored the injection of politics into the issue; but Varela spread oil on the waters by announcing that Catholics were all united, as they ever must be, on a matter so essential to the Faith.

---

[27] John R. G. Hassard, *Life of the Most Reverend John Hughes,* p. 220.
[28] Browne, "Public Support," pp. 30-31, quoting from letter of Hughes to Varela in *Cath. reg.,* June 25, 1840.

Within two weeks of his return to New York, Bishop Hughes had taken over the meetings of the Catholic Association and was himself monopolizing the battle against the Public School Society. He muted not only the Catholic laymen who advocated mixed schools but also the lay leaders in the fight for aid to Catholic schools. John Power left the city for reasons of health. The Reverend Henry J. Browne, who has brought to light many documents concerning the school crisis, credits Varela with "first expounding ideas that were to become the oratorical stock in trade of the campaign later led by the bishop."[29] But it should be noted that, while many of the ideas were those of Varela, the method of campaign was one hundred per cent Hughes. The Bishop was determined to break the monopoly of the Public School Society, which stood in the way of aid to parish schools; and in return he would promise not to teach religion during regular school hours. More important, he wished to subdue once and for all the fractious laity who had caused his predecessor so much heartache, and he declared what he called a "holy war" on the *Truth Teller* editors— "miserable traffickers" in Catholic "credulity" and on their "vile print."[30]

So vigorous were the Bishop's denunciations of the Society, so vociferous the demonstrations he harangued, that the prime questions at issue—Was religion essential in good education? Should church-related schools therefore receive public aid?—were blurred in the controversy. Hatred, already instigated by the libelous bestseller entitled *Awful disclosures of Maria Monk,* now overwhelmed the community's good sense. The Public School Society, forced to yield place to an elected Board of Education, dragged down with itself the hope of public funds for elementary schools which taught religion; and the generation of the Know-Nothings—anti-Hughes, anti-papist, rabidly anti-Catholic—was spawned. The Catholics of New York had achieved a unity of front under a belligerent and capable spokesman; but they paid a high price in the upsurge of public hostility and in the loss of lay leadership.[31]

---

[29]"Public Support," p. 41.
[30]*Ibid.*, pp. 35-36. Browne quotes from Hughes' letter to Seward, N.Y., Nov. 29, 1840, in Univ. of Rochester Library, William H. Seward Papers.
[31]Joseph J. McCadden, "Bishop Hughes Versus the Public School Society of New York."

Varela, who saw religion as necessary in education and wanted only to eliminate anti-Catholic bias, faded out of the educational conflict as Bishop Hughes took over. The Cuban is not listed among the prominent laymen and clerics who silently flanked the Bishop as he harangued the Board of Aldermen on the offenses of the Public School Society. His *Catholic Register* was absorbed in January 1841 into the *Freeman's Journal,* with Bishop Hughes editorially endorsing the merger. For a time, Varela continued to write for the "Register" section of the enlarged *Freeman's Journal.*

In April 1841 Varela began another vehicle, *The Catholic expositor and literary magazine: a monthly magazine.* His collaborator on this publication was the Reverend Dr. Charles Constantine Pise, poet, playwright, novelist, and only Catholic priest ever to serve as chaplain to Congress. A decade earlier, Pise had edited in Baltimore, for the one year of its existence, the *Metropolitan,* a highly literate publication which has been called the first Catholic magazine in America.[32]

Taking its tone from the editors, the *Expositor* was literary and philosophical. Pise was translating for the magazine *Les soirées de St. Pétersbourgh,* published 1821 by the royalist, ultramontane Count Joseph Marie de Maistre. Coeditor Varela, who felt that Maistre's antagonism to materialism had pushed him to extremes on "innate ideas," balanced this work with an essay "Concerning the Origin of Our Ideas."[33] He also wrote critiques of the ultraliberal ideas of de Lamennais, whose condemnation by the Pope in 1832 had led him into virulent attacks on Rome,[34] and of the transcendentalism of Immanuel Kant, which admits material and metaphysical realities only in terms of our perception of them. The Cuban evaluated the German philosopher as a great thinker who had built a magnificent, coherent system on the impracticable premise that things can never be known as they actually exist, that all knowledge is relative to the eyes and mind of the beholder. More than a century later, in 1944, Cuban historians would republish, in their own language, these essays of their philosopher.

---

[32]Sheerin, p. 7.
[33]*Cath. expositor,* Jan. 1842. For discussion of this essay and of Varela's "Letter of an Italian . . . on the Doctrines of M. de Lamennais" and "Essay on the Doctrine of Kant," 1841-43, cf. *Reforma filosófica,* pp. 125-58.
[34]Cf. Farley, pp. 114-17.

The scholarly bent of Father Varela had caused him to pursue his textual comparisons of various Bibles. Dissenter sects among Protestants in that day (Presbyterians, Methodists, Baptists, Unitarians, Quakers) held that a man's salvation depended, among other factors, on the reading of the Scriptures, through which God spoke to the receptive individual. They had actively sponsored universal education, in Sabbath schools and free public schools, so that "every child might learn to read the Bible" and interpret it for himself. Scripture lessons used in the Quaker-and-Presbyterian-oriented New York Public School Society's classes bore on the title-page the words "without notes or comment," stressing the fact that no Church, with its claims of authority, should come between the reader and his personal inspiration. The Roman Catholic Church was not, as Protestant fundamentalists often charged, anti-Bible and therefore anti-God; but it upheld the importance of tradition and authority and deemed that the untrained laity were not always capable of interpreting the Divine Word correctly. Varela had pointed out to the Public School Society trustees that the principle "without notes or comment" went to the root of the Protestant-Catholic division; and they, out of respect for his sincerity, had made the tremendous concession of expunging the phrase from their textbooks. They restored it, however, in the heat of their controversy with Bishop Hughes.

For the *Expositor,* Varela wrote "The Five Different Bibles Distributed and Sold by the American Bible Society"—a work not so much of Scriptural exegesis as of textual comparison, implemented by his adeptness as theologian and philologist. He showed, for example, that the Spanish Bible distributed by the Society was a translation of the accepted Catholic version; and that some of the Bibles were rejecting as uninspired or unauthentic whole books which were included in others. The message received by the individual reader would, he emphasized, depend on the particular edition which he consulted—being, therefore, relative, how could it be endowed with the certainty of revelation?[35]

Along with this heady intellectual fare, Varela treated *Expositor*

---

[35]*Cath. expos. and lit. mag.*, 1 (July 1841): 137-45, "The Five Different Bibles, Distributed and Sold by the American Bible Society. Compared by the Very Rev. Felix Varela, D.D.;" continued in subsequent issues, Aug.-Dec., 1841. Varela makes a comparison of the five biblical texts.

readers to lucid answers on problems of general and immediate concern. Catholics in New York, as elsewhere in the United States, were widely accused of placing fealty to the Pope above the demands of American citizenship. In the 1840's and '50's, the fear that the Pope and his priests were plotting a despotic takeover of free America mounted into a political mania. Félix Varela knew love of country and love of God as children of one mother. In "Religion and Patriotism," he affirmed that true patriotism is always religious; and that if a Catholic sovereign attacked the United States, even if he were the Pope as ruler of the Papal States, American Catholics would repel him with the same fighting spirit they had shown against England, "contributing with their lives and their goods to the preservation of national independence."[36]

In 1844, when a request for public aid to parish schools in Philadelphia resulted in riots in which several Catholic churches and a valuable library were burned and many persons lost their lives, Félix Varela counselled his readers to keep their heads and counter hatred with love. While Bishop Hughes was calling on Catholic men to defend their churches with arms if necessary, the Cuban priest sought to calm the waters in an *Expositor* editorial: "And, who knows but, that out of the smouldering ruins of our Churches and edifices, may spring up a monument which, while it records the horrors of fanaticism, will stand as a warning and a caution to future generations. As for us Catholics, 'let us,' following the good advice of the *Catholic Herald* [founded by Hughes when he was a priest in Philadelphia], 'forget and forgive, and in Christian love, show the happy influence of Religion, which, even in the face of an enemy, discovers a brother.'" We know, continued Varela wishfully, that no one will join more heartily in this sentiment than will Bishop Hughes.[37]

To his sister in Cuba, worried about the American church-burnings, he wrote consolingly: "This now has passed, and has only served to augment the number of converts to the Church."[38]

The *Expositor* endured for almost four years—a remarkable span, in view of its uncompromisingly high intellectual caliber and

---

[36] Quoted from *Cath. expos.* in *El padre Varela*, p. 440.
[37] *Cath. expos.*, 6 (June 1844): 240, "Editorial Observations."
[38] "Cartas Inéditas," p. 71, letter dated "Nueva York 26 de julio de 1844."

the general impoverishment and illiteracy of New York's Catholic populace—especially of its inpouring immigrant sector. During several of these years, Varela was also editing the *Young Catholic's magazine,* successor to his popular *Children's Catholic magazine.*

Félix Varela was now a recognized leader among American Catholics. His works were quoted in the *United States Catholic miscellany* of Charleston, a pioneer Catholic weekly.[39] He served as Vicar General of New York continuously, under Bishops Dubois and Hughes, from 1837 to his death in 1853. In 1841, he was awarded the degree of Doctor of Sacred Theology by St. Mary's Seminary, Baltimore. Thus was made official the title of "Dr. Varela" which New Yorkers had long accorded him. Also in 1841, he published from New York a fifth, up-dated edition of his most demanded work, the *Lecciones de filosofía.*

When New York's first diocesan synod was convoked in St. Patrick's Cathedral, on Sunday, August 28, 1842, with nearly 70 priests in attendance, Bishop Hughes offered the Holy Sacrifice and "the promoters were the Very Rev. Drs. Power and Varela."[40] On March 10, 1844, when John McCloskey, Brooklyn-born former parishioner of St. Peter's and first president of St. John's College, Fordham, was consecrated bishop in the Cathedral, with Bishops John Hughes, Richard Whelan of Richmond, and Benedict Fenwick of Boston presiding, "the assistant priest"—to quote a later American cardinal—"was the famous Cuban patriot, Father Felix Varela."[41] Two other New York priests were elevated to the prelacy at the same time—Fathers Andrew Byrne, pastor of St. James (offspring of Varela's Christ Church), and William Quarter of old St. Mary's, and "the effect was heightened by the eloquent discourse of John Power."[42] Varela and Power, the Vicars General, two bulwarks of Catholicity, beloved leaders of their flocks, who, for reasons of state, would never themselves become bishops. In 1846, Varela attended as theologian for Bishop Hughes, along

---

[39] Aug. 9, 1834, p. 45, "Answer to the Arguments Contained in the Extract of a Letter from the Late Charles Butler to Dr. Fletcher, on the Proper Method of Finding the True Religion. Published in the *Birmingham Catholic Magazine,* and inserted in the last number of the *Register.* By the Rev. Felix Varela."
[40] Shea, *Catholic churches,* p. 96.
[41] Farley, p. 147.
[42] Shea, *Hist. of the Catholic Church,* 4: 105.

with Bishop (later American's first Cardinal) McCloskey, at the Sixth Provincial Council of Baltimore.

Among his personal friends, Varela numbered many of New York's leading Catholic laymen: the merchant John Baptist Lasala; Joseph O'Connor and his son-in-law, Edward Shortell, builders of churches; the Delmonico family, restaurateurs; and the family of André Parmentier, noted Belgian horticulturist and founder of the Botanic Garden in Brooklyn. He was also responsible for several religious vocations, notably that of Adelaide O'Sullivan, who on his advice was received into the Convent of the Discalced Carmelites in Havana and who later founded her own convent in Spain.[43] It was her brother, John L. O'Sullivan, who brought Orestes A. Brownson to New York.

Varela remained keenly alert and, when need be, critical, to popular currents of thought. His Cuban compatriot, Mariano Cubí y Soler, founder of the periodical *Revista bimestre cubana*, had become a phrenology enthusiast. After lecturing and writing on the subject to eager audiences in New England, he had established a school of phrenology in France. Varela analyzed this fad in an appendix to the fifth (1841) edition of his *Lecciones*, remarking that, although it called itself a science, he considered it an aberration. He had already assailed it in the *Miscelánea filosófica*, and treated it now only because of its renewed popularity. It was an absurdity of materialism to dismiss the brilliant talents of a Voltaire, or to excuse the crimes of an assassin, as consequences of cranial configuration. Not only was phrenology useless (for who can change the shape of a skull?); it was also illogical, deducing invalidly from superficial likenesses.[44]

Varela's *Lecciones de filosofía* and other texts remained standard in the Cuban seminaries of learning; for, although the man and his *Habanero* had been banned, his scholarly works had not. His disciples in Havana, using his books and expounding the philosophical principles he had set forth, continued to seek his opinion on moot questions. On October 22, 1840, he discussed in a long letter problems which José de la Luz, Francisco Ruiz, and Manuel González del Valle, the latter the initiator of modern philosophy

---

[43] Ryan, *Old St. Peter's*, pp. 124-25.
[44] Varela, *Lecciones de filosofía*, 1: 308-25.

in the University of Havana, had laid before him. He had hesitated to reply to them, for he had been so far removed from philosophic pursuits; but their insistence could no longer be disregarded. He took up, accordingly, three controversial matters.

(1) Should the teaching of philosophy begin with logic or with physical science? His answer was that the two are interrelated and may well be taught together. Logic is necessary for correct scientific conclusions; but students prefer physics, finding it more enjoyable, and often learn logic through this study without realizing it. Although Varela continued to place logic first in his *Lecciones,* the professor was at liberty to begin with the second volume, which dealt with science.

(2) Should utility be allowed as the principle and standard of behavior? To this question, Varela pointed out that there had never been a philosopher who dared deny that a *real good* is *true utility* and that *seeming good* is *false utility*. The *real good* is that which conforms to the nature of things and therefore to the Divine Will which is their origin. Actions which have as their object the *real good* are just, those which are directed toward a *seeming utility* are evil. Basically, both the Utilitarians and their opponents agree on this; and the dispute hinges mainly on semantics.

(3) Should the system of Cousin be adopted? Educational circles in Havana were then agog with the teachings of Victor Cousin, France's renowned minister of public instruction. Cousin, like Varela, was an eclectic, a believer in universal education and in freedom of thought; but he taught that truth could be grasped through intuition, whereas Varela stressed the importance of sensory experience, observation, and reasoning. In his student days at San Carlos, said Varela, all the disciples of José Agustín Caballero had been *cousinianos*—although Cousin was yet an inarticulate youth—because they learned the extreme Cartesian theory of innate ideas. O'Gavan, on the other hand, had stressed sense learning. What, now, asked Varela, was all the excitement about? Cousin and his followers would eventually become but names in history. Both the *innatista* and the *sensualista* must direct instruction toward the acquisition of sciences, and whose system was correct would become a matter of philosophic curiosity. Although Cousin might be termed a pantheist, let us not, Varela

concluded, alarm ourselves if others follow his system. Let us, avoiding these futile divisions, get on with the important business of education.

Alluding, in a postscript to this epistle, to phrenology, Varela commented that "it was passing, like all fads." He marvelled that José de la Luz y Caballero and José de la Luz Hernández seemed to have taken it seriously. If he himself ever served as a phrenological specimen, quipped the learned priest, they would find on him an anti-phrenological bump, or a most prominent convolution of phrenological incredulity.[45]

Félix Varela's own philosophy aimed at being selective, progressive, open to new ideas but not unhinged by them; comprehensive, well-balanced; tempered by observation, meditation, and reason, and by an understanding of man's individual and social needs. As an eclectic, he took truth where he found it and eschewed the building of an imposing thought system. If he never attained fame among American thinkers, it was partly because the English-speaking world did not in that epoch look to Spanish Catholics for wisdom; and partly because his cogitation was so calmly many-sided and undramatic.

Increasingly, the priest's far-ranging mind was applying itself to the practical and immediate. Cares of his parish occupied his hours and monopolized his thoughts. His collaborator on the *Catholic expositor and literary register,* Dr. Pise, departed for Europe, and the magazine was discontinued in 1844. Thereafter Varela wrote no further philosophic essays in his adopted tongue.

Spiritually, the Church of the Transfiguration was thriving. Financially, it was in turbulent water. The Report of the Trustees, December 1, 1840, showed an annual deficit of $1,103.75 on operating expenses of $4,753.75.[46]

Félix Varela had poured his patrimony into its purchase and maintenance, no one could know to what extent. His personal friends, Spanish, Irish, French, Swiss, and established American, had been more than generous. Yet, in the liberal tradition of the young Republic, he had left the management to elected laymen. In

---

[45]Mestre y Domínguez, pp. 93-110.
[46]MS signed by Thomas S. Scanlon, president of the board of trustees of Transfiguration Church, and by Edward P. McGloin; AANY, Church Records, Church of the Transfiguration, "Dec. 1st 1840."

other churches, Bishop Hughes had found it necessary to checkmate the trustees when, buttressed by state law, they sought to stand up against ecclesiastical authority. In the Church of the Transfiguration, however, members of the lay board petitioned their pastor to meet with them; when he assented, they elected him President.

Varela was a man of hope. "Never mind—go on," he was wont to say. "The sun shines for all without distinction."[47] Times were desperately hard for Catholics of New York. Their victory over the Public School Society had backfired in clouds of calumny and hate. Nativists were assailing them—economically, socially, politically. Haggard hordes of famine victims were arriving from Ireland—starved, unlettered, penniless, plague-ridden. For them, too, the church and its works of mercy had to be kept going.

St. Peter's, with its fine new edifice in Barclay Street, was snatched from the auction block only by the vigorous action of Bishop Hughes. Lawyer John Jay, who had early sought a constitutional clause to disfranchise Catholics, threatened in 1843 to offer for sale at a discount the bonds on which St. James, Transfiguration's sister church, was defaulting.[48] Through his Church Debt Association, and through monies obtained abroad, the Bishop bought this and others of his diocesan churches as they teetered on bankruptcy.

At Transfiguration, the people and Father Varela continued to work a miracle of survival. His wants were simple—men wondered how he existed—but parish needs were insatiable. Records at Transfiguration show him spiriting up funds to save the choir from extinction; paying $225 for repairs to a stained glass window and refusing reimbursement; heeding a call for relief of hard-pressed creditors; accepting title to some of the church's sacred utensils in lieu of $600—a full year's salary—owed him; persuading Nicholas Cádiz to take a "mortgage" on the church organ; requesting, vainly, a loan from a society in Holland which had succored St. Peter's in Barclay Street; and receiving a vote of thanks from the trustees "for his late very great exertions to

---

[47]"Father Felix Varela," p. 474.
[48]ALS, John Jay to Bp. Hughes, "New York May 18th 1843, Law Office No. 55 Wall Street," AANY, AHP, A-16.

sustain the church by soliciting voluntary contributions in aid of it."[49] Some of the contributions had come from Havana, in response to a campaign by his young curate, Bernardo Antonio Llaneza.

Still the demands for repayment of loans continued, and the trustees could think of no better solution than further borrowing. This course Bishop Hughes sternly forbade. The corporation of Varela's former parish, now located at Christ (or St. James) Church in James Street, was in a legal snarl for taking out one mortgage too many; and not wanting the error repeated, Hughes indited this warning to the Board at Transfiguration:

> Having understood that you are about to make or obtain a loan by bond & mortgage on Transfiguration church, I wish to say that I regard that course as unprofitable in a fiscal point of view, and more than doubtful in regard to its morality. Every note hitherto given out by the Trustees to poor creditors for small sums, you are bound to regard as if it were a mortgage—& I do not see how you can admit new credit on that which is already pledged to the whole of its value. If you can by a loan pay *all*, very well. If you can and will substitute your own or some other security for the difference between what the church owes, and the amount of the loan, I have no objection. But I admonish you again—not a proceeding that cannot extricate the church, and which will only pay some all, and leave the rest nothing. This was done at St. James's & was regarded as dishonest & disgraceful. If all cannot be paid, at least let all share the loss pro rata alike. It is thus alone you can save all that remains the honour of your board.[50]

Finally, on Easter Monday, April 8, 1844, the congregation assembled in the basement of Transfiguration Church, heard a full report of the trustees on receipts, expenditures, and indebtedness, and solemnly requested Félix Varela to act as sole trustee. This move had received an advance nod from Bishop Hughes. Varela accepted, and a week later the laymen conveyed the whole property and the whole debt "to our beloved Pastor .... as a Corpora-

---

[49]Cf. MS Minutes at Transfiguration Church, 1840-1843, *passim*. The vote of thanks is dated Feb. 8, 1843.
[50]Copy of letter of John, Bishop of New York, from "New York Octr. 23rd, 1843," to the Trustees of Transfiguration and St. Peter's Churches, AANY, AHP, A-10.

tion sole, or Trustee for the Benefit of the Roman Catholic Congregation worshiping in said church."[51]

The financial report of November 1, 1844 revealed a precariously balanced budget, with $3.37 in cash-on-hand. The debt had been reduced by $3,812.97 during this year, and claims of $222.60 had been surrendered, leaving a capital indebtedness of almost $46,000. Varela asked his creditors to be patient, and to desist from incurring the added costs of judgments against the church.[52] Records at this period show Varela at one time "loaning" Transfiguration $467.50, while his "donations" to it topped $612.00.

Ladies of the parish, already occupied with the Half-Orphan Asylum's needy, came to the help of their hard-pressed pastor. They ran a week-long fair to reduce the debt, raising in some years over $2,000. In 1845, rumor had it that Transfiguration was in bondage to the sum of $64,000; Varela, fearing that the fair would be dismissed as a futile gesture, advertised in the *Freeman's Journal* to set the record straight: the amount was under $39,000.[53] Again, the distaff efforts brought substantial results.

During 1845 the receipts included $200 in donations from Havana and $150 from gifts to Father Varela. The report of June 22, 1846, showed the church debt down to $36,322.62.[54] Varela was making headway in the financial struggle, but it was heavy going for a man prone to regard money as of small consequence.

Nature had endowed Félix Varela with a frail body and a seemingly infinite reserve of nervous energy. His delicate Latin physique never became inured to the harsh New York climatic changes. From his first winter in Manhattan, he had suffered a hacking cough. But in his obsession to serve man and God, he disregarded the stop-signs of illness. Night and day, in all weather, he was on call for the sick and the poor. He went always on foot, often without protection against the elements. While others

---

[51]MS Minutes, Apr. 15, 1844.
[52]Printed circular, "Receipts and Expenditures of Transfiguration Church from October 10th, 1843, to November 1, 1844," with five paragraphs of comment and appeal by the pastor. AANY, Church Records.
[53]*Freeman's jrnl. and Catholic reg.*, Nov. 29, 1845.
[54]Printed report, Transfiguration Church, signed by the pastor, dated "New-York, June 22d, 1846; from April 17, 1844." AANY, Church Records.

slept, he was busy with his pen; for writing was more essential to him than rest. His mind remained keen, his spirits defied weariness.

"Three or four ailments," he jested, "are contending to pull me down." His cough worsened—people whispered the dread word, "Consumption!" Asthmatic seizures stifled his breath—held him paralyzed for long minutes. Twice, as early as 1839, the Havana papers carried reports of his death—the third time, he said, the report would be true.[55] When he reached the point of exhaustion, he traveled to Saratoga Springs, finding his energies renewed by the mineral waters.[56]

The third report of his death must have come in 1845; for on March 12 of that year he wrote to his sister in Havana, saying that, far from being dead, he felt stronger than ever and believed he would reach a tough old age.[57]

In 1846, he went with Bishop Hughes to the Provincial Council in Baltimore, serving as theologian. Returning to New York, he was caught up at once in the hectic activity of his pastorate. "Transfiguration Church," wrote his young curate, the Reverend William McClellan, on August 26, 1846, "is already famous for the multiplicity of its business, sick calls, confessions, duns, confraternities, &c." As to Dr. Varela, "He is as usual jogging along at the same pace, and with the same peculiarities."[58]

But the aging priest could not keep his self-assigned pace. He was visibly unwell—his smile, his luminous eyes had become a mask for suffering. His lungs, it was said, had collapsed. As winter set in, friends, fearing for his life, removed him to Florida, to his old haunts at St. Augustine, whose salubrious climate was already attracting the invalid and the aged.

A few months in the old Spanish city eased Father Varela's pain. Apparently recovered, he journeyed back to New York with the spring, resuming the feverish routine in disregard of his

---

[55]Varela to his sisters, "Nueva York enero 20 de 39," in "Cartas Inéditas," p. 67.
[56]To his sister, María de Jesús Varela, "Nueva York 26 de julio de 1844," in "Cartas Inéditas," p. 71.
[57]*Ibid.*, p. 72.
[58]McClellan to "Rev. & Dear Friend;" Archives of Univ. of Notre Dame, photostat in Browne Collection. McClellan, fresh from seminary, succeeded the venerated Father Muppietti as Varela's assistant.

physical frailties. Winter again forced him South, for a longer stay. From St. Augustine, he kept in touch with his church, which McClellan administered in his absence.

By the summer of 1849, a surge of renewed energy induced him to follow his heart back to Transfiguration, where the Cuban fellowship in New York, ever loyal to "el padrecito" ("little father"), rejoiced that he had returned to them revitalized. "I never would have believed it," wrote Gaspar Betancourt Cisneros to José Antonio Saco, "if with my own eyes I had not seen it. When he left for Florida, I would not bet a pinch of snuff on his life; you could not hear his words from chair to chair. Now he talks like seven, and how he laughs and jests is a delight." Betancourt Cisneros voiced but one complaint; although Varela inquired often after Saco and other disciples, he was "entirely and exclusively devoted to his Church and his Irishmen."[59]

Soon the reaction set in. The priest's eagerness to resume his post had betrayed him. His tormented body would no longer follow his spirit's bidding. With the onset of winter, he was smitten again. Rigid with pain, choking with every breath, he could neither lie down nor recline. In 1850 he deeded the Church of the Transfiguration to Bishop Hughes, who became New York's first Archbishop in that year, and said what proved a final farewell to those in New York who loved him as friend and mentor.

He would end his years in St. Augustine, serving as priest there as long as the Lord gave him strength to breathe.

He was back among the scenes of his childhood—San Marcos Castle, the Tolomato Cemetery where Rita Morales and other kinfolk reposed, where a sepulchre enclosed the mortal remains of his old teacher, the Reverend Michael O'Reilly. The Florida peninsula had now been American for a generation: the old Spanish families were fled, the narrow streets had taken on English names; but the Spanish Church of St. Augustine, built by Michael O'Reilly of coquina and of the ruins of mission chapels, dominated the square, and the column erected in jubilation over Spain's liberal Constitution of 1812 still held its head high, the Spanish inhabitants, in 1818, having disregarded Ferdinand's

---

[59]Letters, Gaspar Betancourt Cisneros to Saco from N. Y., June 3 and July 17, 1849; *Medio siglo*, pp. 111-19.

order to demolish it. Félix Varela, the expatriate who had given half his life to New York's unwanted, could here feel the soft breath of home.

He was a day or two's journey from Cuba, whose citizenship he had never renounced; yet he sought no return to his native land. The prophet of her liberation would not cringe to the realities of the island's fate. Slavery, which he had harangued the Cortes to outlaw, was more than ever entrenched. Bishop Espada was dead, and interred with him was his program of social progress. His successors, taking their cue from Madrid, had veered toward reaction. The Chair of the Constitution was a dubious memory at San Carlos; and in 1841, Governor Gerónimo Váldez had activated an old law for the seizure of monasteries. Even the Economic Society—formerly the Patriotic Society of Friends of the Fatherland—under the once-liberal O'Gavan had turned its back on change. The fervent lyrical voice of José María Heredia, whom Saco and Varela had defended in *El Mensagero* against government partisans, lay muted in a Mexican grave. The Cortes in Spain had rejected Saco and other Cuban delegates, declaring the island a mere possession, its colonial inhabitants not entitled to representation as citizens. General Leopoldo O'Donnell y Jorris, most execrated in a line of tyrants sent from Madrid, had become, in 1844, Captain General in Havana and governor of the island; to the cruelty of a Tacón he and his lady added corruption and remorseless cupidity. Among the orders of O'Donnell was a new decree of condemnation of Félix Varela.

Friends of the island were torn among themselves. There were those who pressed for revolt from within and those who feared this would lead to the self-enthronement of a ruthless caudillo. The Negro insurrection of 1844 and the separationist conspiracy of Narciso López (1849-51) both resulted in fearful reprisal and a tightening of the vise.

Cristóbal Madan and fellow-expatriates clamored more loudly than ever for absorption into the United States as the only avenue to democracy. Encouraged by their representations, and by the desire of Southerners to add another slave state, President James Polk in 1848 offered to purchase Cuba for $100,000. But, unlike Florida a generation earlier, the Pearl of the Antilles was not for sale. José Antonio Saco, who clung to hope for amelioration under the Spanish connection, editorialized from New York in *La Verdad* against annexation, especially if it involved perpetuation of slavery; and Madan published broadsides against him. Outshouted as to the best recourse for Cuba, Saco, leaving *La Verdad* to the annexationists, traded America for Europe, where—concentrating on another aspect of freedom—he prepared a monumental history of slavery. Luz y Caballero, also true to his master's teachings, sought the slow, sure means of liberation—through principles instilled by education.

Félix Varela clung to his premise: The great mass of Cubans wanted to be free; some day they would be free. But the race of upstanding, intelligent, patriotic *habaneros* he had envisioned would not arise in his lifetime. The leaven must have time to work. Meanwhile, his feeble hand would yet hold the torch in the land where, despite animosities and injustice, the law proclaimed all citizens equal.

CHAPTER V

The Flame Burns Low

Father Varela's priestly services in St. Augustine, twice interrupted by return trips to New York, extended through six years. Available records remain scant. There is evidence, however, that, as assistant to the Reverend Edmond Aubril at the Church of St. Augustine, he took his religion, as at Transfiguration, directly to the people, instructing, consoling, and inspiring them. Like his northern parishioners, the poor Catholics of the ancient Florida town believed that the Lord had sent them one of His elect.

A present-day historian of the early days of the Catholic Church in Florida lists Félix Varela's as one of the three important names during the mid-nineteenth century; the other two denoted Floridian natives from the Minorcan colony who became bishops in 1874.[1]

A priest in Savannah, where he sojourned while traveling down from New York, described Varela's sudden appearance after Mass one day at St. John the Baptist Church:

> While [I was] disrobing in the sacristy, a plain man, rather diminutive in size, walked in, slightly wet from rain, with the ease and freedom of one who felt at home in the *adytum*, not entirely warranted by his *personnel* [sic]. His dress was thin and seedy, his shoes heavy and not unlike small coffins, reminding one of Napoleon's first appearance in military boots, his figure attenuated, face sharp and fleshless, with an olive complexion bordering on the Indian. A pair of gold spectacles bridging a prominent nose riveted my attention and seemed not in keeping with the *tout ensemble*. In a sweet, subdued voice he answered the silent enquiry of my glance, 'I wish to say Mass. I am one Varela.'[2]

Father Jeremiah J. O'Connell, the young priest of this encounter, remarked many years later: "I have never been more agreeably disappointed in the personal appearance of a man than in this instance. . . . In Savannah and among those islands his memory is held in deep veneration by the faithful and all who

---

[1]Michael V. Gannon, *The cross in the sand*, pp. 156-57.
[2]Jeremiah J. O'Connell, O.S.B., *Catholicity in the Carolinas and Georgia*, p. 510.

made his acquaintance. How he lived was a wonder to his friends, for he gave everything he had to the poor."

Savannah, like St. Augustine, was then administered from Charleston. Father Jeremiah F. O'Neill (called Sr., to distinguish him from his nephew, of the same name, who, until his premature death, labored in the same diocese), pastor of the sole Catholic church in the Georgia city, was an Irishman, a fiery Repealer,[3] and a champion of the rights of Irish laborers building American railroads. He had recovered from an ailment similar to Varela's by wintering in Cuba and Florida. Moreover, he was already acquainted with the pastor of Transfiguration, having lectured on Repeal in New York. To have so eminent a priest as Varela on the Florida mission he regarded as an honor to the diocese.

After more than two decades of Protestant American rule, Spanish-speaking inhabitants were "amazed and delighted" to hear again Catholic sermons in their ancestral tongue. The good news of Varela's presence traveled all the way to New Orleans, and from the periodical *La Patria* in that city it was reprinted in the *Diario de la Marina* of Havana.[4]

A fellow-countryman, Alejandro Angulo y Guridi, who called on Varela in St. Augustine in 1851, found him in clerical habit—black trousers and coat, with blue and white neckpiece, and reported him to be of medium stature, brownish, very thin, with eyes at once penetrating and kindly, "as was his soul."[5]

It was a quiet community in which the once-dynamic Cuban philosopher was ending his laborious years. The once-flourishing Franciscan Convent overlooking the bay on the fringe of town had served as barracks for both British and Americans and was now in ruins. St. Augustine's Catholics were Minorcan, Spanish, Indian, Negro, with a sprinkling of Irish colonists from New York. The city lay between the mild Atlantic, warmed by the

---

[3]"Repeal" was an Irish movement, supported by many Americans, to revoke the political union of Britain and Ireland effected in 1801 through abolition of the Parliament of Ireland. Though periodically renewed on both sides of the Atlantic, the hope for Irish freedom was not realized until the establishment of the Irish Free State in the 1920's.
[4]"Cartas Inéditas," p. 64, quoting from the *Diario de la marina* of Jan. 14, 1847, about Varela's sermon at St. Augustine on the 27th of the preceding month.
[5]Quoted in "Más Que Humano," p. 21.

Gulf Stream, and the secret, interminable Everglades. "It almost seems a city separated from the rest of the world," wrote Varela. "There is a continuous silence because of the small population and because the streets are not paved but are covered with sand. In other words, he who has a headache can come and cure himself in this good climate and this most silent town."[6]

Life was simple and easy, the climate not conducive to ambition. A visiting priest who preached "mission services" for a week in the town, four years after Varela's time, reported that, although fishing was the chief industry, not a fish was available in market on the Friday of that week. "The people seemed literally to have nothing whatever to do; the fort and barracks were garrisoned by one soldier with his wife and children; the government of the place was a sinecure; the mails came only twice a week. . . . Although it was midwinter, the weather was commonly as pleasant and the sun as warm as it is in New England in the month of June. I have never witnessed such a scene of dreamy, listless, sunshiny indolence."[7]

Varela's associates in the divine service were both, like him, down from New York for their health. One, the Reverend Stephen Sheridan, was but a few years out of the seminary and was destined to die young. The pastor, Father Aubril, a French priest of the Fathers of Mercy, became Varela's special friend and protector, "the preserver of my life." Only Aubril, of the three now in St. Augustine, was later able to resume his ministry in New York, where he was to serve for many years as pastor of the Church of St. Vincent de Paul.

Less than 100 miles from Cuba, which he still regarded as his country, Varela made no effort to return there. He was too exhausted to beat against the stone wall of Spanish rule. He continued to reject suggestions of amnesty. His Cuban friends and

---

[6]Letter from "San Agustín de la Florida 20 de julio 1848," in "Cartas Inéditas," p. 72.
[7]Augustine F. Hewit, *Life of the Rev. Francis A. Baker,* p. 164.

A "mission" is a type of periodic religious revival in which Varela is said to have pioneered while pastor in New York, and which came to be widespread in Catholic parishes in the United States. For a week or more, special services are held in a given church, by priests trained for the purpose, to recall parishioners to their spiritual duties, to renew the promises made in baptism, and to make resolutions for better conduct for the future.

associates in the exile colony in New York—Cristóbal Madan, Gaspar Betancourt Cisneros, Lorenzo de Allo, José Luis Alfonso, Miguel Del Monte, and others—almost unanimously desired annexation of their native isle by the United States. Such a move would have pleased the South, for Cuba was slave territory; but both Varela and José Antonio Saco opposed annexation without abolition, for they deemed slavery of black men to *criollos* as objectionable as subjection of Cubans to Spaniards.[8] Moreover, Varela, who seemed to know the thought-trends of the aggressive North American republic more intimately than did his fellow expatriates, had reasons of his own to hold out for complete Cuban independence.

When, in 1850, Cristóbal Madan, the perennial harborer of refugees in New York, wrote to him for a copy of his 1823 *Proposals for the Government of the Ultramarine Provinces*, for publication, Varela replied sadly. The first liberation expedition of Narciso López against Cuba had recently failed. This gave point to the priest's response that the appearance of his work now would serve no useful purpose. Moreover, he averred he could not send the plan even if he wished; for his copy had disappeared, *en route* from New York to St. Augustine, along with many of his other papers. "If the Spanish government wishes to make use of any of the Ideas, it has the Proposals in its archives or could easily obtain them." Then he added, "I am not very well, and, were it not for this climate, I would be worse. In New York, I would probably have died."[9]

The Archdiocese of New York, absorbed in its own growing pains, made no provision for broken-down priests, not even for him whom the various issues of the *Catholic Directory*, year after year until the end, termed Vicar General. Quite the contrary. He

---

[8]The bearing of the slavery question during this period on the movements for annexing Cuba to the United States is clearly brought out in Portell Vilá's *Historia de Cuba en sus relaciones con los Estados Unidos y España*, I: 347-483. Cf. also Richard Burleigh Kimball's annexationist *Cuba and the Cubans*, 1850, in which Kimball tried to justify, *passim*, the continuance of slavery; also his Appendix No. III, pp. 214-51, in which Cristóbal Madan, under an alias, tried to demolish the objections of the abolitionist José Antonio Saco to annexation. For Varela's pioneering against slavery, cf. *supra*, Chapter II.
[9]JIRP, Varela to Madan, from St. Augustine, July 11, 1850.

had sunk his patrimony and the revenues from his books into the Church of the Transfiguration, had kept the parish going with gifts from friends in New York and Cuba, from his relatives in Havana. Before his last departure from New York, he had arranged to convey title on the church to the Archbishop, who, the following year, obtained a Supreme Court order commanding the lay trustees to release all their rights.[10] Now, in his illness and poverty, Varela received harassing reminders of the persistent debt and the unhappiness of the laymen; and exaggerated reports of proposed "manipulations" by Archbishop Hughes made him fear for his own reputation for integrity. Anxiously he wrote for details. Dr. Hernández Travieso says he "demanded, across the wall of assistants, secretaries, and coadjutors with which Hughes immured himself, to know clearly what all the trouble was about."[11] Actually, Hughes had no such corps of assistants; but communication difficulties made it impossible for the ailing and absent pastor of Transfiguration to find out how matters really stood.

The making over of the deed for St. James Church to Hughes in 1844 had, because of its involved mortgage situation, created legal headaches for all concerned, culminating in lawsuits and in decisions adverse to Hughes and the church by the Vice Chancellor in 1846 and by the Court of Appeals in April 1850.[12] Aware of these long-drawn-out and distasteful proceedings, Varela dreaded lest he become similarly involved. But he was feeble and far from the scene of action; and no way was offered to shake off this gnawing concern.

A third mortgage for $10,000, held by John Delmonico, was paid off, but no receipt for the sum was sent to Varela as mortgagee. Because of technicalities, a second deed to Transfiguration was forwarded to St. Augustine, for him to sign and convey. Wearily he complied:

> I return the Deed signed and authorized, but I fear that you will be obliged to send me a *third* one.—It is not mentioned

---

[10] Shea, *Catholic churches*, p. 791.
[11] *El padre Varela*, p. 447.
[12] See letters of Charles F. Grim to Hughes, 1844-1850, AANY, AHP, A-16.

> in what capacity I sell the Church, and nothing is said about the mortgages; on the contrary, it is given to understand that there is none—Moreover if the first Deed is already recorded, the second cannot be also recorded; because it would appear that I had sold the property twice to the same person, without stating how it came again to be mine. . . .
> I must have a receipt either from Delmonico or from you, for the $10,000 you paid him; and let the Bishop give you the mortgage on the Church—I will not be free from responsability [sic] unless all the payments are made by me.[13]

He had escaped the rigors of New York weather, but not the worries of his pastorate, and the mild Florida climate, as he went on to say, could afford only partial relief:

> My asthma is not much better, and I may say that from some days since is getting worse, but I am accustomed to its alternatives, & I hope that the pure air of this city will relieve me.

Father Aubril assigned him a room behind the parochial school in St. Augustine. Here he received those who sought his consolation. Here, too, he instructed the children, played the violin for them, gave them his benediction, and in delighting them, charmed away his nostalgia.[14] He became an institution, a living legend, in the ancient Florida town.

When health permitted, he said Mass. But often a choking cough bent him double, and he was loath to ascend the altar. He had gone with Aubril to Tolomato—there they visited the tomb of Father O'Reilly, and Varela pointed out the grave of Rita Morales. Beside her, his "second mother," in the Spanish town that now belonged to the States, he wished to be buried.

Contact with Félix Varela for the Cubans in New York and Havana petered out during 1852. Along the intercourse axis between the two cities there was concern for the beloved cleric and a need for reassurance from him.

Lorenzo de Allo, alumnus of San Carlos, collaborator on *La Verdad*, and a co-founder of the Democratic Atheneum of New York, the "cultural symbol of the criollo emigration,"[15] was travel-

---
[13]ALS, Varela to "Revd. dear Sir," dated "St. Augustine E Florida April 24th 1850," AANY, AHP, A-13.
[14]*El padre Varela*, p. 447.
[15]*Ibid.*, p. 452.

ing to Charleston, S. C., on business for a countryman. Infirm, prematurely aged, expatriate, poor, discouraged by the failure of the López liberation attempts, he decided to stretch the journey to include St. Augustine. He felt the need, he said, to kiss the hand of El Padre Varela. It was the Feast of the Nativity. What better time for a reunion of friends, for a blessing from his old master!

Ten A.M., Christmas Day, Señor Allo attended Solemn High Mass at the Church of St. Augustine, expecting to find Father Varela officiating. The Cuban priest was not in the church. After Mass, Allo inquired of a Negress and was led behind the school to a little room, no larger than a seminarian's cell, where a frail, venerable old man with faraway, mystic gaze reclined on a couch.

The pupil recognized his master at once and bent in humble salute. Varela stared, unrecognizing, until Allo identified himself. Then a flood of memory came over the invalid. He recalled Allo—he inquired for other disciples—for Father Francisco Ruiz, for Bermúdez, for José María Casal, for Luz y Caballero. What a feast of reminiscence ensued! The visitor marveled that Varela, after 31 years, held fresh the minutiae of persons and bygone events at San Carlos.

Allo restrained himself from weeping as he took in the details of his master's situation: the bare wooden room, devoid of books and maps and writing materials, furnished with two pictures of saints on the wall and a miserable little bell on the fireplace mantel. Varela was propped up by three cushions—only in this posture could he breathe, and Allo implored him not to stir. He had, he explained, three or four ailments contending to finish his life; he could not see to read nor hold a pen to write. Allo noted that, remarkably for a man of his age—he was 64—his hair and his teeth were intact, and his mind was incisive as ever. Father Aubril, said Varela, was the soul of kindness; were it not for the French cleric, he would not now be alive.

That very day, December 25, 1852, Lorenzo de Allo wrote to Francisco Ruiz, a successor of Varela in the chair of philosophy at San Carlos.[16]

---

[16]The entire letter is given in *Vida*, pp. 227-28; also, in slightly different form, in Valverde, *La muerte del padre Varela*, pp. 45-47.

> It does not seem possible that a man of such wisdom and such virtues should be reduced to living in a foreign country, and to being kept alive by the piety of a man who is also an alien. Is it not extraordinary that among his many disciples, some of them well-to-do, there is not one who has extended a loving hand? Varela can not live much longer. Could not his followers, at least those who have means, assign him a small stipend for his few remaining months of life? Could they not at least raise a small subscription? Alas, it wrenches the soul to see a saint perish without succor. Never have I lamented my poverty as I do today.

Allo assured Ruiz that life in the United States had not altered the qualities which his followers revered in their master:

> Varela has not lost his Cuban gestures and mannerisms. His expression does not look English except when he talks English, a language which he has mastered as well as his own. All the world admires and loves him, but no one, except Fr. Aubril, gives him the hand of friendship. How incomprehensible is this mound of earth which calls itself the world! . . . Poor priest—his life is to suffer and vegetate. His words are of peace, of love, of religion; if they were printed, they would enrich the field of science and ethics. His brain has lost nothing; but his remarkable talent only would serve to make more lamentable his situation were it not that his faith and his virtues are more remarkable.

This heartbreaking missive, arriving after a week in transit, aroused immediate action from Havana. Señor Gonzalo Alfonso sent a gift of 200 pesos to Varela, remitting it through John Baptist Lasala of New York. Hearing of his friend's plight, Lasala went straight to Archbishop Hughes to deplore the neglect of the devoted priest. Hughes protested that he had been uninformed of Varela's circumstances. He detailed his plan to sell Transfiguration Church and purchase a less expensive edifice for the congregation. Out of the profit, a pension could be assigned to the ailing pastor.[17] Within a month, Hughes made a down payment of $3,000 on the selected building,[18] but this move in no way benefited the dying pastor of Transfiguration.

---

[17] Valverde, *La muerte*, pp. 48-49, Lasala to Gonzalo Alfonso, N.Y., Feb. 12, 1853.
[18] *The Church journal*, (N.Y.C.), 1, no. 2 (Feb. 12, 1853): 12.

Meanwhile, in Varela's native city, Señor Alfonso assembled a crowd of the faithful to a reunion at his home; and the *habaneros* agreed to provide for their prophet. They pledged a fund to return him to Cuba: surely, no tyrant would harm him now. But if he clung to his exile, they would make him comfortable in whatever location he chose.

As bearer of their token of love, they nominated the most eminent disciple, José de la Luz y Caballero, the bold, brilliant, amiable giant who, though he had abandoned the practice of his faith, declared, "I have always been on good terms with God." Less intense than Varela, less outspoken, beloved "Pepe" had managed to survive under despotism and yet keep burning in the pupils of his celebrated academy the flame which his priestly predecessor had kindled. Luz it was who, a decade earlier, in answer to a belittling of Varela's influence by a "Citizen of the World" from Trinidad, had vigorously proclaimed the priest-philosopher as pioneer in the emancipation of Cuban thought, ending with the now-famous epigram, "Thus when we think in the Island of Cuba, we will think of him who first taught us to think."[19]

But Luz in January 1853 was in poor health; and grief at the recent loss of his only daughter held him immobilized. He was willing to gather subscriptions for his dying fellow-philosopher, but he could not make the journey.

The choice then fell on José María Casal, a disciple after Varela's heart: lawyer, counsellor, Economic Society member; active in the erecting of schools and the improvement of existing ones, in building railroads, establishing factories, introducing new industries, reforming the asylum for foundlings and poor children, and setting up the Lyceum of arts and literature for the recreation of youth. Casal accepted the charge; and on February 23, 1853, he and his Señora left Havana on the steamboat *Isabel*, bound for Savannah and Charleston. It was agreed that their visit to Varela should seem casual, so as not to injure his pride. So feelingly did his disciples love him!

But it was not granted to his Cuban followers, or to their ambassador, to behold again the animate face of their brave philosopher.

---

[19] Luz to *Gaceta de Puerto Príncipe*, from "Puerto Príncipe, April 28, 1840," printed in full in *Vida*, App. V, pp. 252-55.

Félix Varela remarked, on the morning of February 17, 1853, that he felt uncommonly feeble. Yet he walked the several rods from his sleeping quarters to the little rear room of the schoolhouse where he passed his days. The next morning, Friday the 18th and an Ember Day, debility so encompassed him that he asked Father Aubril for the Sacraments:

> He spoke of his approaching dissolution with so much fortitude, firmness, self-possession that we could scarcely believe that he realized it, or that he would not recover from this attack as he had from so many others. When Rev. Mr. Aubril was about to give him the Viaticum he interrupted him, saying: 'I now wish to fulfil a promise which I made long ago, to make a profession of faith—at death as in life—in the real presence of Jesus Christ in the Blessed Eucharist;' and looking steadfastly at the elevated Host, he said: 'I firmly believe that the Host which you hold in your hand is the Body of Jesus Christ under the appearance of bread.'[20]

"¡Venid a mi, Señor!" ("Lord, come to me!") concluded his final earthly communion.

At noon, the doctor confirmed his awareness that death hovered near. "As soon as it was known that he was in danger, many of the congregation flocked to the Church to pray for him, whilst others continued to pray around his bed, almost without intermission, as long as he continued to live." He could no longer see, but his mind remained alert. A Protestant woman of eminent family asked his benediction on her two sons. He requested they be brought near him, held their small hands in one of his, prayed for them and her, and imparted his blessing. Said the woman, departing: "My sons will be fortunate. They have been blessed by the saint, Varela."[21] At 8:30 in the evening, without a struggle, he surrendered his spirit—departing this life, becomingly, surrounded by the poor of mixed races, in a room behind a school, in the shadow of Michael O'Reilly's coquina church in the Republic's most ancient city.

---

[20] Stephen Sheridan to Abp. Hughes, from "St. Augustine, Feb. 26th, 1853," *Freeman's jrnl.*, Mar. 12, 1853, p. 4. The date of Varela's death has been questioned by Cuban scholars, who place it on Feb. 18 or Feb. 25, 1853.

[21] José María Casal's "La Muerte de Un Justo" is on pp. 88-96 of Valverde, *La muerte;* the incident is recounted on p. 90. Sheridan, writing to Abp. Hughes, who disapproved of "Protestant priests," tells the story somewhat differently.

The church tower in St. Augustine, says a contemporary traveler, "has a chime of small bells, which are rung in a most joyous, clashing style, according to the Spanish custom, for festival occasions, and with a peculiarly plaintive peal for deaths and funerals."[22] Now they tolled dolorously—and among them the voice of the ancient bell from an Indian-ravaged mission—to lament the passing of a lover of all God's people.

Days pace slowly in St. Augustine. The unambitious fisherfolk —the Minorcans and Negroes and Irishmen and Spanish half-castes—took time for a proper farewell to their beloved cleric. Reverent hands prepared his body. A pious woman trimmed his hair, and the shorn strands were eagerly sought as relics. Crowding, they venerated his mortal remains—praying about him, women, and children, some loudly weeping. The room where he lay was narrow, packed to overflowing, and mourners had to be forcibly restrained from pushing their way in. "Let me in," one woman is quoted as saying: "Let me in. I seek only to look upon him again, and I will look upon him again and again while his body is with us; and after I can no longer behold him with the eyes of my face I will see him with the eyes of my soul, on which are engraven his image and his good works." And the crowd fell to talking about his deeds of benevolence, whose fame had spread even from New York.[23]

Then, at 5 in the evening, Friday, February 25—on the day when the Mass observed the "Office of the Spear and Nails of Our Lord," they eulogized him in the Church of St. Augustine; they said his Requiem; and they interred him, as he had desired, simply and without time-defying coffin, in the earth near his Morales forbears in Tolomato. Rodríguez tells us that men vied for the honor of bearing his corpse, and that, walking wordless in two's in the doleful procession to the cemetery on the city's outskirts were all the clergy of the area, the children of the boys' and girls' schools, and a huge concourse of the populace, hundreds of mourners "without distinction of age, sex, color, or condition."[24]

A Cuban bystander related that there were seven orators at the

---

[22]Hewit, p. 163.
[23]*Ilus. amer.*, 3 (Nov. 12, 1867): 59.
[24]*Vida*, p. 234.

graveside; and that he himself, learning tardily the identity of the deceased, rushed up to behold the pale face of the beloved teacher of his youth, kissed the rigid fingers, and fell in a faint across the lifeless body.[25]

So was Father Varela's tormented frame returned to earth—his soul winged aloft with many a prayer.

On March 3, after a journey of eight days from Havana, José María Casal reached St. Augustine on his belated errand of mercy. The steamship *Isabel,* prevented by stormy weather from making port at Savannah, had carried him north to Charleston. Casal bore over $1,000 subscribed by Cubans for the relief of Varela, along with letters from Rafael Díaz and Francisco Ruiz imploring the expatriate priest to return to his fatherland.

Father Stephen Sheridan sent an eye-witness account of the death and burial to New York in a letter to Archbishop Hughes dated February 26. When, in the leisurely tempo of the coastal mail, the missive arrived, the prelate already had the unhappy tidings from John Baptist Lasala, whose sources of information were more urgent. The *Freeman's Journal,* on March 12, 1853, printed Sheridan's letter, enclosed in heavy black border, deferring for a week the obituary *vita* which Hughes, with details supplied by Lasala and Agustín Morales, had been preparing.[26]

The honors due a departed Vicar General were accorded in the metropolis. A solemn pontifical Mass of Requiem was celebrated in the Cathedral of St. Patrick on Mulberry Street. A lithograph likeness of Varela, taken from a daguerreotype, was offered for sale in the Metropolitan Catholic Bookstore, 556 Broadway, between Spring and Prince Streets.[27] An account of the deceased's life and good works was published in the *Freeman's Journal* on March 19, 1853.[28] It glossed over his Cortes activities and his philosophical eminence; it stressed his heroism in the cholera epi-

---

[25] *Ilus. amer.,* loc. cit.
[26] ALS, John B. Lasala to Abp. Hughes, dated New York, March 7, 1853; also memorandum signed A. J. Morales, March 1853, n. pl., n. addressee, but undoubtedly intended for Hughes; both in AANY, AHP. These two items supply facts on the life of Varela.
[27] *Freeman's jrnl.,* Apr. 2, 1853. This was probably the portrait used by Rodríguez as frontispiece in *Vida.*
[28] "Father Felix Varela," p. 465, gives the year as 1856, and several writers have copied this misprint.

demic, his charity to the poor, and his exhaustion of personal funds in providing churches for New York. The obituary also contained, as is the way with such hasty compositions, several factual misstatements which have been perpetuated by later writers.

The Reverend James Roosevelt Bayley, secretary to the Archbishop of New York, paying tribute to the beloved Cuban in a book published the year of his death, cited "that career of charity and self-devotion which has made his name one of benediction in the City of New-York."[29]

The secular metropolitan press, not noted for tenderness to Catholics in that Know-Nothing era, bade gentle farewell to Father Varela. While "friends of religious freedom" rallied and protested over the imprisonment of the Madiai group in Catholic Italy, while Archbishop Hughes and various Protestants argued the matter in columns sometimes acrimonious, while comparatively moderate papers like the new *Church Journal* (New York City, Episcopalian), consistently spoke of clerical and lay converts to Catholicism as "perverts" guilty of "perversion,"[30] while Congress fumed because Spain had detained an American mail steamer in Havana, while a military commission in Cuba condemned ten patriots to "the garrote," Henry J. Raymond's *New-York Daily Times* marked thus the passing of the Cuban-born Vicar General of New York:

> His death will be sincerely regretted in New-York, where he had been stationed for several years as Pastor of Transfiguration Church, where he was almost universally known as a man of irreproachable life, of great piety and zeal, and of a most benevolent disposition. The benedictions of the poor will rest upon his memory.[31]

When John Power died in 1849, Archbishop Hughes declared that St. Peter's was now more than ever "a millstone around our necks."[32] Such was not to be the fate of Transfiguration. In the issue of *Freeman's Journal* that carried the official obituary, there was an account of a meeting on March 15, 1853, of the clergy and

---

[29] Bayley, p. 98.
[30] Cf. 1 (Feb. 5, 1853-Jan. 26, 1854), *passim*.
[31] Mar. 8, 1853, p. 6.
[32] Letter to Abp. of Baltimore, Samuel Eccleston, from "New York, April 16th, 1849." Browne Collection.

laity of New York in the basement of Transfiguration Church, under the aegis of the Archbishop. Resolutions were adopted expressing admiration and sympathy for the Archbishop of Santa Fé de Bogotá, Manuel José Mosquera, banished from New Granada and now resident in New York, and for Dr. John Henry Newman, convicted of libel in a bigoted Court of the Queen's Bench, London. It was also decided that the Church of the Transfiguration should be sold and the congregation moved to another location—to the building for which Archbishop Hughes had already contracted, paying $3,000 down and promising the remainder by May 1. Varela's favorite charity, his "crèches" for the children of working widows and widowers—known as the Half-Orphan Asylum—had already been legally absorbed, by Act of April 13, 1852, into the Roman Catholic Orphan Asylum,[33] and Archbishop Hughes arranged for its buildings and site to be taken over by the Sisters of Charity for St. Vincent's Hospital.[34]

Much had been made, over the years, of the debt on Transfiguration, which Félix Varela had tangled with so persistently. But when the building on Chambers Street was sold, a few weeks after his death, it brought $75,000—enabling Archbishop Hughes to pay off the remaining mortgage, to buy a church on Mott and Cross Streets for $30,000, and to have a reserve for further contingencies.[35] The new home of the parish was dedicated on April 30, 1853—two months after Varela's burial.

On its Mott Street site, the Church of the Transfiguration has maintained much of the missionary character imparted by its founding pastor. Like Varela's earlier churches, the building was a convert from Protestantism: originally the house of worship of English Lutherans, it was Episcopalian when bought under the name of Zion Church by the Catholic Archbishop. It was located close to the notorious "Five Points," the most noisome slum in Manhattan, and the Episcopalians grieved at having to abandon to Roman Catholics this focus for doing good.[36]

Unlike many other churches in the metropolitan area, Trans-

---
[33]Bayley, p. 156.
[34]12-page letter, unsigned, to "My Dear Mr. O'Donnell," n.d., n. pl., AANY, Letters from Abp. Hughes, A-6.
[35]Shea, *Catholic churches,* p. 693.
[36]*The church journal,* 1 (Feb. 13 and 26, 1853).

figuration has never manifested a clannishness of national origins: as successive waves of immigration have made its congregation predominantly Irish (under William McClellan, Varela's immediate successor), or predominantly Italian (under the Salesian Fathers of St. John Bosco, at the turn of the century) or predominantly Chinese (it is now staffed by Maryknoll), the spirit and tradition of Félix Varela has pervaded it. Schools for boys and girls continued to flourish as did the many organizations he had encouraged among the laity, such as the Temperance Society and the women's sodalities. A quarter century after his death, it was recorded: "The Rosary Society, one of the oldest connected with the church, meets every evening, and still remembers in its prayers the Rev. Dr. Varela and Rev. Mr. Muppietti."[37] José Ignacio Rodríguez noted, in an article published in 1883, that one elderly parishioner, who had retired to country living in Harlem, still made an annual pilgrimage to the grave of Varela in St. Augustine.[38]

Varela's extensive library of learned books—his "companions of the night"—was auctioned off in New York in 1880. It included rare and valuable editions in Greek and Latin, ecclesiastical histories, theological treatises both Protestant and Catholic, 243 unsold copies of Volume 2 of *Cartas a Elpidio,* 62 volumes of *Oeuvres completes de Bossuet* (wanting volume 37), a Hebrew Bible in vellum, Homer's *Iliad,* etc., to a total of 506 separate titles, item 507 being "A Galvanic Battery with Apparatus, &c."[39] But mementoes of his priesthood were long cherished by the faithful. Rodríguez, 30 years after his death, spoke of persons in New York who jealously guarded a bit of his cassock or a lock of his hair.[40]

"Seventy years ago, on July 15th, 1827, our parish was founded by the saintly Father Félix Varela." So stated the *Souvenir history of Transfiguration parish, Mott Street, N.Y., 1827-1897,*[41] tracing its origin to Varela's purchase of Christ Church in Ann Street. "The silver Crucifix on the high altar of our church and

---

[37]*Catholic churches,* p. 696.
[38]"Father Felix Varela," p. 464.
[39]*Valuable theological library. Catalog . . . of the library of the late Rev. Father Varela.*
[40]"Father Felix Varela," p. 464.
[41]Pp. 3, 9, 10.

the silver sanctuary lamp that hangs before the Tabernacle were presented to the church by him, and his picture hangs over the old desk used by him in the little sitting room of the presbytery." In use at the Rectory was a solid silver soup ladle which by his housekeeper's vigilance had escaped the fate of his table silver.

It was for his charity, his zeal, his selfless devotion, his spirit of love, that the people of New York remembered Félix Varela. Official Catholic histories commended him as a learned and zealous priest; but popularly the fact that he was a spiritual and intellectual pioneer escaped notice or was successfully hidden: the community was too young culturally and too hard-pressed by material concerns to appreciate him as philosopher. Professor Morales of the New York Free Academy (from which developed the City College of the College of the City of New York) included his little moral homilies, written four decades earlier for the Patriotic Society in Cuba, in Morales' *Progressive Spanish reader,* published in 1856. An unnamed writer in Frank Leslie's *Illustración Americana* recalled the episodes of his donating his spoons to a beggar woman and thrusting his cloak on the shoulders of a freezing mother on an icy street, and he recreated the emotional scenes of his burial in St. Augustine. "Dr. Varela's name is now a household word with our clergy," wrote the Catholic bibliographer, Reverend Joseph Maria Finotti, in 1875.[42] The *Souvenir History,* 1897, stressed the subterfuges to which his housekeeper had resorted to keep him decently clothed, while the brochure of Transfiguration's *Centennial and jubilee celebrations, 1827-1927,* described him as "a priest of boundless zeal and tact, courtly manners, unusual acumen, varied intellectual endowments, and possessed of an appreciable patrimony which he expended exclusively in behalf of God's Church and His poor."[43]

In the same centennial year, 1927, just 100 years after the founding of Christ Church, the first article in English on Varela by a non-Cuban appeared in the *Records* of the American Catholic Historical Society of Philadelphia. Its author, the Reverend William F. Blakeslee, C.S.P., assessed Félix Varela for a man of many talents and great Catholic liberalism:

---

[42] Finotti to Rodríguez, Oct. 19, 1875; quoted in *Vida,* p. 220.
[43] Pamphlet in archives of Transfiguration Church, p. 1.

Few men have accomplished so much good: few have left behind them a record of such pleasant memories. Félix Varela was indeed "All things to all men." To the scholar he was a scholar, to the poor he was poor, to those who suffered he was ever in sympathy. Whether we view him in the light of the Professor of Philosophy in the College of San Carlos, or as a member of the ill-fated Spanish Cortes, or as a priest laboring earnestly for the salvation of souls, his great liberal spirit must ever stand in the foreground.[44]

When this belated clerical study of one of New York's most distinguished priests made its appearance, the bones of Father Varela were no longer in the United States. His Cubans, who knew and loved him best, had finally had their way and had brought him home to Havana. But for many years the project of transferring him was blocked by the affairs of nations, and Varela's Cuban disciples had to be content with honoring his mortal remains in St. Augustine.

> O may not Heaven permit, sweet Cuba,
> That the blow of Death should surprise me
> Far from your fields of delight.
> I wish that when I surrender existence
> The last light which my eyes behold
> May be the same which shone on my brow
> When my cries announced that I was born.
> I wish to return to you the being you gave me.
> I wish my grave where is my cradle.

Thus did the circumstances of Varela's death move Pedro Angel Castellón, Cuban poet, rebel, and exile, a patriot proscribed, like Varela, by the Spanish government and destined to be interred in an unknown foreign grave.[45] Castellón's "To Cuba, on the Death of Varela," expressed the feeling of the philosopher-priest's countrymen, that for a Cuban no fate could be worse than to lie forever under foreign soil. Unanimously, the *varelistas* agreed with Castellón—all, that is, except Varela himself, whose life so loudly proclaimed that lasting exile is preferable to subjection to tyranny.

José María Casal, coming to succor Félix Varela in St. Augus-

---

[44] "Félix Varela, 1788-1853," p. 46.
[45] Cf. José Manuel Carbonell, *Los poetas de "El Laúd del Desterrado,"* pp. 121-33. Castellón died in exile in 1856, and his manner of death and place of burial are unknown.

tine, found him already laid in the ground. Father Edmond Aubril led the shocked Cuban to Tolomato, pointed to the bare, unsettled earth, and said: "There rests Father Varela." Two crude wooden crosses and a circle of straggly shrubs marked the place. The French priest and the Cuban philanthropist stood in silence.

"After we had prayed like Catholics," says Casal, "we pondered like philosophers; then we wept as men."[46] Casal had been commissioned to take his master back to Havana. Now the waiting disciples would never see their teacher alive again; but their mystic Iberian minds would demand his remains for their fatherland. This Casal knew, and he so informed Aubril. He said the body must be quickly exhumed; it must be preserved in a suitable vault until preparations could be completed for a ceremonial transfer to Cuba. He insisted that whatever the cost, it would be but a *centavo* to the debt that Cubans owed Félix Varela.

Aubril, although moved by Casal's ardor, foresaw as pastor and ecclesiastical superior the difficulties. New York had, it was true, practically surrendered its Vicar General to the Floridians, and they had in their turn taken him to their souls. They had given him not only harbor but reverence. Already they venerated him as one worthy of canonization. They had almost rioted to remain near his corpse. They had vied for the sacred privilege of carrying his body the long stretch to the grave. They cherished the bits of his hair in their amulets. They would not lightly yield him now to the place of his birth.

Moreover, Varela had requested to be buried in Tolomato. He had died a Cuban, yet true to his determination never to leave his adopted land. His wishes, as confided to Aubril, must be honored.

Public opinion bore out Aubril's forecast only too well. Violence threatened when the rumor circulated of Casal's plans. "A saint has died in our midst, and we shall keep his body here to bring God's blessing upon us."[47] There was also the political complication—Spain would take it unkindly if the States sent the rebel priest's remains to Cuba. The situation was too delicate for Casal to press his demand.

Looking about Tolomato, the Cuban emissary had noticed that,

---

[46]*Vida*, pp. 235f.
[47]*Souvenir history*, p. 9.

unlike other Spanish cemeteries, it contained no chapel. Why not build one, he proposed, as a memorial to Varela? There the priest might be fittingly sepulchred until he could be returned to Havana. The chapel might then remain as a house of prayer, a place of pilgrimage, an eternal monument for the Catholics of St. Augustine.[48]

This plan Aubril approved. He remarked that Varela had often commented on the absence of a chapel, and had been hindered from building one only by lack of funds.

Casal lost no time in purchasing a plot adjacent to the cemetery, in engaging an architect, in contacting builders. Since speed was of the essence, the contract called for completing the chapel within thirty days. Casal reported his plans to Havana, and his associates approved. On suggestion of Lorenzo de Allo, it was decided that the altar be made, not in New York, as originally proposed, but in Cuba, of native mahogany and by native craftsmen. It was to be a replica of the altar in the Cathedral of Havana before which Varela had been ordained priest by Bishop Espada.

The cornerstone-laying took place on March 22, 1853. Again the townsfolk of St. Augustine gathered in their church for the solemn journey to Tolomato. At the head of the procession they bore the Cross; then followed, in order, the boys of the Catholic school, the men of the congregation, the church wardens, Father Aubril, Father Sheridan of the Archdiocese of New York, the girls from the Catholic school, and a large concourse of women. Father O'Neill blessed the land and pronounced a eulogy in English. Casal, in Spanish, spoke for the Cubans, with David D. Griswold translating. The crowd responded with sobs and tears. Both discourses, along with an account of the ceremonies, were deposited in a metal box in the cornerstone. The events were recorded for posterity in a pamphlet published in Charleston: *Ceremonies at the laying of the corner stone of a chapel in the Roman Catholic Cemetery in the City of St. Augustine, Florida, dedicated to the memory of the Very Rev. Félix Varela, late Vicar General of New York.*[49]

---

[48]Casal, "La Muerte de Un Justo," in Valverde's *La muerte;* p. 93.
[49]Printed by Councell & Phynney, 1853.

Señor Casal used the occasion to explain to the townsfolk why Cubans were erecting the chapel:

> He who loves always is loved. Varela loved all men, and Varela has been loved by all. But Cubans owe Varela not only love, but profound veneration. They owe him their education. They owe him what they are today. And had it not been for his extraordinary genius, his perseverance, his wisdom, his selflessness, then their learning today would be burdened with the weight of authority of men who wrote in ages long past....
> If Varela should be cherished by all men for his love of the human race, Cubans ought to cherish him as a father, because he gave life to their intellect and unbound their spirit that it might soar free of error and approach better the throne of the Most High, from which it proceeds.

The Cuban emissary left the way open for the eventual transfer of Varela's bones, although he admitted that circumstances prevented their immediate removal to his native land:

> I have wished to carry with me to Havana these precious relics, that the grave of Varela might be beside his cradle, that Cubans might guard them with due respect and veneration, that they might have the consolation of possessing the body of their master and friend who could not spend among them the last thirty years of his life. . .But my desire, gentlemen, as I understand, distresses many of the people here who love him tenderly; and I know that if I now removed these honored remains, I would cause deep grief to those friends who here lament him, and especially to those persons who companioned and consoled him in his last days. . . .And so I have believed it my duty to erect a monument where these remains may be deposited and guarded by the Catholics of this city until the occasion offers for returning them to that place which has the honor of having witnessed the birth of this worthy man for whom we weep.
> No monument, gentlemen, is more fitting for the sanctity of this place, and for the eminent virtues of Varela, than a chapel wherein we may celebrate the bloodless sacrifice of the Mass.[50]

Casal intended (1) that Varela's remains should soon be re-

---
[50] The Spanish text of Casal's speech is in *Vida,* pp. 239f.

moved to Havana; and (2) that the chapel should be used for all time as a memorial house of worship. He could not foresee how Fate would turn his purpose awry.

Two days after the ceremony, Casal returned to Havana, and Francisco Ruiz and José de la Luz y Caballero were named a committee to pursue the project. An altar was fashioned of mahogany and marble, with a cabinet for storing the sacred vessels; also a magnificent black cross of rosewood inlaid with silver, two candelabra and two lecterns of mahogany. Two slabs of white marble were inscribed, one to be embedded in the wall of the chapel, the other to cover the sepulchre in its floor. The latter bore, in Spanish, the simple legend: "To Father Varela—The Cubans —Died February 25, 1853."[51] The Cubans also arranged to provide a rug for the chapel and a large painting of the Transfiguration of Our Lord.

Built in the popular Federal style, this building resembled a miniature Roman temple, thick walled, fronted with four columns, and surmounted by a simple cross. On April 13, 1853, construction being sufficiently advanced, the transfer of Varela's remains was effected.[52] The chapel stood near a spot where, in the days of Spanish exploration, a missionary had been murdered by Indians for whom he had often said Mass. Now as they laid the mortal relics of their present-day saint under the flagstone, the people of St. Augustine, Negro and white and Indian, wept before the Cuban's tomb, while the French priest, Edmond Aubril, said the first Solemn Mass in the shrine of Félix Varela.

"Be assured," wrote Aubril to Casal, "that the good Priest will never be forgotten in St. Augustine. . . . And I hope that if some day his remains are transferred to the Island of Cuba, some of them will be left behind in this chapel."[53]

---

[51] The date probably should have read Feb. 18. But cf. Francisco González del Valle, "Rectificación de Dos Fechas: Las de Nacimiento y Muerte del Padre Varela," citing Feb. 25 as the correct date.

[52] Valverde, *La muerte,* dates this event as Apr. 13, 1855. Rodríguez, who knew both Casal and Aubril personally, gives the year as 1853, as does Hernández Travieso, who cites inscriptions in the chapel (*El padre Varela,* pp. 452-53). Since the contract called for haste in erecting the chapel, because Varela's body had been laid directly in the earth, 1853 seems the more likely date. The altar and other equipment for the interior are known to have arrived later from Havana.

[53] Translated from the Spanish as found in *Vida,* p. 241. Rodríguez dates

For a time, the chapel in Tolomato served its dual purpose. A mission priest in St. Augustine in 1857 commented on its beauty, on its impressive altar, and on the "heavy marble slab in the center of the pavement, containing the simple but eloquent inscription."[54] To implement Aubril's promise that the city would always remember Father Varela, a committee of women proceeded to the cemetery every Monday to pray in the little memorial church.

A quarter century later, when St. Augustine had become an episcopal see with a bishop of its own, José Ignacio Rodríguez noted that the women's "Oratorical Society" continued its regular weekly visits, imploring God's mercy on the living and the dead, keeping ever renewed the flowers which adorned the chapel of Cuba's torch-bearer.[55] But Father Aubril, Varela's protector and kindred spirit, was now stationed in New York; and the Cuban's biographer seems not to have known that, since the French priest's departure from St. Augustine, the vault in Tolomato had been violated in a manner which Varela's countrymen would find it difficult to forgive.

---

this letter April 13, 1853. In Casal's "La Muerte de Un Justo," however, the year is given as 1855 or 1857; cf. Valverde, p. 94.

[54] Hewit, p. 163.
[55] *Vida,* p. 242.

CHAPTER VI

HIS TORCH BECOMES A BEACON

To the Cubans, Varela was a living and a growing memory.

Those who had learned from his lips were dying off. Escobedo was gone, and Heredia, and Govantes, and Bermúdez. Lorenzo de Allo survived him by only a year, having been spared, says one author, just long enough to accomplish his masterstroke: the awakening of the Cuban conscience, by his letter of December 26, 1852, to the debt it owed Varela.[1]

But a new generation was arising, of Cubans instructed by the educator Luz y Caballero, by the anti-slavery journalist Saco, by public men like Madan and Casal. These younger men used Varela's writings as texts, and they learned from their elders of his life without blame, of his liberation of intellect, of his conviction that Cuba must one day be free. As with the followers of most great teachers, many distorted his gospel: they forgot that he had decried religion without social conscience, freedom without faith, revolution without responsibility. He would have grieved to see the purposes to which some in later generations put his doctrines. Yet, steadily, Cuban lore enhanced his halo: he was the wise man, the unblemished, whom no one except the crown minions would dare accuse.

Fate had arranged that José Martí be born in January, 1853, the month before Varela died. Martí was reared in the liberal tradition of Varela and Luz and Mendive. In many attitudes, he differed from the priest-philosopher; he was anti-clerical, critical of the United States of America, and committed to revolution by force of arms. Yet like his predecessor, he was more dreamer than statesman, more Cuban patriot than server of self, ready with every sacrifice, even the ultimate, to free his fellow-Cubans. Varela and Martí—they were bracketed together, they were called, by many, precursor and activator, seer and "Apóstol."

José María Casal contributed to the growing Varela legend with a volume of Varela speeches, published in Matanzas in 1860, to which he prefaced his own "La Muerte de Un Justo"[2]—"The Death

---

[1] Valverde, *La muerte,* p. 10.
[2] Casal, *Discursos del Padre Varela.*

of a Just Man." This account of Varela's last days and of the subsequent events was reprinted, in abridged form, in the *Libro cuarto de lectura* (*Fourth Reader*) of Eusebio Guiteras (Matanzas, 1868), and became an inspiration to schoolboys.[3]

Luz y Caballero, forming the minds of the young élite in his academy, named Varela as originator of modern thought in Cuba. Antonio Bachiller y Morales, "Patriarch of Cuban letters," historiographer, bibliographer, and fecund journalist, devoted a chapter to Varela in the "Galaxy of Famous Men" in his three-volume *Apuntes para la historia de las letras y de la instrucción pública en la isla de Cuba, 1859-61*. He noted that the priest, who might be compared to Socrates and Descartes, was the pioneer Cuban philosopher, that in destroying the grip of scholasticism he opened the way to scientific thought, and that in the *Cartas* he had expressed the hope "to make with my last breath a protestation of my firm faith and a fervent prayer for the happiness of my fatherland."[4]

Francisco Calgano, Cuban biographer, published a brief life of Varela in Volume 2 of *Revista de Cuba* in 1877—a sketch later reproduced in his *Diccionario biográfico cubano*. Then, in 1878, twenty-five years after Varela's death, José Ignacio Rodríguez published the first book-length biography. Although he called himself "a disciple of Father Varela, actuated by a feeling of gratitude and patriotism," Rodríguez had been influenced not through personal contact with the philosopher-priest (whom he probably never met), but through reading Varela's works and listening to Luz and other followers. Rodríguez, scholar, teacher, lawyer, public servant, and associate of Bachiller y Morales, had emigrated to the United States in 1869, when his anti-slavery pronouncements (he had translated *Uncle Tom's Cabin* into Spanish)[5] and his involvement in the 1868 rebellion made life in Cuba hazardous. Like Varela, he was a sincere Catholic and an ardent patriot. He studied

---

[3]Cf. Valverde, *La muerte*, p. 5.
[4]Varela's biography is in 3: 138-51; quotation is from p. 150.
[5]The translation, entitled "La cabaña del Tío Tomás," was suppressed because the Cubans in New York to whom he had consigned it for publication were annexationists who thought that as a slave state Cuba stood a good chance of joining the U.S.A. Cf. Juan Miguel Dihigo y Mestre, *José Ignacio Rodríguez*, p. 21.

law under Caleb Cushing, the jurist and statesman from Massachusetts, was admitted to practice in Washington, and attained eminence both as historian and as international jurist. His long service as secretary and translator for the Bureau of American Republics in Washington was directed toward reducing the North Americans' "amazing ignorance" of their Latin-American neighbors.

Rodríguez had been acquainted in Cuba with Casal and his coterie of *varelista* intellectuals. He had come to New York "consigned" to Cristóbal Madan, as had Varela in 1823. While becoming established in the United States, he wrote a monumental biography of Luz y Caballero, which prompted the faithful to clamor for a similar work on Félix Varela.

The *Vida del presbítero don Félix Varela* of José I. Rodríguez, published in New York in 1878 on the press of *O novo mundo,* a Portuguese periodical issuing from the Times Building, represented an eager collaboration of many followers of the beloved Cuban priest. From Casal, who died before the work was completed, the author had notes, materials, and "memories." Dr. Vidal Morales y Morales, a former pupil in Rodríguez's schools in Havana, claimed to have initiated the project in an anonymous letter to his erstwhile principal, in which he proffered his services as researcher and amanuensis if the biographer of Luz would now write on Varela. Vidal Morales worked indefatigably to furnish necessary documents from Cuba, as did also Dr. Eusebio Valdés Domínguez. Dr. Raimundo de Menocal y Menocal, another Cuban, cooperated from Madrid. Dr. Agustín José Morales, professor of Spanish at New York (City) College and first cousin to Varela,[6] supplied geneological data as well as letters, books, and unpublished Varela manuscripts. Cristóbal Madan, now a successful merchant and owner of vast land holdings in Louisiana, gave details of Varela's life in New York and a transcript of a Varela sermon which he had committed to memory some 30 years past.[7]

Among non-Cubans, Rodríguez' principal encouragement came

---

[6]Dr. Morales' father was Bartolomé Morales y Morales, brother to Varela's mother.

[7]Hundreds of MS letters to Rodríguez in JIRP, Library of Congress, from Valdés, Vidal Morales, Agustín Morales, Madan, and others, during 1875-79, attest to widespread interest in the Varela biography.

from the Reverend Joseph Maria Finotti, a distinguished American Catholic bibliographer. He gave leads on rare copies of the *Truth Teller,* which carried Varela's first writings in English, and on the six volumes of *Catholic Expositor,* 1841-44, the Cuban philosopher's most ambitious publication in his adopted tongue. Finotti urged Rodríguez to present the Varela *Life* in English, because Americans had most need of such a book. "His name is now a household word with our clergy. Ten years hence, the growing generation will have forgotten him."[8]

Notwithstanding Finotti's plea, Dr. Rodríguez wrote the *Vida* of Father Varela in Spanish, dedicating it to the youth of Cuba, who held in their hands the fate of their country. The bibliographer now pressed for an immediate version in English. He said it would be

> interesting, especially, for that portion of Catholic readers in the U. S. who have any connection with our Literary Institutions; which, without distinction or exception, are all at the very lowest degree of perfection. To such, the reading of what V. has done to revive belles-lettres and sciences in Cuba will be of the greatest profit. By all means let us have an unabridged translation.[9]

But difficulties arose regarding translation and publication. As a compromise, Rodríguez himself compressed the essential materials into an article for the *American Catholic quarterly review.*

Rodríguez's *Vida del presbítero don Félix Varela* aimed at "recalling to the memory of the Cuban people the fruitful example of private and public virtue given by the great priest, and preventing his teachings from being lost at the very critical moment of the political reconstruction of the country, after the convulsions of the struggle through which Cuba had passed."[10] The biography was well-documented, informative, and reverent. It was highly acclaimed, especially in Varela's native land. "Your grateful fatherland will always hold in its memory," wrote Vidal Morales y Morales to the author, "your name eternally united with those of the immortal Cubans called Luz and Varela. What an enviable

---

[8]ALS, Finotti to Rodríguez, from "St. Malachi's Arlington Mass.," Oct. 19, 1875, JIRP, Box 7.
[9]ALS, "Central City Colo. October 6th 1878;" JIRP, Box 7.
[10]Cf. "Father Felix Varela," p. 463.

glory to live forever associated with such outstanding names!"[11]

Finotti reviewed the book at considerable length for the *Catholic Telegraph* of Cincinnati, commenting that Cubans must be pleased at the value which Americans set on "that distinguished Habanero to whom the Church in the United States is so much indebted."[12]

A legion of subsequent writers on Varela have used Rodríguez as their starting point—quoting from him, checking on his accuracy, and enlarging upon his assessment of the priest as a Cuban national figure.

Thus the Varela historiography expanded, and it was noteworthy that as researchers probed the memories of men and the letters and writings pertinent to his life, they could find no flaw in the patriot-priest. Except for the Spanish authorities whose misrule he had denounced, Varela, man of many friends, had never incurred an open enemy. The verdict was unanimous: his ways were saintly, his wisdom sweet-tempered, his insights profound, his charities unbounded.

What was perhaps the only critical note came in 1885 from Bachiller y Morales, who had spent in the United States the period of Cuba's unsuccessful Ten Years' War for independence.[13] During this period, many exiles agitated for help from Washington in overthrowing Spain, even at the cost of the annexation of Cuba by the United States as a slave state. Bachiller y Morales, like Varela, was an anti-slavery liberal; but unlike the priest, he doubted that education and the force of destiny alone could give the island independence. In an essay for Enrique José Varona's *Revista cubana,* entitled "Error Político de Don Félix Varela: Los Contemporáneos y La Posteridad,"[14] Bachiller y Morales pointed out that the priest had hoped to accomplish by peaceful evolution what really required a bloody revolution. Perhaps, he said, had not Varela and others like him frowned on invasion of Cuba from the mainland, and had not the United States vetoed such military action, the cause of freedom for the island could have been won in

---

[11]ALS, "Habana, 20 de Julio de 1877," JIRP, Box 24.
[12]ALS, Finotti to Rodríguez, "Central City, Colo. Dec. 3, 78," JIRP, Box 7.
[13]He fled to New York in 1869, in the same "wave" as José Ignacio Rodríguez.
[14]2 (Oct., 1885): 289-94.

the 1840's or 1850's. But this, the author admitted, was in the area of guesswork; and no one could deny the sincerity of Varela's principles in seeking liberty without bloodshed.

When the ties with Spain were finally cut, at the close of the century, Cubans would lament the belated intervention from Washington, which substituted a new, more subtle master for the Spanish military machine. Then they would discover that Félix Varela really spoke for them when he stated that their nation wanted complete independence, beholden to no major power.

* * * * *

The priest Félix Varela had not been accorded the rank of Bishop; but a Roman Catholic bishop now lay in Varela's tomb.

Rodríguez did not know of the disturbing of Varela's remains when he wrote the book and the article in which he rhapsodized over the loving attention given to the chapel by the ladies of St. Augustine. But he was soon to be informed.

St. Augustine, originally attached to the Diocese of Santiago de Cuba, next an ecclesiastical no-man's-land between New Orleans and Havana, then successively administered from Mobile, Alabama, and from Savannah, Georgia, became an episcopal see in 1870. Augustin Verot, Bishop of Savannah, was transferred to the new post, having requested it "because St. Augustine and Florida are the place where I was first sent, and also because in Florida there is more holy poverty as well as more good to be done in building churches and founding schools."[15]

Verot, born in a lace-making town in south central France, trained in a seminary near Paris, had joined the Sulpicians and taught mathematics in St. Mary's College, Baltimore. He had been made Vicar Apostolic of Florida, with the title of Bishop, in 1858, and, in addition, Bishop of Savannah in 1861. During the Civil War era, he distinguished himself by his ringing defense of the institution of slavery on theological grounds, his courageous concern for the Union prisoners in the notorious stockade at Andersonville, his consistent support of the Confederacy, and his efforts to assist and educate emancipated Negroes. During Vatican Council

---

[15]Letter of Verot from Rome, May 2, 1870, quoted in Michael V. Gannon, *Rebel bishop*, p. 228.

I, in 1870, he was the American *enfant terrible* who opposed the definition at that time of the doctrine of papal infallibility.

Verot, although a Frenchman, was interested in the Spanish antiquities of St. Augustine. He redecorated and restored Father O'Reilly's church, now a cathedral, raising funds for the purpose on a tour of Baltimore, Brooklyn, and Augusta. He journeyed to Cuba in successful quest of the city's earliest parochial records, dating back to June 25, 1594. He excavated at the site of Nombre de Dios and restored there the ancient chapel of Nuestra Señora de la Leche. He built churches and a convent, opened "a sort of seminary" to train priests, published a tiny diocesan weekly, sent a missionary to the Indians in the Everglades, and finally wore himself out in a rugged visitation of his sparsely civilized diocese.[16]

The intrepid Bishop died on a hot June 10, 1876. His body was packed in ice and hastily buried two days later in Tolomato. There being no accommodation prepared in St. Augustine for the reception of such worthy remains, they were placed under the slab in the floor of Father Varela's chapel. The Cuban priest's bones were moved to make room for Verot's in the single vault. The Oratorical Society protested vehemently; but what could the plaints of women avail against a decision of the officiating clergy? On June 16, the official eulogy of the prelate was spoken before a large assemblage in the cathedral of St. Augustine.[17]

A prominent bronze plaque commemorating the interment of Augustin Verot was placed on an outer wall of the chapel.

No one bothered to alert the Cubans to the second occupant of Félix Varela's tomb. But in 1883—the year in which Rodríguez's article appeared in the *American Catholic quarterly review*—the biographer received in Washington a letter from Agustín Morales in New York. Morales was informed, by his wife's niece living in St. Augustine, that, when Verot was buried, a Mrs. A. L. de Medicis had placed Varela's bones in a pillowcase and left them to one side in the tomb. Morales wrote to Mrs. de Medicis, who answered that the remains of Varela had indeed been gathered into an embroidered pillowcase by a devout lady and deposited in a corner of the vault. She declared that she herself had not par-

---

[16]*Rebel bishop*, pp. 233-47.
[17]*Ibid.*, p. 248.

ticipated in or witnessed the act. Morales enclosed her letter with his own to Dr. Rodríguez.[18]

Rodríguez did not make this correspondence public. He must have known that the incident, if broadcast, would give fuel to anti-clerical and anti-American sentiment in his native land. It would vitiate the benevolent, enlightening effect of his recent publications on Varela. He was a sincere Catholic and he wanted to promote better understanding among American neighbors. Rodríguez filed the letters from Morales and Mrs. de Medicis among his papers and said nothing. When he died, in 1907, after long service in inter-American affairs, he left his document files to the Library of Congress in Washington, D. C.

Cuba, during the latter 19th century, continued to draw moral sustenance from the life and works of Félix Varela. But the desired removal of his bones to his native land had to bide its time. The remains of his friend and patron, Bishop Espada y Landa, were exhumed in 1881, examined for identification by a Technical Commission and solemnly reinterred in a fitting mausoleum in the Cementario de Cristóbal Colón.[19] But in the case of Varela there was always the ready excuse: St. Augustine and New York had so loved him that they would not consent. An Irish priest in Florida was said to have declared that no one in St. Augustine, either Catholic or Protestant or heretic, would permit that they part with a single hair of his head.[20]

However, the basic reason for delay was political.

The transfer would have to initiate through diplomatic channels. The restive island belonged to Spain; and Varela, deceased, was even more of an embarrassment to the royal government than he had been in his lifetime. Spain did not want him back in Cuba, and the United States could not act on the matter without her consent.

An article in the Trinidad *El Telégrafo* in 1888 lamented that the mausoleum of the illustrious *habanero* in St. Augustine was "in ruins." The account must have been second-hand, for it exaggerated the state of disrepair and evidently showed no awareness of the presence of Bishop Verot therein. Enrique José Varona

---

[18]Julio Morales Coello *et al., Los restos del padre Varela,* pp. 9-11.
[19]Valverde, *Documentos relativos al obispo Espada,* pp. 20ff.
[20]Raimundo Cabrera, "Nuestro Homenaje a Varela," p. 476.

y Pera, Cuba's leading *pensador* of that era and an ardent nationalist, a man of great intellect but wavering faith, called the story to the attention of his countrymen in *Revista cubana:*

> This monument was constructed by Cubans, in homage to a man wise and good, who crowned with the aureole of exile a whole life consecrated primarily to the prosperity and progress of his country. Indeed, to no one does Cuba owe more— a patriot, he chose to die in a foreign land rather than to witness the serfdom of his own. . . .
> The pious thought of transporting to Cuba the ashes of the great Cuban philosopher perished with those who had cherished him in their love and enthusiasm. The monument which gave testimony to strangers of the gratitude of our people, forgotten, abandoned, is yielding to the onslaughts of time and will soon be no more. The virtues and the works of Félix Varela do not in truth need the record of bronze or marble; but it is very sad, none the less, that we do not even know how to conserve that which our predecessors built for us.[21]

Although the intention was there, the time was not yet. On the insistence of Alfred Zayas and others, the Economic Society appointed a Commission in 1891. But the pangs of the island's long birth struggle were approaching a climax, and the transfer of bones had to wait.

Cuba's economy collapsed in the 1890's. José Martí, journalist, poet, patriot, organized in New York in 1892 a Revolutionary Junta which was ready to invade by 1895. Spain, after futile efforts to appease the *criollos,* sent General Valeriano Weyler, "The Butcher," to suppress revolt. Martí died in action in May, giving the Cuban *independientes* an authentic martyr. The rebel leaders asked recognition from the United States government and received military intervention instead. With the turn of the century, the unhappy island changed from a Spanish dominion to a Yankee protectorate. After several more years, Cuba elected a president and legislature, which functioned, however, in the omnipresent shadow of Washington.

In 1909, Cuba had as president José Miguel Gómez, a liberal, and the United States had withdrawn its administrator. The

---

[21]"La Capilla del P. Varela," *Rev. cub.*, 8 (1888): 380-84.

centenary was approaching of Félix Varela's ordination as priest and of his appointment to modernize philosophy at San Carlos. The anniversary seemed a fitting occasion to accomplish the long-projected return of his remains.

Havana archivists had cooperated with Verot and later dignitaries in restoring to St. Augustine her ancient Spanish records, the bulk of which, dating back to 1594, were delivered in 1906.[22] In November 1911 it was the City of St. Augustine's turn to reciprocate. A commission had been appointed in Havana, funds procured, officials contacted. By authorization of Bishop William J. Kenny of St. Augustine, a mortician was employed to lift the marble slab in the chapel at Tolomato. Bones wrapped in white linen were packed in fragrant cedar pine shavings, hermetically sealed in a large zinc container and delivered to Dr. Manuel Landa González, president of the High Court of Piñar del Rio, and Julio Rodríguez Embil, Cuban consul in Jacksonville.[23]

No mention was made, at the time, of the second occupant of the vault. The zinc box, reaching Havana before completion of Varela's new resting place, was deposited provisionally in the ancient and dilapidated Zoological Museum in Havana.

The return of the remains to Havana merited much sentimental recall and expansive eulogy. There was a funeral oration in the Cathedral; there were discourses in the University and in the Department of Elementary Education. At the meeting of the Economic Society on November 17, 1911, the historian and Cuban nationalist Raimundo Cabrera delivered "Our Tribute to Varela," expressing satisfaction that "those beloved remains lie now in the bosom of his free and devoted fatherland." Dr. Fernando Ortiz, president of the Section on Education, to which Varela had belonged, spoke on "Félix Varela, Friend of His Country;" while Rafael Montoro, former president of the Economic Society, depicted Varela as priest, educator and political autonomist.[24]

Finally, there was a solemn convocation in the University of Havana on August 22, 1912. Atop a pedestal in the Aula Magna (Great Hall), in a marble urn, they placed the bones received

---

[22] *Rebel bishop*, p. 235.
[23] *Los restos*, pp. 6f, 19.
[24] "En Memoria de Félix Varela," a series of articles, *Rev. bim. cub.*, 6 (Nov.-Dec. 1911) : 473-97.

from St. Augustine. Since the zinc container was too large, the linen packet had been transferred, intact, into a smaller metal box.

In addition to the mortuary urn on its column, the University of Havana had a marble bust of Félix Varela in its Great Hall, while, at a busy crossroads in the city, the conjunction of Dragones, Zanja, and Finlay Streets, there was placed an imposing monument to the philosopher-priest. It represented the Youth of Cuba looking up in awe at the inspiring teacher.

Dr. Antonio L. Valverde y Maruri, historian, jurist, scientist, and president of the Economic Society's Section of History, Geography, and Statistics, published in 1924 an examination of numerous documents which might settle the uncertainty as to the exact dates of Varela's death, burial, and re-interment in the chapel in Tolomato.[25] Valverde's research, which was painstaking and considerable, did not prove conclusive. More important, it did not reveal the fact of Bishop Verot's presence in Varela's vault.

In his book, Valverde criticized the location of the Varela memorials. The public monument to so holy and learned a man ought not be located in the midst of traffic, but rather in the Cathedral plaza or near the site of the Seminary of San Carlos and San Ambrosio. Moreover, the priest's last resting place should not stand in a center of constant concourse in a University where there was no longer any religion but much that was irreverent. In the very month of Valverde's writing, there was a student demonstration because the Rector of the University had refused the use of the Great Hall for an anti-religious assemblage.[26]

President Gerardo Machado, seeking to suppress unrest by despotism, declared martial law in 1930. He closed the University of Havana and the secondary schools, and the intense intellectual activity of the times seethed underground. After more than 50 years of extraordinary literary fecundity and frequent involvement in public life, Enrique José Varona y Pera died in 1933. He had traveled the long parabola from youthful reformer to disillusioned sceptic; and his passing seemed to mark the end of an era of travail toward Cuban independence and the inception of a time of national competence.

---
[25]Cf. *La muerte.*
[26]*Ibid.,* p. 43, n. 57.

For almost two decades beginning in 1933, when the ruthless Machado was ousted, nationalist and reform elements dominated Cuban politics. Fulgencio Batista was emerging as the man of power, with a reformist program that included a minimum wage law, the eight-hour day for labor, tariff reductions, economic stabilization, the vote for women, rural schools and health measures, business stability, legalization of the Communist Party, and cancellation of the hated Platt Amendment which—execrated by practically all Cuban writers—gave the United States the right to interfere in Cuban internal affairs. In July 1940, Batista was legitimately elected President, under a new Constitution, with coalition support from the Democratic, Liberal, and Communist Parties. The University had been reopened and the perennial "opposition" in the island was trained on the Falangists, whom Batista also denounced. Cubans took sides during the Spanish Civil War, the most vocal support going to the Loyalist Left. In World War II, the island endorsed the cause of the Allies.

This period of relative progress and seemingly responsible government witnessed a reawakening of interest in Félix Varela, whose principles were activating the civic-minded. In 1935 graduate students at the University dedicated a circulating library to his name,[27] and selections from his works, under the title *Education and patriotism,* were published by the Havana Office of Culture.[28]

Up to this time, Varela had been honored by Cubans as teacher, priest, and intellectual liberator; his service as deputy in the Cortes had been glossed over largely as a mission that ended in exile. Now the emphasis shifted. José María Chacón y Calvo had discovered that Varela's "Project for the Economic and Political Government of the Ultramarine Provinces," 1823, which Rodríguez had declared lost or buried, was readily available—as Varela had told Madan in 1850—in the Archives of the Indies, File 1523, and that the *Diario de La Habana* had carried excerpts from it in July 1823. Chacón y Calvo published his findings in the Secretariat of Education's official *Homenaje,* or *Tribute,* to José Enrique Varona; he evaluated Varela's "Project" as a pioneer plan for colonial autonomy, and he reprinted its Preamble, which declared

---

[27]Chacón y Calvo, "Varela y la Universidad."
[28]Félix Varela y Morales, *Educación y patriotismo,* 1935.

that Cubans and other Latin Americans must be treated as free, responsible citizens, not as mere subjects of exploitation. He also printed from the Archives the 1825-1830 correspondence between Philadelphia, New York, Madrid, and Rome relative to Varela's allegedly revolutionary activities in the United States and his bruited nomination as bishop. Varela, said Chacón y Calvo, suffered persecution "as the mighty theorist of our liberties."[29]

The historian Herminio Portell Vilá, in *Revista cubana*, 1935, pursued the same theme, portraying Varela as the prophetic political ideologist of Cuba.[30] Portell Vilá had unearthed the Varela letters in the Poinsett Papers in Philadelphia, and he showed that the philosopher-priest, though seeming to flirt briefly with the possibility of help from the United States, had sought above all the freedom and well-being of Cuba as an independent nation. A few months later, Francisco González del Valle, also in *Revista cubana*, revealed in "Father Varela and the Independence of Hispanic America" another long-hidden document—Varela's proposal to the Cortes of 1823 for recognition of the independence of the newly liberated American republics.[31]

A synthesis of Varela's political ideals, based on selections from his projects submitted to the Cortes, his *El Habanero*, and his *Miscelánea filosófica*, and portraying him as the ideological father of the Cuban Republic, appeared early in 1936 under the byline of Enrique Gay Calbó.[32] The following year Gay Calbó excerpted, analyzed, and eulogized all three "Proyectos" which Varela had submitted to the Cortes, including the heretofore little-known plan for the abolition of slavery.[33] His studies and those of his contemporaries, bringing to light out of Spain's *Archives of the Indies* and the writings of Varela himself the liberal and far-sighted political proposals, greatly enhanced the reputation of the philosopher-priest as social visionary and prophet.

Varela, the holy priest, the progressive educator, was taking on

---

[29] "La Autonomía Colonial."
[30] *Op. cit.*, 1 (Feb.-Mar. 1935): 243-65, "Sobre el Ideario Político del Padre Varela."
[31] *Op. cit.*, 4 (Oct.-Dec. 1935): 27-45, "El Padre Varela y la Independencia de la América Hispana." Cf. also, 5 (Jan.-Feb. 1936): 191-92, "Homenaje a Varela," by Chacón y Calvo.
[32] *Ibid.*, 5 (Jan.-Feb. 1936): 23-47, "El Ideario Político de Varela."
[33] "El Padre Varela en las Cortes Españolas de 1822 y 1823."

the color of the times as Varela, humanitarian reformer and Cuban nationalist. The same trend was manifested a few years later, when the University of Havana reissued *El Habanero* (1945) with commentaries by Enrique Gay Calbó and Emilio Roig de Leuchsenring that pointed up Varela's uncompromising denunciation of Spanish misrule.

Less politically-oriented was "Father Varela, 'the First Who Taught Us to Think,' " by Roberto Agramonte, professor of sociology at the University of Havana.[34] A book by Antonio Hernández Travieso entitled *Varela and philosophical reform in the island of Cuba,* with an introduction by Portell Vilá, was published in Spanish in Havana in 1942. A picture-history of Cuba for young pupils, 1932, carried the likeness of Varela and described him as the fountainhead of modern Cuba's intellectual life.[35] On the university level, Dr. Medardo Vitier inaugurated in May 1938 a course on "Philosophy in Cuba," which stressed Varela's reforms in philosophical substance and method and in scientific approach and his contribution to incipient Cuban nationalism.[36]

The Cuban Society for Historical and International Studies and the Office of the Historian of the City of Havana together arranged in 1942 a "cycle of conferences" devoted entirely to Félix Varela. In these, the work of the priest-philosopher was analyzed from many angles by men whose liberalism ranged all the way from Catholic to Communist. The titles alone[37] show the scope of interest in the beloved Cuban patriot: "Varela, More than Human;" "Philosophical Evaluation of Varela;" "Varela's Position as a Philosopher;" "Varela as Writer;" "Varela as Teacher;" "Varela as Revolutionary;" "Varela as Scientist;" "Civic Actions and Ideology of Varela." These studies were printed, under the title *Vida y pensamiento de Félix Varela, (Life and thought of Félix Varela),* as volume 5 of *Colección histórica cubana y americana,* published in 1945 under direction of Emilio Roig de Leuchsenring, City Historian. Also in this volume were three additional articles: "The Theological Concept in the Personality of Father Félix Varela," by Domingo Villamil; "Varela in 'El Habanero,'

---

[34] Agramonte, "El Padre Varela, 'El Primer que Nos Enseñó a Pensar.' "
[35] Heriberto Portell y Vilá, *Historia de Cuba gráfica,* p. 95.
[36] "El Curso del Dr. Vitier," *Rev. cub.,* 12 (Apr. 1938): 271-73.
[37] The original titles are, of course, in Spanish.

Precursor of the Cuban Revolution," by Roig de Leuchsenring; and, by Monseñor Eduardo Martínez Dalmau, "The Philosophical and Political Orthodoxy of the Patriotic Thought of Father Félix Varela."

Up to this time, the Church had maintained a customary if marked official silence on the merits of the Cuban priest. The Vatican of Pope Pius IX and the Spanish hierarchy may well have accepted the verdict of the Spaniard, Marcelino Menéndez y Pelayo, that Varela's mind was clouded by contemporary political and philosophic errors.[38] Men like Casal and Rodríguez and Valverde had extolled him; but to others he had been, in his rejection of the methodology of scholasticism and his liberal social tenets, misguided and perhaps a Jacobin, best honored in the forgetting. Before independence, most prelates in Cuba, having been chosen between Madrid and Rome, sided with the Spanish governors; and during the twentieth century, religious education in the island had diminished to the point where the majority of priests were supplied from Spain. Not until the 1930's did the Catholic Church in Cuba reawaken to the kind of social consciousness which had sparked the effectiveness of Bishop Espada and of Father Varela a century earlier. A lay Catholic Action group was organized in 1929 and the mildly reformist Christian Social Democracy movement appeared in 1942.

There now emerged a champion for Varela among the higher clergy. Monseñor Eduardo Martínez Dalmau, a native Cuban, Bishop of the southern coastal city of Cienfuegos, having participated in the 1942 colloquium on Varela in Havana, projected a series of philosophical studies on the Cuban patriot-priest.

Martínez Dalmau became in 1943 the center of a noisy controversy. On his admission to the Academy of Cuban History on May 28, he delivered a paper on the weaknesses of Spanish colonial and foreign policy, with emphasis on the capture of Havana by the British in 1762. He criticized the Austrian and Bourbon rulers of Spain, including the renowned Philip II and excepting only Charles III, who had expelled the Jesuits from Spain and her

---

[38]Menéndez y Pelayo, "Historia de los Heterodoxos Españoles," 6: 365-68, ftn. 1. In this footnote, closing the chapter "De la Filosofía Heterodoxa Desde 1834 a 1868," the author discusses Varela and Luz.

dependencies. Martínez Dalmau also condemned the Inquisition, racism, imperialism, colonial exploitation, and self-serving despotism.[39] Ambassador Spruille Braden of the United States was among the many to congratulate him on his forceful presentation.

A writer in the conservative *Diario de la Marina* attacked Martínez Dalmau, calling him a slipshod historian, a friend to the enemies of the Church and especially to the Communists. Instantly, led by the popular weekly *Bohemia*, a legion of champions sprang to the Bishop's defense: among them, Aníbal Escalante, editor of *Hoy*, the Communist Party organ; Emilio Roig de Leuchsenring, who amplified the Party line in two letters to *Hoy;* Pastor González in *Acción;* the Secretary of the Academy of Colonial History; Roger Fernández Calleja, in an editorial in *Orientación Masónica;* José Antonio Portuondo, also in *Hoy;* the civic-minded historian, Herminio Portell Vilá; and Raimundo Lazo, professor of literature at the University, expert on Martí and Christian liberal in the advanced Varela tradition, who could find no paper willing to print his piece. Several of his defenders—Escalante, González, Roig, Portuondo—called Bishop Martínez Dalmau a modern-day Félix Varela. Roig shouted that the real authors of the attack must be two Jesuit Falangist priests—a charge which other *Hoy* contributors and the Masonic organ eagerly echoed. Messages of tribute poured in on the Bishop from the Mayor of Cienfuegos, the Atheneum, the Veterans of Independence of Cienfuegos, and the National Antifascist Front.[40]

At the Second National Congress of History, organized by Roig de Leuchsenring and held in Havana in October 1943, Martínez Dalmau not only received felicitations on his recent discourse; he also served as presiding officer and featured speaker. His topic was "Father Félix Varela's Democratic and Pro-Independence Position," and he claimed for Varela unequivocal primacy in many fields:

> Father Varela was, at least chronologically speaking, the FIRST REVOLUTIONARY, in addition to being the Cubans' first thinker and first teacher. The name of FATHER

---

[39] Eduardo Martínez Dalmau, *La política colonial y extranjera.*
[40] Cf. Sociedad Cubana de Estudios Históricos e Internacionales, *El obispo Martínez Dalmau y la reacción anticubana.*

OF THE FATHERLAND, on the inscription which adorns the base of the modest monument erected to him in the Great Hall of our University, is not an exaggeration but an act of strict justice. . . . The merit of Varela as educator and thinker has already been duly appreciated. That of Varela as apostle, missionary, and man of outstanding priestly worth is being explored. But Varela as Father of the Fatherland and magnificent pioneer of the Cuban Revolution has not been properly gauged. . . . To confound totalitarian arrogance, and to know ourselves happy to have been born in the democratic Americas, we need but remember Washington, Bolívar, Varela, and Martí.[41]

The Congress passed many resolutions after Martínez Dalmau had finished his oration. Among them was this decision:

To render tribute of exceptional veneration to the figure of the great thinker and Cuban patriot Father Félix Varela y Morales, proclaiming him the first revolutionary of Cuba because he enunciated for the first time in our history the necessity of absolute independence; to recognize that his personality and accomplishments should gain greater popular acknowledgment and acclaim, and with this object to commission the Cuban Society of Historical and International Studies to take steps necessary to publish a national edition of the *Complete works of Father Félix Varela,* including a translation of his English writings recently discovered; and to solicit from the Government of the Republic an issue of stamps reproducing the likeness of this outstanding Cuban.[42]

The Library of Cuban Studies, Havana, now put out (1944) a second edition of Rodríguez's *Vida del presbítero don Félix Varela,* updated with footnotes and an Appendix of recently discovered documents. The dedication by the editor, Bishop Eduardo Martínez Dalmau, was to Fulgencio Batista, "President of the Republic . . . whose efforts for the culture of the Cuban People have made possible this volume on the first who taught us to think." This dedication was to prove disastrous later for its author, when Batista emerged as a despot from under his liberal cloak and the Communists marked for destruction all who had endorsed him.

---

[41]Martínez Dalmau, "La Posición Democrática e Independentista del Pbro. Félix Varela," Sociedad Cubana de Estudios Históricos e Internacionales, *Historia y cubanidad,* pp. 21-36. The running quotation is from pp. 23, 35, 36.
[42]*Ibid.,* p. 55.

The Prologue, by Martínez Dalmau, contained hard words about the neglect of the saintly priest by his Church:

> If reverence to Varela, priest and teacher, has not been and is not now duly encouraged among Catholic Cubans, at least as much as it should be; if the life of this eminent Cuban priest is almost completely unknown to the immense majority of the clergy of the Catholic Church in Cuba; if, when we try to set before our young aspirants to the priesthood models of conduct and inspiration, we hardly ever mention the deeds and writings of so illustrious a servant of the Lord; all this is due to the unjustified charge that he did not adhere rigidly to the canons of Catholic orthodoxy and that his writings and his conduct were distorted by philosophical concepts and political norms which do not fit perfectly within the limits of thought and feeling of Holy Mother Church. It is urgent, as we shall see, to clear away this insidious falsehood, so that the life of the noble Cuban may serve as an example to Catholics and non-Catholics, priests and laymen alike.[43]

Martínez Dalmau stressed that Varela had never strayed from orthodoxy; that those who accused him of heresy were blinded by ignorance or bigotry. He had battered at scholasticism because its dominant methodology stood in the way of scientific progress. In declaring the right of subjects to revolt, as a last resort, against a despotic government, he had followed in the Catholic tradition of Thomas Aquinas, Suárez, and Bellarmine. When from the pages of *El Habanero* he incited to revolution in order to gain complete independence for Cuba, it was because the despotic regime in Spain was not serving the general good of the people and therefore was not worthy of the submission of rational beings.

"Few Republics in America and few nations of the earth," concluded the Bishop, "can glory in having had among their sons a man in whom were joined in such eminent and unusual form both intelligence and virtue, honor and patriotism. For Cuba, our loved Fatherland, to possess him, is one of her greatest glories."[44]

Further to implement the resolution of the Congress of History for the publication of Varela's works, the energetic Bishop began a series in the *Boletín de las provincias eclesiásticas de la república de Cuba,* on the subject, "Father Varela as a Catholic Apologist."

[43] *Op. cit.,* pp. ix-x.
[44] P. xxv.

The writings of Varela in the *Catholic Register, Catholic Expositor,* and other New York periodicals were collected, with help from a professor at St. John's University, Brooklyn, and translated for their first appearance in Spanish, in a seven-volume collection.[45]

In accordance with the same resolution, Varela's writings in Spanish were also reproduced, as part of the *Library of Cuban Authors* series of the University of Havana. The series began with his *Observaciones sobre la constitución política de la monarquía española,* with a Supplement embracing his other political works (1944). It included also his *Miscelánea filosófica* (1944), to which were appended Spanish versions of his two "Essays on the Origin of Ideas," his "Letter of an Italian to a Frenchman on the Doctrines of M. de Lamennais" and "Essay on the Doctrines of Kant," translated by Agramonte and others from the *Catholic Expositor* of 1841-42. *El Habanero,* with introductory comments by Roig de Leuchsenring and Enrique Gay Calbó, appeared in 1945; *Cartas a Elpidio,* volumes 1 and 2, in 1944-45; and volume 1, "Lógica," of his *Instituciones de filosofía ecléctica* in 1952. The series contained, in addition, three titles by Father José Agustín Caballero and thirteen by Luz y Caballero. Number 24 was *Lecciones de filosofía,* fifth edition, volume 1, by Félix Varela. Unlike earlier works in the *Library of Cuban Authors,* number 24 was bare of commentary, introduction, or supplement, and it carried no names of modern-day editors. This edition of *Lecciones* was published in 1961, more than two years after Fidel Castro captured the ship of state.

Antonio Hernández Travieso was contemplating a twentieth-century life of Félix Varela. His earlier work, *Varela and philosophical reform in the island of Cuba,*[46] with prologue by Professor Herminio Portell Vilá of the University of Havana, was largely biographical, covering the priest's Cuban years. After publishing this volume, he visited the States on a Guggenheim grant, researching in St. Augustine, Washington, and New York. In the Library of Congress, he pored through the Rodríguez Papers. There he

---

[45]Cf. Chacón y Calvo, *Rev. cub.,* 18 (Jan.-Dec. 1944): 211-13, "El Padre Varela como Apologista Católico."
[46]*Reforma filosófica.*

HIS TORCH BECOMES A BEACON   165

came upon the incriminating letters of 1883 from Agustín Morales and Mrs. de Medicis. Rodríguez had long been accused of suppressing matter which did not suit his purpose.[47] Here was further evidence, of startling import.

Hernández Travieso released the results of his studies as *El padre Varela; biografía del forjador de la conciencia cubana* (*Father Varela; biography of the forger of the Cuban conscience*) in 1949.[48] He used the style prevalent in semi-fictionalized biographies of the period, introducing so much background, so many human and imaginative touches, that his story reads like a novel. He did not clutter his pages with documentation. In the concluding paragraphs, however, he planted a blast of dynamite.

When the Bishop of St. Augustine died in 1876, said Hernández Travieso, he was buried in the vault of Tolomato chapel without regard to its inscription: "This chapel was erected by the Cubans in the year 1853 to preserve the ashes of Father Varela." Those who committed this profanation placed the bones of the *criollo* in a pillow case and left them in the corner of the chapel, from which they had since disappeared. In 1911, Bishop Kenny exhumed and gave to the unsuspecting Cubans the remains of Augustin Verot. Since then, concluded the writer, the University of Havana had unwittingly enshrined in its Great Hall "the product of the worldly preoccupations of the foreign clergy who in 1876 desecrated the grave of Varela."[49]

Hernández Travieso did not identify in his book the documents which prompted his conclusions.

His statements caused consternation on both sides of the Florida Straits. The clergy of St. Augustine, who had cooperated in his research, found their predecessors accused of desecration and deceit. In Havana, savants who had paid homage to Varela in the Great Hall of the University were faced with the humiliating thought that they had been honoring the bones of another man. It did not save face for them to have Hernández Travieso remark, in effect: "It really doesn't matter, except to point up the barbarous

---

[47]*E.g.*, Valverde, *La muerte*, pp. 6, 7, 13, 14, 16ff.
[48]Havana, Montero.
[49]*Op. cit.*, pp. 453-54.

tradition of robbing the earth of perishable bodily remains, not allowing them to accomplish their final and noble function of making fertile the dust from which they came."[50]

The *habaneros* decided that a commission must be appointed to sift Hernández Travieso's charges. Assigned to the task were a group of eminent scholars and scientists from the University of Havana: Julio Morales Coello, president; Dr. Luis Felipe LeRoy Gálvez, secretary; Carlos García Robiou, Esteban Valdés-Castillo Moreira, and Elías Entralgo Vallina.[51] Their number included a professor of Cuban history, a doctor and toxicologist, a chemist, and two anthropologists. They were to visit St. Augustine, to check pertinent records, and to examine for evidence of identity the bones in the urn in their own Aula Magna.

Meanwhile, the uncertainty was not allowed to interfere with celebration of a double anniversary in 1953: the centenary of the death of Varela and the birth of José Martí. The observance was important to the restless "outs" on the Cuban political scene. Fulgencio Batista, with army support, had seized power in a bloodless *coup* the year before, forestalling the anticipated election to the presidency of Roberto Agramonte, candidate of the reformist *Ortodoxo* Party.[52] Agramonte was a *varelista* from long since. In the study entitled "Father Varela, the 'First Who Taught Us to Think,'" written in 1937 for the Department of University Interchange under auspices of the Havana municipal government, he had stressed that in Varela, as in Mexico's rebel-priest Hidalgo, religion was a motive force toward humane legislation, human progress, enlightenment, and liberty.[53] A reprint of Varela's *Lecciones de filosofía,* Philadelphia 1824 edition, was edited for the University of Havana by the same scholar, who also wrote the Prologue.[54]

Batista had become a living example of the maxim, "Power corrupts." The Cuban patriot intelligentsia, shackled with yet another ruthless dictator—and one who had climbed to power on the

---

[50]*Ibid.,* p. 454.
[51]*Los restos,* p. 3.
[52]Cf. Wyatt MacGaffey and Clifford R. Barnett, *Cuba: its people, its society, its culture.*
[53]Agramonte, "El Padre Varela."
[54]Biblioteca de la Revista de la Universidad de La Havana.

ladder of welfare legislation—hugged their national heroes to their hearts and planned for other days. Among the congressional candidates of Agramonte's frustrated Ortodoxo Party in 1952 had been Fidel Castro, a young lawyer who would on July 26, 1953, announce his revolutionary intentions by attacking an army post at Santiago de Cuba; his following thereafter called itself the Twenty-Sixth of July Movement and appropriated Martí, who had died on the battlefield of revolt, as its hero.

In the public sessions in Havana on February 25, 1953, "for the purpose of observing the centenary of the death of Félix Varela" in "the year of the centenary of Martí's birth," the accent was on revolution. Dr. Bernardo González read a paper entitled "The Cuban Revolution from Buenos Aires,"[55] which was essentially a paean to José Martí and to "Cuba Libre." Dr. Diego González Gutiérrez spoke on "The Continuity of Revolutionary Ideas from Varela to Martí." Varela, he said, after his disillusioning experiences in Spain, became progressively more convinced of the need for Cuban freedom; and although in his later years he eschewed politics, he was still essentially the patriot, "the most holy and wise of Cuba's sons," who handed the torch of liberty to Martí.[56] Emilio Roig de Leuchsenring had his say with *Cuban ideologist: Félix Varela; precursor of the Cuban independence revolution.*[57] Martí, to be sure, was anticlerical, and he had spoken of the United States as "the monster;" but in his disregard of material gain, his burning patriotism, his love of liberty, and his readiness to immolate self for a vision, his countrymen could trace an ideological heritage from the patriot-philosopher-priest. For, along with their tradition of conspiratorial intellectuality, Cubans have often shown a quasi-religious mysticism. Félix Varela had touched their tenderest nerve, as, after Varela, had Martí. Summing up sentiment toward Varela for the Cuban National Commission of UNESCO on April 17, 1953, at the Atheneum of Havana, José María Chacón y Calvo reiterated: "Do we not sense, behind this simple narrative,

---

[55] Publ. by Academia de la Historia de Cuba as *La revolución cubana desde Buenos Aires.*
[56] González Gutiérrez, *La continuidad revolucionaria de Varela en las ideas de Martí,* separately publ.
[57] *Ideario cubano Félix Varela, precursor de la revolución libertadora cubana.*

the wise priest, the creative patriot, the illustrious master with that radiant crown which God has designated for His elect?"[58]

Anti-Yankee sentiment found natural fuel when, soon after the Varela-Martí centenary, the Commission on the remains in the Aula Magna urn reported its proceedings.

Dr. Luis F. LeRoy Gálvez had devoted his summer vacation to investigating the matter stateside. In St. Augustine, he encountered cool courtesy and no conclusive evidence. The Sisters of Saint Joseph allowed him duplicates of their portraits of Bishop Verot. The mortuary establishment which had handled the 1911 transfer was now under other management; but a check of its records indicated the exhumation of Félix Varela's remains. Julio Rodríguez Embil, to whom the zinc box had been delivered in 1911, was still at his post as Cuban consul in nearby Jacksonville. He remembered after 43 years that the slab in the floor of the chapel had been lifted, but he could not recall what had been in the vault beneath.

Dr. LeRoy Gálvez petitioned the diocesan authorities for permission to examine Tolomato chapel. The Chancellor, John W. Love, delegated the undertaker, Rondal L. Bennett, to conduct him to the cemetery. Here he saw the Cubans' monument, with the bronze plaque to Augustin Verot at its entrance. He saw the mahogany altar where Mass was no longer celebrated. He read the two inscriptions on the floor, one over the vault, the other at its head, reminding the ignorant that Cubans had constructed this place of worship to preserve the remains and honor the memory of Félix Varela.

One point Dr. LeRoy Gálvez urged especially: if he could but look beneath the slab and see that Bishop Verot remained interred there, the question could be settled once and for all. This request, however, Bennett said he was not authorized to grant, nor did he believe one should question the carefulness of the late Bishop Kenny, who had given the certificate of transfer in 1911. LeRoy Gálvez tried to call on Chancellor Love directly, or to get permission from him to open the grave, but Love declined. As a last resort, he sought an interview with the Bishop, Love's superior, but was informed that Archbishop Hurley and Bishop McDonough were both absent in the north for an indefinite period.

---

[58]Chacón y Calvo, *El padre Varela y su apostolado*.

The findings of the technical arm of the Commission, led by Dr. Julio Morales Coello, now assumed paramount importance. The packet had been removed from the urn in the Aula Magna. Scientists had studied the bones, teeth, and pieces of crucifix it contained; had measured, analyzed, photographed, and assembled them, fragment by fragment, and assessed them as belonging to only one man. Comparing them with descriptions and pictures of Varela and Verot, the commissioners had concluded that the one man was probably Varela.

But what of Dr. Hernández Travieso's statement that the priest's bones had been left outside the grave—eventually to disappear—at the time of Verot's burial? A re-examination of the Morales letters in the Rodríguez Papers showed that they had not said "a corner of the chapel," but, rather, "a corner of the tomb." Hernández Travieso had given the word "tomb" its loosest connotation to mean the entire mortuary building; but the Commission concluded it signified rather the actual burial crypt in the pavement.

The Commission, and the Cubans whom it represented, were satisfied. They had saved face; they had convinced themselves that it was really their national hero to whom they had raised their eyes these 40-plus years in the Aula Magna. On the morning of December 17, 1954, the now-certified remains were solemnly delivered to the venerable Cardinal Manuel Arteaga y Betancourt, who bore them in procession to the pillar which held aloft the urn, their former and, hopefully, their final resting-place. The oratory on this solemn occasion glossed over the unfortunate incidents in St. Augustine and placed the emphasis where it belonged—on the living heritage from Félix Varela. Said Dr. Jorge Mañach, Harvard-trained scientist, poet, politician, professor of history of philosophy in the University of Havana, and biographer of Martí: "For Cuban youth he [Varela] wrote those memorable *Cartas a Elpidio,* which tried to preserve for his people faith without blindness, convictions without intolerance, charity without hypocrisy, human dignity without egotism."[59]

Professor Julio Morales Coello, president of the Technical Commission, emphasized the indestructability of Varela's flame:

---

[59] *Los restos,* "Presencia y Exilio de Varela," p. 76.

> It happens symbolically that the event of his death took place in the same year in which Martí was born, perhaps to indicate that Varela is the precursor of El Apóstol. Both loved Cuba intensely, and each offered his life, the first in exile, unable to behold the radiant landscape of his Fatherland, the second facing the sun, right on a Cuban battlefield, fighting for liberty. . . .
>
> May the worthy priest rest in Peace, while the recollection of him grows and spreads throughout the Cuban Fatherland, and may our beloved University guard always with respect, honor, and reverence his mortal remains . . . while his immortal spirit continues to guide our course and point for us the way.[60]

The Report of the Commission, with reprints of letters, certificates, and speeches, with photographs and engravings and photostats, was sent to press on November, 20, 1955, "the 167th anniversary of the birth of Father Varela." When it appeared in book form, it contained, side by side, two significant documents. One was the carefully drafted "Memorial which Shows the Necessity for the Abolition of Negro Slavery in the Island of Cuba," submitted by Félix Varela to the Spanish Cortes in 1823. It told why slavery must be abolished, and was accompanied by the "Projected Resolution" for freeing Cuban slaves without drastic social or economic upheaval. "I am glad to be able to tell the Cortes," Varela had stated, "that the inhabitants of the Island of Cuba view with horror this same enslavement of the Africans. . . . I can further assure you that the general will of the people of the Island of Cuba is that there be no slaves."[61]

The other document was a sermon by the French Catholic bishop who now occupied Father Varela's memorial chapel in the United States. Delivered January 4, 1861, at St. Augustine, on a day of national humiliation, fasting, and prayer proclaimed by President James Buchanan, Verot's speech offered biblical and theological sanction for the institution of slavery:

> We find that God, in the Old Testament, under the law of nature, and under the law of Moses, not only did not prohibit Slavery, but sanctioned it, regulated it, and specified the rights of masters and the duties of slaves. . . . Indeed, it seems that

---
[60] *Ibid.*, pp. 61f.
[61] *Ibid.*, pp. 189-209; quotation is on pp. 191-92.

every page of Holy Writ contains some statement to demolish the false and unjust principles of Abolitionism. Those men must be ignorant even of the Ten Commandments of God; for the Tenth Commandment also forbids coveting our neighbor's property, 'nor his servant, nor his handmaid, nor his ox.' . . . The modern fanatics not only desire, but actually take iniquitous means to release servants from their masters, in defiance of the plainest laws of God. . . . Can there be anything, then, more unscriptural than Abolitionism, and if this country be . . . the country of the Bible, as some have asserted, Abolitionism must then be of exotic growth.[62]

There was no mention of the fact that Augustin Verot was an angel of mercy to war prisoners; that in 1863 he promoted "a simultaneous effort and union of prayers throughout the land North and South in order to obtain peace;"[63] that he supported the Confederacy on the liberal principle of the Southern people's rights to determine their own government; and that he, like Varela, saw dangers in too broad an emphasis on papal infallibility. The Franco-Yankee in Varela's grave had defended slavery, and that made his intrusion—though through no fault of his own—even more ironic.

"A rather weird book," comments the biographer of Augustin Verot.[64] A Report, one might add, symptomatic of the Cubans' atomizing analysis of their long-moribund body politic, of the force at once unifying and distintegrating in their self-centered individualistic patriotism, and of their yearning for a miracle-worker to raise them to the dignity of a nation of free men. The man in the urn, their voice from afar, offered exile rather than serfdom, service rather than profit, dedication rather than dependence on others. It was hard counsel on which to unite a restive people whose richly endowed island had been so long despoiled.

Selections from Varela's *Cartas a Elpidio,* dealing with education and patriotism, were issued from Havana in 1960, when Castro had been in power more than a year; they constituted volume 3 of the Popular Library of Classical Cubans.[65] Varela's complete

---

[62]Verot, *A tract for the times,* in *Los Restos,* pp. 123-25.
[63]ALS by "Augustin Verot, Bish. Savan, ord. à Fla.," to "Most rev. Dear Sir," dated: "St. Augustine Fla. Sep. 22d 1863;" AANY, AHP, A-12.
[64]*Rebel bishop,* p. 248.
[65]*Cartas a Elpidio; (selección) educación y patriotismo,* Havana, Lex, 1960.

Lecciones de filosofía was republished in his native city in 1961. His monument continued to mark the crossroads. His urn still stood uplifted in the hall of learning.

Fidel Castro's first and only attempt at an individual political ideology, enunciated in New York in April 1959, was borrowed from Cuba's *varelista* "humanist" movement, its so-called Catholic Left: "Government of the people without dictatorship and without oligarchy, liberty with bread and without terror—that is humanism."[66] Roberto Agramonte, who had written in praise of Varela and had headed the Ortodoxo Party against Batista, was Castro's first foreign minister, while the jurist and scholar, Dr. Manuel Urrutia Lleó, served as first provisional president.

Soon, however, those who believed, with Varela, that government must have respect for human dignity, that power without moral restraint is tyranny, that the masses of the Cuban people want to be *free,* began to be disillusioned. Agramonte resigned his post, which fell to Raúl Roa, and became a teacher at an American university. Mañach also went into exile. Bishop Eduardo Martínez Dalmau and thousands of others found haven in Florida. Herminio Portell Vilá settled in Washington, where Antonio Hernández Travieso also established headquarters. President Urrutia, who had begun to scent Communist influence, resigned under pressure in July 1960. His subsequent book, *Fidel Castro & company: communist tyranny in Cuba,* quotes "the admirable words of Cuba's patriot Félix Varela" on the citizen's duty to defend his countrymen even though they malign him.[67] Of the eminent eulogizers of Varela, only the aged Roig de Leuchsenring, who exalted him as the first Cuban revolutionary, Dr. Julio Morales Coello, who identified his remains, and Chacón y Calvo lingered on into the Castro era. Roig is now deceased.

And what of Félix Varela today? His controversial bones remain atop their pedestal.[68] Students who have sat at the base of the

---

[66] Quoted in Theodore Draper, *Castroism, theory and practice,* p. 39.
[67] Urrutia Lleó, *op. cit.,* p. ix.
[68] For pictures of the halls where Varela used to walk and teach, see *El Cardinal Arteaga; resplandores de la purpura cubana,* by Raúl del Valle. The old seminary building had become the Archbishop's residence. The Seminary of San Carlos, moved outside the city, now had the name of "El Buen Pastor."

monument talk of him with respect—in Havana and New York and Miami, wherever the latest throes of their beloved isle have cast them. At least two volumes of his major works have been republished in Havana, under government auspices, since the Castro revolution. An American Sister of Charity from the motherhouse near Pittsburgh, Sister Gemma Marie, has written on Varela as Christian liberal at the University of New Mexico. She has researched at St. Augustine, Washington, New York, Madrid, and the Vatican, and has made authentic biographical finds.[69] A Jesuit who analyzed Varela's philosophy for his doctorate in Havana now teaches at the College of San José in San Salvador.[70] An American priest with a French name is wondering if the cause of Varela's canonization might one day be initiated at Vatican City. At Transfiguration Church, where Varela ministered to Spanish and Swiss and Irish immigrants, an Irish-American Maryknoll priest, more than 140 years after the beginning of Varela's mission to New York, has long imparted the ways of Catholic faith and American freedom and brotherhood to young Chinese.

The cemetery at Tolomato has been closed since 1890. The chapel built by the Cubans for "him who taught us to think" is musty, untended, overgrown. His mortal remains have been removed from the city of St. Augustine. No sacrifice of the Mass is offered on the mahogany and marble altar, replica of Bishop Espada's in the Cathedral of Havana. Dust covers all. But in his adopted land, the United States of America, in the ecumenical Church of the *aggiornamento,* and among the loyal sons of Cuba, the spirit of Félix Varela—apostle of intellectual progress, of activist piety, of human dignity, and of free, responsible government—is very much alive.

---

[69] Sr. Gemma Marie Del Duca, S.C., "A Political Portrait: Félix Varela y Morales, 1788-1853," unpub. thesis, University of New Mexico, 1966.
[70] Gustavo Amigó Jansen, S.J., "La Posición Filosófica del Padre Varela."

BIBLIOGRAPHY

ARCHIVES AND COLLECTIONS

American Catholic Historical Society of Philadelphia. Historical Collections; incl. Bp. Conwell Papers, Martin I. J. Griffin Collection, etc.

Archdiocese of Baltimore, Archives. Contain several items relating to Varela.

Archdiocese of New York. Archives. (AANY). Esp. the 20 vv. of Abp. John J. Hughes Papers (AHP) and the records of early churches.

Archivo General de Indias, Seville, Spain. "Papeles de Cuba": Calendar of Documents Photographed in the Archives of the Indies, Seville, for the Carnegie Institution of Washington, Department of Historical Research. Typescript.

British and Foreign State Papers. Esp. vv. 10 and 44.

"Browne Collection of Photostats." Assembled by Henry J. Browne, in Library of St. Joseph's Seminary, Yonkers, N.Y., from Archives of Archdioceses of Baltimore and New York, the University of Notre Dame, the Catholic University of America, etc.

Catholic University of America. Department of Archives and Manuscripts. Reels, "Abp. John Hughes Microfilms."

Colección de libros cubanos. Fernando Órtiz et al. Esp. vv. 12 and 13, *Escritos de Domingo Del Monte; introducción y notas de José A. Fernández de Castro,* Havana, Cultural, S.A., 1929.

Delmonte y Aponte, Domingo. "Collection." Library of Congress, Manuscript Division: documents on Cuba, Louisiana, and Florida in 4 bundles and 2 vv.; those dated after 1853 are in the "Collection" of Leonardo Delmonte y Aponte.

Del Monte, Domingo. *Centón epistolario* ... 7 vv., Havana, "El Siglo XX," 1923-57. (Academia de Historia de Cuba, Havana).

Dihigo y Mestre, Juan M. "Papers." Washington, D.C., National Archives.

Hill, Roscoe R., comp. *Descriptive catalog of the documents relating to the history of the United States in the Papeles procedentes de Cuba deposited in the Archivo general de Indias at Seville.* Washington, Carnegie Institn. of Washington. 1916. (*Publn.* no. 234. Papers of the Department of Hist. Records, J. F. Jameson, ed.).

Hispanic Society of America, New York. Library.

"Joel R. Poinsett Papers." Philadelphia, Historical Society of Pennsylvania Library, Manuscript Division.

"José Ignacio Rodríguez Papers," Library of Congress, Manuscript Division. (JIRP). 180 filing boxes. Others of the Papers in other departments of the Library.

Mission of Nombre de Dios, St. Augustine, Florida. Library and Archives. Several documents on microfilm dealing with Varela; also parish records of second Spanish period.

St. Augustine Historical Society, St. Augustine, Florida. Collections.

Spain. Archivo General de Indias. Seville. *Catálogo de los fondos cubanos del Archivo general de Indias* ... Madrid, Compañía Ibero-Americana de Pub., S.A., 1929-36. 2 vv. in 3. (*Colecc. de documentos inéditos para la historia de Hispano-América,* tomos 7, 12). (Instituto Hispano-Cubano de Historia de América, Seville, *Publicaciones*).

Spain. Cortes. *Diario de las sesiones.* 1810/13 ... 1820/23 ... Cádiz, etc., 1811-1935.

Spain. *Reales cédulas de Indias.* 33 vv., 1773-1808. (Sociedad Económica de Amigos del País, Laguna, Canary Islands).

Transfiguration Church, New York City. MS minutes, parish records, accounts, books and pamphlets. Incl. *Souvenir history of Transfiguration parish, Mott Street, N.Y., 1827-1897.* N.Y., n. auth., Pakenham & Dowling, printers, 1897.

WRITINGS OF VARELA

Books

Cartas a Elpidio; (selección) educación y patriotismo. Havana, Lex, 1960.
Cartas a Elpidio sobre la impiedad, la superstición y el fanatismo en sus relaciones con la sociedad. Tomo 1: "Impiedad;" tomo 2: "Superstición." Havana, Editorial de la Universidad, 1944-45.
Educación y patriotismo. Havana, Dirección de Cultura, Secretario de Educación, 1935.
Elementos de química aplicada a la agricultura, en un curso de lecciones en el Instituto de Agricultura. Tr. from the English; Humphrey Davy's lectures delivered between 1802 and 1812. N.Y., Gray, 1826.
Instituciones de filosofía ecléctica, publicados para uso de la juventud estudiosa. Tomo 1: Lógica, texto latino y traducción castellana por Antonio Regalodo González. Havana, Cultural, S.A., 1952.
Lecciones de filosofía. Several editions, some revised and enlarged by the author; 1818-1961. 1st ed., Havana, 1818-19. 3 vv.
Manual de práctica parlamenteria para el uso del Senado de los Estados Unidos, traducido del inglés y anotado por Félix Varela. N.Y., Newton, 1826—Thomas Jefferson's *Manual.*
Miscelánea filosófica . . . seguida del Ensayo sobre el origen de nuestras ideas, Carta de un italiano a un francés sobre las doctrinas de Lamennais y Ensayo sobre las doctrinas de Kant. Havana, Universidad, 1944. From the 2nd ed., Madrid, 1821, and the 3rd ed., N.Y., 1827.
Observaciones sobre la constitución política de la monarquía española, seguidas de otros trabajos políticos. Havana, Universidad, 1944. Based on the Havana ed., 1821.
Poesías del coronel Don Manuel de Zequeira y Arango, natural de La Habana. Publicadas por un paisano suyo. N. Y., n. publ., 1829.

Magazines Varela Contributed to and/or Edited

The Catholic expositor and literary magazine; a monthly periodical. N.Y. 7 vv. Apr. 1841-Nov. 1844.
The Catholic register. N.Y. 1839-41.
Children's Catholic magazine. N.Y. 1838-40. Succeeded by *The young Catholic's magazine,* N.Y. 1841.
El mensagero semanal. N.Y.; Phila. 3 vv. Aug. 19, 1828-Jan. 29, 1831.
The New-York freeman's journal and Catholic register. N.Y. Began July 4, 1840; absorbed *Catholic register,* Jan. 1841.
New-York weekly register and Catholic diary. N.Y., 1833-37. Succeeded by *The Catholic observer,* N.Y. 1838.
The Protestant's abridger and annotator, N.Y., Bunce, 1830-31.
Revista bimestre cubana. bi-monthly. Havana, Sociedad Económica de Amigos del País. 76 vv. May 1831 ff.
The truth teller. N.Y. 31 vv. 1825-55.
Varela y Morales, Félix. *El habanero, papel político, científico y literario redactado por el dr. Félix Varela . . . seguido de la Apuntaciones sobre El Habanero;* estudios preliminares por Enrique Gay Calbó y Emilio Roig de Leuchsenring. Havana, Universidad, 1945. Lacks no. 7.

La Verdad. N.Y. 6 vv. 1848-53.
The youth's friend; El amigo de la juventud. N.Y. 1825. Bi-lingual.

Works Containing Excerpts from Varela's Writings

Bachiller y Morales, Antonio. *Apuntes para la historia de las letras y de la instrucción pública en la isla de Cuba.* 3 vv. Havana, Massana, 1859-61. Repr., 3 vv., Havana, Cultural, S.A., 1936-37.
Casal, José María. *Discursos del Padre Varela, precididos de una Sucinta relación de lo que pasó en los últimos momentos de su vida, y en su entierro.* Matanzas, Imprenta del Gobierno, 1860.
Chacón y Calvo, José María. "El Padre Varela y la Autonomía Colonial." Cuba, Dirección de Cultura. *Homenaje a Enrique José Varona . . .* Havana, Secretario de Educación, 1935; pp. 451-71. ("La Autonomía Colonial.")
Diario del gobierno constitucional de La Habana. Daily.
Fernández de Castro, José A., ed. *Medio siglo de historia colonial de Cuba; cartas a José Antonio Saco ordenadas y comentadas (de 1823 a 1879).* Havana, Veloso, 1923.
Gay Calbó, Enrique. "El Padre Varela en las Cortes Españolas de 1822 y 1823," *Universidad de La Habana,* 5 (no. 14, Aug.-Sept. 1937) : 109-29. ("Las Cortes").
González del Valle, Francisco. "Cartas Inéditas del Padre Varela," *Rev. bim. cub.,* 50 (July-Aug. 1942) : 61-72.
———. "El Padre Varela y la Independencia de la América Hispana," *Rev. cub.,* 4 (Oct.-Dec. 1935) : 27-45.
———. "Páginas para la Historia de Cuba; Documentos para la Biografía del Padre Félix Varela," *Cuba contemp.,* 29 (July 1922) : 284-92.
Mestre y Domínguez, José Manuel. *De la filosofía en La Habana.* Havana, "La Antilla," 1862.
Morales, Agustín José. *Progressive Spanish reader.* N.Y., Appleton, 1856.
El revisor político y literario. Havana. 1823.
Rodríguez, José Ignacio. *Vida del presbítero don Félix Varela.* N.Y., "O Novo Mundo," 1878. 2nd ed., Havana, Arellano, 1944, with Prólogo by Eduardo Martínez Dalmau. (*Vida*).
———. *Vida de Don José de la Luz y Caballero.* N.Y., "El Mundo Nuevo —La América Ilustrada," 1874.
Roig de Leuchsenring, Emilio. *Ideario cubano Félix Varela, precursor de la revolución libertadora cubana.* Publicado en conmemoración del preclaro habanero. Havana, Municipio, Oficína del Historiador de la Ciudad, 1953. (*Colección,* 12).
United States Catholic miscellany. Charleston, S.C. June 5, 1822ff.

WRITINGS ABOUT VARELA

Academia de la Historia de Cuba. *Expediente de órdenes del Pbro. Félix Varela y Morales.* Havana, 1927.
Agramonte, Roberto. "El Padre Varela, 'El Primer Que Nos Enseñó a Pensar,'" *Universidad de La Habana,* 5 (no. 13, June-July 1937) : 64-87.
Aguayo y Sánchez, Alfredo M. *Ideas pedagógicas del Padre Varela.*
Amigó Jansen, Gustavo, S.J. "La Posición Filosófica del Padre Varela," unpubl. thesis, University of Havana, 1947, for degree of Doctor in Philosophy and Arts.
Bachiller y Morales, Antonio. "Error Político de Don Félix Varela: Los Contemporáneos y La Posteridad: (*El Habanero*)," *Rev. cub.,* 2 (Oct., 1885) : 289-94.

Blakeslee, William Francis, C.S.P. "Felix Varela—1788-1853," Amer. Cath. Hist. Soc. of Phila., *Records,* 38 (1927) : 15-46.
Cabrera, Raimundo. "Nuestro Homenaje a Varela," *Rev. bim. cub.,* 6 (Nov.-Dec. 1911) : 473-97.
Calcagno, Francisco. Brief life of Varela, *Rev. de Cuba,* 2 (1877).
Castellón, Pedro Angel. "A Cuba, en la Muerte de Varela." Poem, 1853. Various publs.
Ceremonies at the laying of the corner stone of a chapel in the Roman Catholic cemetery in the City of St. Augustine, Florida, dedicated to the memory of the Very Rev. Félix Varela, late Vicar General of New York. Charleston, S.C., printed by Councell & Phynney, 1853.
Chacón y Calvo, José María. "Homenaje a Varela," *Rev. cub.,* 5 (Jan.-Feb. 1936) : 191-92.
―――. "El Padre Varela Como Apologista Católico," *Rev. cub.,* 18 (Jan.-Dec. 1944) : 211-13.
―――. *El padre Varela y su apostolado.* Havana, Cuadernos de Divulgación Cultural de la Comisión Nacional Cubana de la UNESCO, 8 (1953).
―――. "Varela y la Universidad," *Rev. cub.,* 1 (Jan. 1935) : 169-73.
Cuevas Zequeira, Sergio. "El Padre Varela; Contribución a la Historia de la Filosofía en Cuba," Havana, Universidad, *Rev. de la Facultad de Letras y Ciencias,* Havana, "Avisador Comercial," 2 (no. 3, May 1906) : 217-20.
"El Curso del Dr. Vitier," *Rev. cub.,* 12 (Apr. 1938) : 271-73.
Del Duca, Gemma Marie, S.C., Sister. "A Political Portrait: Félix Varela y Morales, 1788-1853," unpubl. Ph. D. dissertation, Univ. of New Mexico, 1966.
Los diputados americanos en las Cortes Españolas. Madrid, Alaria, 1880.
"En Memoria de Félix Varela," series of arts., *Rev. bim. cub.,* 6 (Nov.-Dec. 1911) : 473-97.
Entralgo y Vallina, Elías José. *Los diputados por Cuba en las Cortes de España, durante los tres primeros períodos constitucionales* ... Havana, "El Siglo XX," 1945. (Academia de la Historia de Cuba).
Foik, Paul J. *Pioneer Catholic journalism.* N.Y., U.S. Cath. Hist. Soc., *Monograph series,* 11 (1930).
Garcini Guerra, H. J. "Evolución del pensamiento político de Félix Varela," Havana, Universidad, Facultad de Ciencias Sociales y Derecho Público, *Amario,* 1954; pp. 37-59.
Gay Calbó, Enrique. "El Ideario Político de Varela," *Rev. cub.,* 5 (Jan.-Feb. 1936) : 23-47.
González del Valle, Francisco. "Rectificación de Dos Fechas: Las de Nacimiento y Muerte del Padre Varela," *Rev. bim. cub.,* 49 (Jan.-June 1942) : 69-72.
―――. Review of Valverde: *La muerte del Padre Varela,* in *Cuba contemp.,* 36 (no. 141, Sept.-Dec. 1924) : 98-101.
―――. "Varela, Más Que Humano," pp. 7-25 of *Vida y pensamiento de Félix Varela, I,* which is sub-title of: Havana, Historiador, *Cuadernos de hist. haban.,* no. 25 (1944).
González, Diego. "Teoría y práctica pedagógicas de Varela," Havana, Historiador, *Colecc. hist. cub. y amer.,* 5 (1945) : 93-109.
González y Gutierrez, Diego. *La continuidad revolucionaria de Varela en las ideas de Martí.* Havana, "El Siglo XX," 1953. (Academia de la Historia de Cuba).
Griffin, Martin I. J. "'The Children's Catholic Magazine' of New York, 1838-39," Amer. Cath. Hist. Soc. of Phila., *Records,* 15 (1904) : 164-68.

Guardia, Joseph Miguel. "Filósofos Españoles de Cuba: Félix Varela y José de la Luz," *Rev. cub.*, 15 (1892) : 233-47, 412-27, 493-502. Nota y traducción por Alfredo Zayas y Alfonso.
Guardia, Joseph Miguel. "Philosophes Espagnols de Cuba: Félix Varela— José de la Luz," *Revue philosophique de La France et de L'Etranger*, Paris, 33 (Jan.-June 1892) : 50-66, 162-83.
Havana. Biblioteca Municipal. *Memoria*. 1935ff.
———. ———. *Publicaciones*. Series B, "Cultura Popular," nos. 1-6. Havana, 1936-50.
Hernández Travieso, Antonio. "Expediente de Estudios Universitarios del Presbítero Félix Varela, *Rev. bim. cub.*, 49 (Jan.-June 1942) : 388-401. Actual texts, with commentary, of important documents in the life of Varela.
———. *El padre Varela: biografía del forjador de la conciencia cubana*. Havana, Montero, 1949.
———. "Posición Filosófica de Varela," *Vida y pensamiento; Colecc.*, 5 (1945) : 43-67.
———. *Varela y la reforma filosófica en Cuba*. Havana, Montero, 1942. (*Reforma filosófica*).
Ilustración americana de Frank Leslie. N.Y., 3 (no. 56, Nov. 12, 1867) : 59. Contains anon. art., "El Padre Varela. Un episodio para la Historia de Cuba." Some issues of this now-rare Spanish-language weekly, not to be confused with Frank Leslie's *American magazine* or his *Illustrated weekly*, are in Libr. of Congress and in Univ. of Texas Libr. (*Illustr. amer.*).
Lazo, Raimundo. *El P. Varela y las Cartas a Elpidio: epílogo de las Cartas . . . que se han publicado en la Biblioteca de Autores Cubanos de la Editorial de la Universidad*. Havana, Universidad, 1945. 16 pp.
Martínez Dalmau, Eduardo, *Bishop*. "La Ortodoxia Filosófica y Política del Pensamiento Patriótico del Pbro. Félix Varela," Havana, Historiador, *Colecc.*, 5 (1945) : 247-72.
———. "La Posición Democrática e Independista del Pbro. Félix Varela," in Congreso Nacional de Historia (Cuba), 2d., Havana, 1943, *Historia y cubanidad;* Havana, Sociedad Cubana de Estudios Históricos e Internacionales, 1943; pp. 37-62.
McCadden, Joseph J. "The New York-to-Cuba-Axis of Father Varela," *The Americas*, Washington, D.C., Academy of American Franciscan History, 20 (Apr. 1964) : 376-92.
Menéndez y Pelayo, Marcelino. *Historia de los heterodoxos españoles*, 6 vv., Madrid, 1880-82, constituting vv. 35-42 of *Edición nacional de las Obras completas de Menéndez Pelayo . . .* , Santander, Aldus, S. A. de Artes Gráficas, 1948. 62 vv. (Consejo Superior de Investigaciones Científicas, Madrid).
Morales Coello, Julio, *et al. Los restos del padre Varela en la Universidad de La Habana*. Havana, Universidad, 1955. Text in English and Spanish. (*Los restos*).
The New-York freeman's journal and Catholic register. March 19 and 26, 1853.
Peraza Sarausa, Fermín. *Personalidades cubanos (Cuba en el exilio)*. 8 vv. Havana, Ediciones Anuario Bibliográfico Cubano, 1957-65. v. 8, Gainesville, Fla.
Pérez Cabrera, J. M. "Félix Varela," *The new Catholic encyclopedia*, N.Y., McGraw Hill, 1967; 14: 539.
Portell Vilá, Herminio. "Sobre el Ideario Político del Padre Varela," *Rev. cub.*, 1 (Feb.-Mar. 1935) : 243-65. ("Ideario Político").
Portuondo, José Antonio. "Significación Literaria de Varela," Havana. Historiador. *Colecc.*, 5 (1945) : 69-91.

Purcell, Richard J. "Felix Varela y Morales," *Dictionary of American biography*, 19: 225.
Rexach, Rosario. *El pensamiento de Félix Varela y la formación de la conciencia cubana.* Havana. Sociedad Lyceum, 1950.
Rodríguez, José Ignacio. "Father Felix Varela, Vicar General of New York from 1837 to 1853," *Amer. Cath. quart. rev.*, 8 (1883) : 466-76.
Roig de Leuchsenring, Emilio. "Varela en el 'El Habanero,' Precursor de la Revolución Cubana." Havana, Historiador, *Colecc.*, 5 (1945) : 217-45.
Spain, Cortes. *Diputados á cortes por la península para la legislatura de los años de 1822-1823.* Seville, La Viuda de Vasquez y Cía., 1822.
Valuable theological library. Catalogue of the large and valuable collection. . . . Being the library of the late Rev. Father Varela of New York . . . which will be sold by auction by Bangs, Brother & Co. . . . 13 Park Row, on Monday, Oct. 2d. and following day. 19 pp.; 507 numbered items; n.d.
Valverde y Maruri, Antonio L. *La muerte del padre Varela; documentos inéditos coleccionados y comentados.* Havana, "El Siglo XX," 1924.
Varona y Pera, Enrique José, "La Capilla del P. Varela," *Rev. cub.*, 8 (1888) : 380-84.
Vida y pensamiento de Félix Varela, I-IV. Nos. 25-28 of Havana, Historiador, *Cuadernos de hist. habanero.* 1944-45.
Zequeira, Sergio Cuevas. "El Padre Varela; Contribución á la Historia de la Filosofía en Cuba," Havana, Universidad, *Rev. de la Facultad de Letras y Ciencias*, 2 (1906) : 217-20.

BACKGROUND AND RELATED MATERIALS

Books and Pamphlets

Academia de la Historia de Cuba. *La revolución cubana desde Buenos Aires; por . . . Dr. Bernardo González Arrili . . .* Havana, "El Siglo XX," and Brasil, Muñiz, 1953.
Acta et decreta synodorum provincialium Baltimori habitarum ab anno MDCCCXXIX. usque ad annum MDCCCXL. . . . 2nd ed., Roma, S. C. de Propaganda Fide, 1841.
Agüero, P. de. *Biografías de cubanos distinguidos; I: Don José Antonio Saco.* London, Webster, 1858.
Allo, Lorenzo. *Domestic slavery in its relations with wealth.* tr. by D. de Goicouria. N.Y., Tinson, 1855. 16 pp.
Arango y Parreño, Francisco de. *Obras.* 2 vv., ed. by Andrés de Arango. Havana, Howson & Heinen, 1888. Nueva ed., Havana, Dirección de Cultura, Ministerio de Educación, 1952.
Archdiocese of New York. Centenary brochure publ. by the Archdiocese, 1950.
Arciniegas, Germán. *Caribbean, sea of the new world.* Tr. by Harriet de Onís. N.Y., Knopf, 1946.
Arnao, Juan. *Páginas para la historia de la Isla de Cuba.* Havana, Imprenta La Nueva, 1900.
Baldwin, James Mark, ed. *Dictionary of philosophy and theology, including . . . ethics, logic, . . .* New ed., w. corrections, 3 vv. in 4, N.Y., Smith, 1940-49.
Bayley, James Roosevelt. *A brief sketch of the history of the Catholic Church on the island of New-York.* N.Y., Dunigan, 1853; 2nd ed., N.Y., Catholic Publ. Soc., 1870.
Bennett, William H. *Catholic footsteps in old New York.* N.Y., Schwartz, Kirwin, and Fauss, 1909.

Bennett, William H. *Handbook to Catholic historical New York City.* N.Y., Schwartz, Kirwin, and Fauss, 1927.
Biblioteca de autores cubanos. Havana. Universidad. 1944ff.
Billington, Ray Allen. *The Protestant crusade, 1800-1860; a study of the origins of American nativism.* N.Y., Macmillan, 1938.
Bisbé, Manuel. "Los Grandes Movimientos Políticos Cubanos en la Colonia; 2. Independentismo: I. Movimientos Anteriores a 1868." Emilio Roig de Leuchsenring, ed., *Cuadernos de historia habanera,* no. 24 (1943). Havana, Municipio. ("Independentismo").
Bourne, William Oland. *History of the Public School Society of the City of New York.* N.Y., Putnam, 1873.
Brooke, Henry K. *Book of pirates.* Phila., Perry, 1841.
Browne, Henry J. *The diocesan clergy of New York: an historical sketch.* 12 pp. n. pl., n. publ. (Report read at Dunwoodie alumni reunion on Oct. 11, 1950).
Carbonell y Rivero, José Manuel, comp. *Evolución de la cultura cubana (1608-1927)* ... 18 vv. Havana, "El Siglo XX," 1928; vv. 7-17, Montalvo y Cardenas.
―――. *Los poetas de "El Laúd del Desterrado."* Havana, 'Avisador Comercial,' 1930.
Carey, Henry Charles; and Lea, I. *Geographical, statistical, and historical map of Cuba and the Bahama Islands.* Phila., Carey and Lea, 1822.
Carty, Mary Peter, O. S. U., *Mother. Old St. Patrick's; New York's first cathedral.* N.Y., U.S. Cath. Hist. Soc., 1947. (*Monograph series,* 23).
Catholic Almanacs and Directories.
Catholic encyclopedia. 18 vv. N.Y., Universal Knowledge Foundation, and Gilmary Society, 1913-1952.
Conangla Fontanilles, José. *Tomás Gener del hispanismo ingenuo a la cubanía práctica* ... Havana, 1950. (Academia de la Historia de Cuba).
Connors, Edward Michael. *Church-state relationships in education in the State of New York.* Washington, D.C., Cath. Univ. of Amer. Press, 1951. Cath. Univ. of America, *Ed. res. monographs,* 16 (no. 2, March 1, 1951).
Copleston, Frederick, S.J. *A history of philosophy.* 8 vv. London, Burns, Oates and Washbourne, 1946-66.
Córdova, Federico. *Gaspar Betancourt Cisneros, el Lugareño.* Havana, Editorial Trópico, 1938.
Cornelius Heeney, 1754-1848. Brooklyn Benevolent Society, May 8, 1948. pam.
Cuba. Comisión de Estadística. *Cuadro estadisto de la siempre fiel isla de Cuba, correspondiente al año de 1827.* ... Havana, Impresos del Gobiernos y Capitanía General, 1829. (Oficina de la Viudas de Arazoza y Soler). Bound with: Cuba. *Año de 1828: Censo de la siempre fidelísimo ciudad de Habana,* Havana, 1829. Reviewed in *Amer. qu. rev.,* 7 (June 1830) : 475.
Cuba. Comisión Nacional de la UNESCO. *Cuba: educación y cultura.* Havana, 1963.
Cuba. Comisión Para la Formación de Diccionario Histórico Geográfico de la Isla. *Apuntes para la historia de la isla de Cuba correspondientes á la siempre fiel* ... Puerto Principe, Imprenta de Gobierno y Real Hacienda, 1844. 39 pp.
Cuba. Constitution. *Textos de las constituciones de Cuba (1812-1840).* Havana, Editorial Minerva, 1940. (Antonio Barreras, comp.).
Cuba. Intendencia General de Hacienda. *Informe fiscal sobre fomento de la población blanca en la isla de Cuba y emancipación progresiva de la esclava, con una breve reseña* ... Manuel María Yañez Rivadeneyra. Madrid, 1845. Publ. in French, Paris, 1851, with translation of Saco's notes.

Cuba. Ministerio de Educación. *Impresos relativos a Cuba editados en los Estados Unidos de Norteamérica; comp., Lilia Castro de Morales* . . . Havana, Biblioteca Nacional, *Publicaciones,* 1956.
"Cuba. Pamphlets." New York Public Library. Collection of 96 pieces, 1805-94; decrees, proclamations, etc.
Curley, Michael J. *Church and state in the Spanish Floridas, 1783-1822.* Washington, Cath. Univ. of Amer. Press, 1940.
Del Valle, Raúl. *El Cardinal Arteaga: resplandores de la purpura cubana.* Havana, Ramallo, 1954.
Delaney, John J., and Tobin, James Edward. *Dictionary of Catholic biography.* Garden City, N.Y., Doubleday, 1961.
Diccionario biográfico cubano. 11 vv. Havana, Anuario Bibliográfico Cubano, 1951ff. (Biblioteca del Bibliotecario, Fermín Peraza Sarausa, dir.).
Dictionaire général de biographie et d'histoire. Dezobry, Ch.; and Bachelet, Th., eds. Paris, Darsy, 1895.
Dictionary of American biography, under the auspices of the American Council of Learned Societies . . . 20 vv., N.Y., Scribner, 1928ff.
Dihigo y Mestre, Juan Miguel. *Influencia de la Universidad de La Habana en la cultura nacional* . . . Havana, Universidad, 1924.
———. *José Ignacio Rodríguez (Contribución a su biografía).* Havana, Avisador Comercial, 1907.
Dos orientadores de la enseñanza: el Padre José Agustín Caballero y José de la Luz Caballero. anon. Havana, Molina, 1935. 47 pp.
Draper, Theodore. *Castroism, theory and practice.* N.Y., Washington, and London, Praeger, 1965.
Enciclopedia filosofica. 4 vv. Venezia, Roma, Istituto por la Collaborazione Culturale, 1957-58. (Centro di Studi Filosofici di Gallarate).
Espasa, J., and Espasa-Calpe, S. A. [Espasa]. *Enciclopedia universal ilustrada europeo-americana* . . . Bilbao, Madrid, Barcelona; Espasa, 1907-30. 70 vv. in 72. *Apendice,* 10 vv., 1930-33; and *Suplemento anual,* 7 vv. in 8, 1934-52; 1953-54; Bilbao, Espasa-Calpe.
Extract from the records relative to the formation of the Spanish Grand Lodge of Ancient York Masons, at Habana, Island of Cuba. A circular, n. publ., probably 1820.
Fairbanks, George R. *The history and antiquities of the City of St. Augustine, Florida.* N.Y., Norton, 1858.
Farley, John M., *Cardinal, Abp. of New York. History of St. Patrick's Cathedral.* N.Y., Society for the Propagation of the Faith, 1908.
———. *The life of John Cardinal McCloskey, first prince of the Church in America, 1810-1885.* N.Y., London, etc., Longmans, Green, 1918.
Fell, Marie Léonore, S.C., *Sister. The foundations of nativism in American textbooks, 1783-1860* . . . Washington, Cath. Univ. of Amer. Press, 1941.
Figarola-Caneda, Domingo, ed. *José Antonio Saco; documentos para su vida.* Havana, "El Siglo XX," 1921.
Finotti, Joseph M. *Bibliographia Catholica Americana: a list of works written by Catholic authors, and published in the United States. Part I:* 1784-1820. N.Y., The Catholic Publ. House, 1872.
Fremantle (Jackson), Anne, ed. *The papal encyclicals in their historical context.* N.Y., Putnam, 1956.
Fuentes Mares, José. *Poinsett: historia de una gran intrigua.* México, Editorial Jus, 1951.
Gannon, Michael V. *The cross in the sand; the early Catholic Church in Florida, 1513-1870.* Gainesville, Univ. of Florida Press, 1965.
Gannon, Michael V. *Rebel bishop; the life and era of Augustin Verot.* Milwaukee, Bruce, 1964.
García Galán, Gabriel. *La masonería y su actuación en la independencia de Cuba.* Havana, 1938.

Gil, Julian. *Cubanos celebres: José de la Luz y Caballero.* Havana, "La Correspondencia de Cuba," 1887.
González Arrili, Bernardo. *La revolución cubana desde Buenos Aires* . . . Havana, "El Siglo XX," 1953. (Academia de la Historia de Cuba).
González del Valle y Ramirez, Francisco. *La Habana en 1841; obra póstuma ordenada y rev. por Raquel Catalá.* Havana, Oficina del Historiador, 1952. (*Colecc.*, 10).
González, Zephirin, Cardinal. *Histoire de la philosophie.* Tr. into French by R. G. P. de Pascal from the Spanish. Paris, Lethielleux, 1891.
Griffin, Appleton Prentiss Clark. *List of books relating to Cuba* . . . *with a bibliography of maps by P. Lee Phillips.* Washington, Government Printing Office, 1898. (U.S., 55 Congr., 2d Sess., 1897-98, Senate Doc. no. 161).
Guilday, Peter. *History of the Councils of Baltimore, 1791-1884.* N.Y., Macmillan, 1932.
—————. *The national pastorals of the American hierarchy, 1792-1919.* Westminster, Md., Newman, 1954.
Hassard, John R. G. *Life of the Most Reverend John Hughes, D.D., first Archbishop of New York; with extracts from his private correspondence.* N.Y., Appleton, 1866.
Hazard, Paul. *European thought in the eighteenth century from Montesquieu to Lessing.* Tr. from the French . . . by J. Lewis May. Cleveland, N.Y., Meridian Books, World Publ. Co., 1963.
Havana. Historiador. *Colección histórica cubana y americana; dirigida por Emilio Roig de Leuchsenring, historiador de la ciudad de La Habana.* 1938ff. (*Colección*).
Havana. Historiador. *Los grandes movimientos políticos cubanos en la colonia.* 1-2. (*Cuadernos de historia habanera.* nos. 23-24. 1943).
Henríquez Ureña, Max. *Panorama histórico de la literatura cubana.* 2 vv. N.Y., Las Américas Publishing Co., 1963.
Hernández Travieso, Antonio. *La personalidad de José Ignacio Rodríguez.* Havana, Cultural, S.A., 1946.
Hewit, Augustine Francis, C.S.P. *Life of the Rev. Francis A. Baker, priest of the Congregation of St. Paul.* 5th ed. N.Y., Cath. Publ. House, 1868.
Historia de la nación cubana. Publicada bajo la dirección de Ramiro Guerra y Sánchez, *et al.* 10 vv. Havana, Editorial Historia de la Nación Cubana, 1952.
Homenaje al ilustre habanero pbro. dr. José Agustín Caballero y Rodríguez en el centenario de su muerte, 1835-1935. Havana, Historiador, 1935. (*Cuadernos de hist. habanera*, 1).
Humboldt, Alexander de. *Ensayo político sobre la isla de Cuba.* Cuba, Archivo Nacional, 1960. (*Publicaciones*, 1).
Jameson, Robert Francis. *Letters from Havana, during the year 1820; containing an account of the present state of the island of Cuba, and observations on the slave trade.* London, pr. for J. Miller, 1821.
[Kimball, Richard Burleigh]. *Cuba and the Cubans; comprising a history of the island of Cuba, its present social, political, and domestic condition; also, its relation to England and the United States.* By the author of "Letters from Cuba." N.Y., Hueston, 1850.
Le Riverend Brusone, Julio J. *La Habana (biografía de una provincia).* Havana, "El Siglo XX," Muñiz, 1960. (Academia de la Historia de Cuba).
MacGaffey, Wyatt, and Barnett, Clifford R., *et al. Cuba: its people, its society, its culture.* New Haven, The American University, HRAF Press, 1962.
MacGregor, Geddes. *The Vatican revolution.* Boston, Beacon Press, 1957.
Madan, Cristóbal F. *Contestación a un folleto titulado: Ideas sobre la in-*

corporación de Cuba en los Estados Unidos, por Don José Antonio Saco . . . N.Y., "La Verdad," 1849. 23 pp. Signed: León de Pragua Calvo [pseud.].
Martí, José Julian. *Martí obras reunidas por Gonzalo de Quesada.* 15 vv. in 11. Washington, Gonzalo de Quesada, *et al.*, 1900-19.
―――――. *Obras completas.* 73 vv. Havana, Editorial Trópico, 1936ff.
Martínez Dalmau, Eduardo, *Bishop. La política colonial y extranjera de los reyes españoles de la Casa de Austria y de Borbon, y la toma de La Habana por los ingleses* . . . Havana, "El Siglo XX," Muñiz, 1943. (Academia de la Historia de Cuba, Havana).
Matthews, Herbert Lionel. *Cuba.* N.Y., Macmillan, 1964.
Merino y Brito, Eloy G. *José Antonio Saco: su influencia en la cultura y en las ideas políticas de Cuba.* Havana, Molina, 1950.
Millar, Moorhouse F. X., S.J. *Unpopular essays in the philosophy of history.* N.Y., Fordham Univ. Press, 1928.
Mosenthal, Philip F.; and Horne, Charles F. *The City College; memories of sixty years.* . . . N.Y., London, Putnam, 1907.
Mott, Frank Luther. *A history of American magazines, 1741-1885.* 3 vv. Cambridge, Harvard Univ. Press, 1957.
The new Catholic encyclopedia; prepared by an editorial staff at the Catholic Univ. of America. 15 vv. N.Y., McGraw-Hill, 1967.
O'Connell, Jeremiah J., O.S.B. *Catholicity in the Carolinas and Georgia: leaves of its history* . . . *A.D. 1820-A.D. 1878.* N.Y., Sadlier, 1879.
Pacheco, Joaquín Francisco. *O'Gavan.* Madrid, Rivudeneyra, 1848.
Pariseau, Earl J., ed. *Handbook of Latin American studies; no. 27: Social Sciences.* Gainesville, Univ. of Florida Press, 1966.
Pelletier, Victor. *Décrets et canons du Concile oecuménique et général du Vatican, en latin et en français avec les documents qui s'y rattachent* . . . Nouvelle ed. Paris, Palmé, 1873.
Perala, Antonio. *Historia de la guerra civil, y de los partidos liberal y carlista; 2da. edición, refundida, y aumentada con la historia de la Regencia y Espartero.* 6 vv. Madrid, Mellado (later vv.), La Sociedad Española de Crédito Comercial, 1868-70.
Pérez, Luis Marino. *Apuntes de libros y folletos impresos en España y el Extranjero que tratan expresamente de Cuba desde principios del Siglo XVII hasta 1812 y de las disposiciones de gobierno impresas en la Habana desde 1753 hasta 1800.* . . . Havana, Martínez, 1907.
Pierra, Fidel G. *Cuba; physical features of Cuba, her past, present and possible future.* Publ. by the Cuban Delegation in the U.S. N.Y., Figueroa, 1896.
Ponte Domínguez, Francisco J. *La masonería en la independencia de Cuba (1809-1869)* . . . Havana, "Masonic World," 1944.
Portell Vilá, Herminio. *Historia de Cuba, en sus relaciones con los Estados Unidos y España.* 4 vv. Havana, Montero, 1938-41.
―――――. *Vidas de la unidad americana, veinte y cinco biografías de americanos ilustres.* Havana, Editorial Minerva, 1944.
Portell y Vilá, Heriberto. *Historia de Cuba gráfica y sintética en 101 cuadros desde el descubrimiento hasta el inicio de la República.* Havana, Cultural, S.A., 1932.
Power, John. *The laity's directory to the church service; for the year of Our Lord, M, DCCC, XXII.* N.Y., Creagh, 1822.
―――――. *The New Testament, by way of question, and answer* . . . N.Y., Cunningham, 1824.
Ramos, Demetrio. *Historia de las cortes tradicionales de España.* Madrid, Burgos, Editorial Aldecoa, 1944.
Rodríguez, José Ignacio. *Estudio histórico sobre el origen, desenvolvimiento y manifestaciones prácticas de la idea de la anexión de* . . . *Cuba a los*

BIBLIOGRAPHY

Estados Unidos de América. Havana, Propaganda Literaria, 1900.
Roig de Leuchsenring, Emilio. *El americanismo de Martí.* Havana, 1953. 38 pp.
———. *La calle del Obispo de la ciudad de La Habana. Obispo Street in the city of Havana* . . . Havana, Editorial "Promisión del Porvenir," Ponce, P. R., 1940, 26 pp.
———. *Cuba y los Estados Unidos, 1805-1898; historia documentada* . . . Havana, Sociedad Cubana de Estudios Históricos e Internacionales, 1949. (*Publicaciones*).
———. *La Habana; apuntes históricos.* Havana, Municipio, 1939.
———. *Ideario cubano; 1: José Martí.* Havana, Historiador, *Cuadernos de historia habanera,* 6 (1936): 1-157. Also in Havana, Municipio, *Colección hist. cub. y amer.,* 12 (1953).
———. *Los monumentos nacionales de la república de Cuba.* 2 vv. Havana, Junta Nacional de Arquelogia y Etnologica, 1957-59. (*Publicaciones*).
Roth, Benedict, O.S.B. *Brief history of the churches of the diocese of St. Augustine, Florida.* St. Leo, Fla., Abbey Press, 1940.
Ryan, Leo Raymond. *Old St. Peter's, the mother church of Catholic New York, 1785-1835.* N.Y., U.S. Cath. Hist. Soc., 1935. (*Monograph series,* 15).
Sabin, Joseph. *Bibliotheca americana; a dictionary of books relating to America* . . . Begun by Sabin, continued by Wilberforce Eames and completed by R. W. G. Vail for the Bibliographical Society of America. 29 vv. N.Y., 1868-1936.
Saco, José Antonio. *Colección de papeles . . . sobre la Isla de Cuba* . . . 3 vv. Paris, D'Aubusson y Kugelmann, 1858-59. Republ., 1 vol., Havana, Dirección General de Cultura, Ministerio de Educación, 1960.
———. *Memorias varias sobre la Isla de Cuba.* 2 vv. N.Y.
———. *Obras de Don José Antonio Saco . . . por un paisano del autor* . . . 2 vv. N.Y., Lockwood, 1853.
Shea, John Dawson Gilmary. *The Catholic churches of New York City, with sketches of their history and lives of the present pastors.* N.Y., Goulding, 1878.
———. *History of the Catholic Church in the United States . . . 1521-1866.* 4 vv. Akron, McBride, 1886-92.
Smith, John Talbot. *The Catholic Church in New York.* 2 vv. N.Y., Boston, Hall & Locke, 1905.
Sociedad Cubana de Estudios Históricos e Internacionales, Havana. *El obispo Martínez Dalmau y la reacción anticubana.* Havana, Arrow Press, 1943.
Sociedad Económica de Amigos del País, Havana. *Memorias.* 1793-1896.
Souvenir of the blessing of the cornerstone of the new seminary of St. Joseph, by the Most Rev. Michael Augustine Corrigan, D.D., Archbishop of New York, at Valentine Hill, Pentecost Sunday, May 17, 1891. N.Y., Cathedral Library Association, 1891.
Spain. Comisión de Constitución. *Discursos preliminares . . . en las cortes . . .* Cadiz, 1812. Repr. with *Constitución política de la monarquía española,* Barcelona, 1821.
———. Ministerio de Ultramar. *Cuba desde 1850 á 1873; colección de informes, memorias, proyectos y antecedentes sobre el Gobierno de la Isla de Cuba* . . . Madrid, Imprenta Nacional, 1873.
Teilhard de Chardin, Pierre. *The appearance of man.* Tr. from the French by J. M. Cohen. N.Y., Harper and Row, 1966.
Torre, José María de la. *Compendio de geografía, física, política, estadística y comparada de la isla de Cuba.* Havana, Soler, 1854.
Trelles y Govin, Carlos Manuel. *Bibliografía cubana del siglo XIX.* 8 vv. Matanzas, Quiros y Estrada, 1911-15.

———. *Bibliografía cubana del siglo XX.* 2 vv. Matanzas, Quiros y Estrada, 1916-17.
United States. Congress. *Debates and proceedings, 18 Cong., Sess. 1, Dec. 1, 1823-May 27, 1824.* vol. 1. Washington, Gales and Seaton, 1856.
———. Courts. Circuit Court (First Circuit. Massachusetts). *A report of the trial of Pedro Gibert . . . et al. before the U.S. Circuit Court, on an indictment charging them with the commission of an act of piracy, on board the Brig Mexican, of Salem . . .* By a Congressional Stenographer. Boston, Russell, Odiorne & Metcalf; Providence; Salem; 1834.
———. Library of Congress. Division of Bibliography. *List of books relating to Cuba (including references to collected works and periodicals), by A. P. C. Griffin, with a bibliography of maps by P. Lee Phillips.* Washington, Govt. Printg. Off., 1898. (U.S. 55th Congr., Sess. 2, 1897-98, Senate Doc. 161).
———. ———. *A selected list of books on Cuba . . . Jan. 18, 1934.* Washington, 1934. (Sel. list of references, 1305).
United States Catholic Historical Society. *Monograph series.* N.Y., the Society, 1899ff.
Urrutia Lleó, Manuel. *Fidel Castro & company, inc: Communist tyranny in Cuba.* N.Y. and London, Praeger, 1964.
———. *Fidel Castro y compañía, s.a.* Barcelona. Herder, 1963.
Valdés, Antonio José. *Historia de la Isla de Cuba, y en especial de la Habana; impresa en 1813 en la Oficina de la Cena;* in: Cowley, Rafael; and Pago, Andrés, eds., *Los tres primeros historiadores de la isla de Cuba.* Havana, Pago, 1876-77; 3: 1-502. (Real Sociedad Patriótica de Amigos del País).
Valverde y Maruri, Antonio L. *Documentos relativos al obispo Espada . . .* Havana, "La Universal," 1926.
———. *José Antonio Saco: aspectos de su vida.* Havana, "El Universo," S.A., 1930.
Velázquez de la Cadena, Mariano. *Pronouncing dictionary of the Spanish and English languages.* N.Y., Appleton-Century-Crofts, 1962, 1965, etc.
La verdad. A series of articles on the Cuban question published by the editors of "La Verdad." N.Y., 1849.
Vitier, Medardo. *La filosofía en Cuba.* Mexico City, Fondo de Cultura Económica, 1948.
Vollmar, Edward R., S.J. *The Catholic Church in America—an historical bibliography.* 2nd ed., N.Y., Scarecrow Press, 1963.
Wetzer und Weste's Kirchenlexikon oder Encyklopaedie der katholischen Theologie und ihrer Huelfswissenschaften. Begun by Joseph Cardinal Hergenrother; continued by Dr. Franz Kaulen. 13 vv. Freiburg im Breisgau, Herder, 1901ff.

Articles

"The Administrative System in the Floridas, 1781-1821." *Tequesta,* 1 (1942) : 41-62.
Browne, Henry J. "Public Support of Catholic Education in New York, 1825-1842: Some New Aspects." U.S. Cath. Hist. Soc., *Hist. records and studies,* 41 (1953) : 14-41.
Conner, Jeanette Thurber. "The Nine Old Wooden Forts of St. Augustine." Fla. Hist. Soc., *Quarterly,* 4 (1926) : Jan., 102-11; Apr., 170-80.
Herbermann, Charles G. "The Right Reverend John Dubois, D.D., Third Bishop of New York." U. S. Cath. Hist. Soc., *Hist. rec. and stud.,* 1, Pt. II (Jan. 1900) : 278-335.

Lewis, Frank G. "Education in St. Augustine, 1821-1845." *Fla. Hist. Soc., Quarterly*, 30 (July 1951-Apr. 1952) : 230-60.
Lockey, Joseph B. "Public Education in Spanish St. Augustine," *Fla. Hist. Soc., Quarterly*, 15 (Jan. 1937) : 147-68.
McCadden, Joseph J. "Bishop Hughes Versus the Public School Society of New York." *Cath. hist. rev.*, 50 (July 1965) : 188-207.
―――. "Governor Seward's Friendship with Bishop Hughes," *N. Y. hist.*, 47 (Apr. 1966) : 160-84.
Parsons, J. Wilfred, S. J. "Reverend Anthony Kohlmann, S. J. (1771-1836)." *Cath. hist. rev.*, 4 (1918) : 38-51.
Presno, José A. "Homenaje a la Memoria del Doctor Tomás Romay," *Universidad de La Habana*, 15 (Nov.-Dec. 1937) : 18-31.
Sheerin, John B., C.S.P. "The Development of the Catholic Magazine in the History of American Journalism." U.S. Cath. Hist. Soc., *Hist. rec. and stud.*, 41 (1953) : 5-13.
"Story of the Island of Cuba." *The talisman*, (1829) : 163-220.

Periodicals

American Catholic Historical Society of Philadelphia. *American Catholic historical researches*. Pittsburgh, Phila. 29 vv. 1884-1912. Merged into their *Records*.
American Catholic quarterly review. Phila. 49 vv. 1876-1924.
The Americas, a quarterly review of inter-American cultural history. Washington, D.C., Academy of American Franciscan History. July 1944ff.
Anuario bibliográfico cubano. Havana. 16 vv. 1937-52. 1953ff., title became *Bibliografía cubano*.
The church journal. weekly. N.Y. 26 vv. 1853-78. Absorbed the *Gospel messenger*, 1872.
Cuadernos de historia habanera dirigidos por Emilio Roig de Leuchsenring, Historiador de la Ciudad de La Habana. Havana. 1935ff.
Cuba contemporánea. monthly. Havana, Biblioteca Municipal, Departamento de Cultura. 44 vv. 1913-27.
Florida Historical Society, The quarterly periodical of the. Jacksonville, Fla. 1908ff.
The New-York freeman's journal. weekly. 77 vv. 1840ff. Absorbed the *Catholic register*, Jan. 1841.
New York history, qu. Cooperstown, N.Y., New York State Historical Association, 1932-date.
Revista cubana; periódico mensual de ciencias, filosofía, literatura y bellas artes. E. J. Varona, ed. Havana, Biblioteca Municipal, 1885-95. Superseded *Revista de Cuba*.
Revista cubana. monthly. 1935-57. Issued by Cuba, Dirección de Cultura, 1935-52; then by Instituto Nacional de Cultura, Havana, 1956-57. Superseded by *Nueva revista cubana*.
Revista de Cuba; periódico mensual de ciencias, derecho, literatura y bellas artes. Havana. 16 vv. 1877-84.
Revista de la Facultad de filosofía y letres. Havana, Universidad. 1905ff.
Revista de la Facultad de letras y ciencias. Havana, Universidad. 1905ff.
Revue philosophique de la France et de L'Etranger. Paris, 1876ff.
Tequesta; the journal of the Historical Association of Southern Florida. Coral Gables, Fla. 1942ff.
United States Catholic Historical Society, N.Y. *Historical records and studies*. Jan. 1899ff.
United States Catholic miscellany. Charleston, S.C. weekly. 39 vv. 1822-61.
Universidad de La Habana. bi-monthly. Havana, Universidad, Departamento de Intercambio Universitario. 1934ff.

INDEX

Academy of Colonial History, 161
Academy of Cuban History, 160
Adot, Fernando, 39
Agramonte, Roberto, 159, 164, 166, 167, 172
Albani, Giuseppe, cardinal, 81, 82
Alfonso, Gonzalo, 131, 132
Alfonso, José Luis, 127
Alfonso, Silvester, 77
Allo, Lorenzo de, 127, 129-31, 142, 146
Álvarez, Juan, 23
American Bible Society, 83, 111
American Catholic quarterly review, 149
Amigó Jansen, Gustavo, S.J., 173
Angulo y Guridi, Alejandro, 125
Anti-Catholicism. *See* Nativism
Aponte, José Antonio de, 19, 29
Apuntes Filosóficos, 25
Aquinas, Thomas, 14, 20, 22, 163
Aranda, Count of, 9
Arango y Parreño, Francisco de, 32, 33, 44, 52
Argüelles, Agustín, 43, 44, 48-49
Aristotelianism, 13-14, 20-22, 26
Arteaga y Betancourt, Manuel, cardinal, 169
Aubril, Edmond, 124, 126, 129-30, 133, 141-42, 144-46
Bachiller y Morales, Antonio, 147, 148, 150-51
Bacon, Francis, 8, 9, 21, 22, 25
Baltimore, Provincial Councils of, 78, 84, 104, 105, 113-14, 120
Báñez, Domingo, 7
Batista, Fulgencio, 157, 162, 166-67
Bayley, James Roosevelt, 136
Bellarmine, Robert, 48, 163
Bennett, Rondal L., 168
Bermúdez, Anacleto, 48, 130, 146
Betancourt Cisneros, Gaspar, 27, 53, 121, 127
Bibles, comparison of, 111
Bichat, Marie François-Xavier, 8
Billington, Ray Allen, 84, 85
Blakeslee, William F., C.S.P., 139-40
Blanc, Anthony, bp., 105
Bolívar, Simón, 18, 53, 162
Bonaparte, Joseph, 18, 19, 29, 32
Bonaparte, Napoleon, 11, 18
Braden, Spruille, 161
Browne, Henry J., 109

Brownlee, William Craig, 84-86, 89-90
Brownson, Orestes Augustus, 114
Bruté de Rémur, Simon, bp., 83, 105
Buchanan, James, 170
Bulnes, José de, 48
Bureau of American Republics, 148
Byrne, Andrew, bp., 100, 113
Caballero, José Agustín, 13-14, 17, 28, 42, 96, 115, 164
Cabrera, Raimundo, 155, 156
Cádiz, Nicholas, 117
Calgano, Francisco, 147
Cano, Melchior, 7
Cartas a Elpidio, 94-98, 138, 147, 169, 171
Cartesianism, 14, 22
Casa de Beneficencia, 10, 12
Casal, José María, 27, 94, 130, 132, 135, 140-44, 146-48
Casserly, Patrick S., 78
Castellón, Pedro Angel, 140
Castro, Fernando de, 48
Castro, Fidel, 18, 164, 167, 171-73
Catholic Action, 160
Catholic Association, 99, 109
Catholic Emancipation Act, 84
Catholic Expositor (sub-title varies), 110-12, 116, 119, 149, 164
Catholic Herald, 102, 112
Catholic Observer, 78
Catholic Register, 107, 110, 164
Chacón y Calvo, José María, 157-58, 167-68, 172
Charity, Sisters of. *See* Sisters of Charity
Charles III of Spain, 1, 3-5, 7, 9-10, 34, 72, 160
Charles IV of Spain, 1, 2, 11, 18, 32-34
Charleston, S.C., 100, 125, 130
Children's Catholic magazine, 102, 106, 113
Christ Church, 77-79, 86, 99-101
Church Debt Association, 117
Church Journal, 136
Churchman, 102
City College (New York), 139
Clay, Henry, 64-65
Clinton, DeWitt, 91
Condillac, Étienne de, 13, 16, 22, 23, 25, 52
Connolly, John, bp., 51, 73, 75, 81, 83

187

INDEX

Cortes of Spain, 5, 16, 18, 29, 32, 35, 40, 46-48, 117, 122
Cousin, Victor, 115-16
Cuba, and Catholicism, 74; education in, 12-13, 16-17, 26-28; Negro population of, 10, 19, 45-47, 122; reforms in, 9-12, 19, 32-33, 157; repression in, 52-53, 62-63, 93-94, 122-23, 154, 156, 166-67; trade and industry of, 10, 31-32, 44-45, 52; and the United States, 56-57, 127, 150-51, 154; unrest in, 19, 40, 50, 53-57, 68-69, 122-23, 127, 150, 154, 172
Cuban Society for Historical and International Studies, 159, 162
Cubí y Soler, Mariano, 50, 66, 70, 114
Cuevas, José de la, 39
Cullen, Paul, 83
Cushing, Caleb, 148
Davy, Humphrey, 70
Del Duca, Gemma Marie, S.C., 173
Del Monte, Miguel, 127
Delmonte, Domingo, 48
Delmonico, John, 100-01, 114, 128-29
Denman, William, 75
El Desafío, 15
Descartes, René, 14, 22, 113, 147
Destutt, Antoine, Comte de Tracy, 22, 25
El diario de La Habana, 10, 13, 29, 42, 125, 157, 161
Diario de la marina, 161
Díaz, Rafael, 135
Dubois, Jean, bp., 76-83 *passim,* 87, 90-91, 105-06
Duns Scotus, John, 22
Echavarría y O'Gavan, Bernardo, 48
Economic Society (Havana). *See* Royal Patriotic Society.
Elenco, 24
Emmitsburg, Md., 76
England, John, bp., 75, 105
Epicurus, 22
Escalante, Aníbal, 161
Escobedo, Nicolás de, 27, 38, 146
Espada y Fernández de Landa, Juan, bp., death of, 93, 96; as reformer, 11-13, 16-17, 19, 28-29, 35-36, 52-53; reinterment of, 153; replica of his altar in St. Augustine, 142, 144, 173; and Varela, 15-17, 19-20, 24-35, 38, 52, 68, 74
Evening Post, 86
Everard, François, 101
Everard, John, 99

Feijóo y Montenegro, Benito-Gerónimo, 8-9, 14, 51
Fenwick, Benedict Joseph, bp., 74 n., 92, 113
Ferdinand VII of Spain, death of, 93; persecution of Varela by, 49, 55, 60-64; rebellions against, 29, 35, 39-40, 43-44, 47-49; repression by, 16-19, 34-35, 49, 52, 62-63; Varela's "eulogy" of, 32-33, 56, 58
Fernández Calleja, Roger, 161
Ferrety, Juan Agustín de, 58
Finney, Charles G., 83
Finotti, Joseph Maria, 139, 149-50
"Five Points," (New York City), 137
Florida, 3, 18, 35, 122
Freeman's journal and Catholic register, 102, 107, 110, 119, 135-36
Freemasons, 11, 53, 66-67, 68 n., 161
Freitas, John, 101
Galileo Galilei, 22
Gannon, Michael V., 124
García, Francisco de la O., 53, 77
García, John P., 101
Gardoqui, Diego de, 72
Gassendi, Pierre, 22
Gay Calbó, Enrique, 159
Gener y Bohigas, Tomás, 39, 47-50, 93
Gibert, Pedro, 92
Godoy, Manuel, 12
Gómez, José Miguel, 154
Gómez Pereira, Antonio, 9, 22
González, Bernardo, 167
González del Valle, Manuel, 27, 114-16, 158
González Gutiérrez, Diego, 167
González Salmón, Manuel, 80-82
Goodhue, Jonathan, 50
Gorostiola, Pedro, 39
Govantes, José Agustín, 146
Griswold, David D., 142
Guardia, Joseph-Miguel, 51
Guía de Forasteros, 10
Guiteras, Eusebio, 147
El Habanero, 54-65, 73, 159, 163
Haiti, 10, 19, 46
Half-Orphan Asylum, 79, 101, 119, 137
Hassett, Thomas, 2, 3, 4, 5
Havana, City of, Academy of Literature in, 93; Age of Enlightenment in, 7-13; cathedral of, 12, 34, 155; Convent of Discalced Carmelites in, 114; Department of Elementary

INDEX

Education of, 155; and Francisco de Arango, 32-33, 44; memorial service for José Valiente, 31; monuments to Varela in, 156; Philharmonic Society of, 15; Office of Historian of, 159-60; Zoological Museum of, 155
Havana, University of, closed by Machado, 156-57; in eighteenth century, 13-14, 17; examines Varela's bones, 165, 168-71; modern philosophy in, 115; receives Varela's remains, 155-56; reissues Varela's works, 24-25, 159, 164, 166, 171-72
"He Who First Taught Cubans to Think," 28, 37, 132
Heeney, Cornelius, 79
Henry, Patrick, 90
Heredia y Campazano, José María de, 53, 69, 70 n., 93, 122, 146
Hernández, Miguel, O.P., 1
Hernández Travieso, Antonio, 14 n., 58, 85, 128, 159, 164-66, 169, 172
Hibernian Benevolent Society, 79
Hidalgo y Costilla, Miguel, 36, 68, 166
Hobbes, Thomas, 37
Holy Alliance, 32, 47
Hughes, John J., abp., 83 n., 87; and the School Aid Crisis, 105-112 *passim*; and Varela, 107-110, 113, 117-18, 120-21, 131, 135-37
Hurley, Joseph P., abp., 168
Ideas, origin of, 110
Infallibility of the Pope. *See* Papal Infallibility
Innate ideas, 110, 114
Inquisition, in Mexico, 16-17; in Spain, 16, 35, 52
Isabella II of Spain, 19
Institutiones philosophiae eclecticae, 24
Jackson, Andrew, 91
James I of England, 8
Jay, John, 117
Jefferson, Thomas, 66, 70
Jesuit colleges in Havana, 12, 13, 160
Journal of Commerce, 86
Jovellanos, Gaspar Melchior de, 51
Junta to Promote the Liberty of Cuba, 68-69
Kant, Immanuel, 110
Kenny, William J., bp., 155, 165
Kenrick, Francis Patrick, bp., 105
Kepler, Johann, 40

Kindelán, Sebastian, 52
"Know-Nothing" movement. *See* Nativism
Kohlmann, Anthony, S.J., 83
Laguardia's *Spanish Grammar*, 30
Lamennais, Robert de, 110
Lancasterian (monitorial) instruction, 11
Landa González, Manuel, 155
Las Casas, Bartolomé de, bp., 44
Las Casas y Aragorri, Luis de, 9-10, 19, 29, 31, 51
Lasala, John Baptist, 77, 114, 131, 135
Lay trustees, 74, 77, 80, 90, 100, 109, 116-19
Lazo, Raimundo, 161
Lección Preliminar, 25
Lecciones de filosofía, 25, 77
Leibnitz, Gottfried Wilhelm von, 17, 22
Leo XIII, pope, 20
LeRoy Gálvez, Luis Felipe, 168
Les Misérables, 103
Levins, Thomas C., 86, 90
Library of Cuban Authors, 164
Library of Cuban Studies, 162, 164
Llaneza, Bernardo Antonio, 101, 118
Locke, John, 14, 16, 22, 52
López, Narciso, 122, 127, 130
Love, John W., 168
Luz y Caballero, José de la, biography of, 148-49; as disciple of Varela, 27-28, 37, 48, 114-16, 130; as philosopher-teacher, 51, 53, 123, 132; and phrenology, 116; republication of writings of, 164; and *Revista bimestre cubana*, 70; as transmitter of Varela's ideas, 18, 57, 132, 146-47; and Varela's *Cartas a Elpidio*, 94, 96; and Varela's death and burial, 132, 144
Luz Hernández, José de la, 116
Lynch, Dominick, 61
McClellan, William, 101, 120, 121
McCloskey, John, cardinal, 83, 113, 114
McDonough, Thomas Joseph, bp., 168
Machado, Gerardo, 156-57
McKeon, Robert, 99
Maclay, Archibald, 85
Macneven, William, 99
Madan, Cristóbal, 27, 50, 52, 104-05, 122-23, 127, 146, 148, 157
Madison, James, 66, 90-91

INDEX

Mahy, Nicolás, 52
Maistre, Joseph Marie de, 110
Maria Isabella of Spain, 93
Maria Louisa Theresa of Parma, 18
"Maria Monk," 86-87, 95, 109
Martí, José, 18, 28, 57, 146, 154, 161-62, 166-70
Martínez, Martin, 9, 51
Martínez Dalmau, Eduardo, bp., 160-64, 172
Masonic Order. *See* Freemasons
Matamoras, Mariano, 68
Materialism, 110, 114
Maynooth, seminary at, 75
Medicis, Mrs. A. L. de, 152-53, 165
Mendive, Rafael María de, 18, 28, 57, 146
Menéndez y Pelayo, Marcelino, 160
Menocal y Menocal, Raimundo, 148
El mensagero semanal, 70, 77, 122
Metropolitan, 110
Mexico, 40, 53, 66, 68-69
Minorcans, 3
Miranda, Francisco, 18, 29
Miscelánea Filosófica, 25
Missions, parish, 102, 126
Molina, Luis de, 7
Monroe, James, 19, 49-50
Monroe Doctrine, 18-19, 49-50, 66
Montoro, Rafael, 155
Morejón, "One-Eyed," 59-60
Morales, Agustín José, 30, 135, 139, 148, 152-53, 165, 169
Morales, Buenaventura, 39
Morales, María (Mother Natividad de María), 2, 6, 16
Morales, Rita, 2, 6, 16
Morales, Rita Josefa, 1, 4, 6, 121, 129, 134
Morales Coello, Julio, 166, 169-70, 172
Morales y Morales, Bartolomé, 1, 39, 148 n
Morales y Morales, Vidal, 148-50
Morales y Remírez, Bartolomé, 1-4, 6, 7, 15-16
Morelos, José María, 68
Morse, Samuel B., 85
Mosquera, Manuel José, abp., 137
Mulledy, Thomas F., S.J., 83
Muppietti, Alexander, 101, 120 n., 138
National Congress of History, Second, 161, 164
National Gazette, 86
Nativism, 83-91, 109, 112, 117, 136

New York, Diocese of, 51-52, 72-92, 101
New York Bible Society, 86
New York City Board of Education, 109
New York City Hospital, 103
New-York Daily Times, 136
New York Free Academy (later The City College), 139
New York Observer, 85-86
New York Orphan Asylum, 74
New York Protestant Association, 84
New York weekly register and Catholic diary, 78, 86-87, 107
Newman, John Henry, cardinal, 137
Newton, Isaac, 8, 22, 40
"No Popery." *See* Nativism
Nombre de Dios, 152
Nuestra Señora de la Leche, 2, 3, 152
Nugent, Andrew, 72
Nyack, N.Y., seminary at, 87, 91
Obregón, Pablo, 68, 69
O'Brien, William, 73
Observaciones sobre la constitución, 35-37
Ockham, William of, 22
O'Connell, Jeremiah J., 124
O'Connell, John, 72
O'Connor, Joseph, 114
O'Donnell, Enrique, 48-51
O'Donnell y Jorris, Leopoldo, 48, 51, 122
O'Gavan y Guerra, Juan Bernardo, and the Patriotic Society, 16, 93, 122; and Pestalozzianism, 11-12, 16; and the Spanish government, 16, 32, 39, 52; as teacher of Varela, 13-14, 17, 115
O'Neil, Felix, 101
O'Neill, Henry, 103
O'Neill, Jeremiah, Jr., 125
O'Neill, Jeremiah F., Sr., 125, 142
Oratorical Society, 145, 152
O'Reilly, Felipe, 3, 51
O'Reilly, Michael, 3-6, 51, 121, 129, 133, 152
Órtiz, Fernando, 155
O'Sullivan, Adelaide, 114
O'Sullivan, John L., 114
Pantheism, 116
Papal Infallibility, 89-90, 152, 171
Papel Periodico, 10, 13. *See also El diario de La Habana*
Pardow, George, 75
Parmentier, André, 114
Patriotic Society of Friends of the

INDEX

Fatherland. *See* Royal Patriotic (Economic) Society
Pestalozzi, Johann Heinrich, 11-12, 16, 52
Philharmonic Society of Havana, 15, 39
Philip II of Spain, 160
Phrenology, 114, 116
Piñar del Rio, 155
Pise, Charles Constantine, 83, 101, 110, 116
Pius IX, pope, 160
Plato, 21
Poey y Aloy, Felipe, 27
Poinsett, Joel Roberts, 65-69
Polk, James, 122
Popular Library of Classical Cubans, 171
Portell Vilá, Herminio, 158, 159, 161, 164, 172
Portell y Vilá, Heriberto, 159
Porter, David, 67, 69
Portuondo, José Antonio, 161
Power, John, and Dubois, 76, 83; and the episcopacy, 73-74, 80, 83, 105, 113; and Hughes, 105, 109, 113, 136; and Nativism, 83-86; as pastor of St. Peter's, 52, 73-74, 91; and the School Aid Crisis, 106-09; as Vicar General, 73-80, 82-86, 105-09
Progressive Spanish reader, 30, 149
Propositiones Variae, 23
Protestant, 84, 87, 88-90
Protestant Vindicator, 102
Protestant's abridger and annotator, 88-90
Provincial Councils of the Bishops of the United States. *See* Baltimore, Provincial Councils of
Public School Society of New York, 74, 91-92, 102, 106-11, 117
Puerto Rico, 19
Quarter, William, bp., 113
Quesada, Adolfo, 39
Randolphs of Virginia, 91
Rayos y Soles de Bolívar, 53, 56, 58
Real Sociedad Patriótica de Amigos del País. *See* Royal Patriotic (Economic) Society
Reformed Scotch Presbyterian Church, 100
"Repeal" for Ireland, 125
Repertorio médico habanero, 71
Revista bimestre cubana, 66, 70, 77, 93, 114, 144
Revista Cubana, 150, 154

Ricafort, Mariano, 92
Riego, Rafael del, 35, 39-40, 48-49
Rivas y Salmón, Hilario de, 60-62
Roa, Raúl, 172
Rodríguez, José Ignacio, his biography of Luz y Caballero, 148-49; his "Father Felix Varela," xiv, 24, 138, 149, 152; and *El Habanero*, 65; and Varela's remains, 145, 152-53, 164-65; his *Vida* of Varela, xiv, 1 n., 44, 144 n., 147-50, 157, 162-63
Rodríguez, Juan Francisco, 48
Rodríguez Embil, Julio, 155, 156, 158
Rodríguez Papers, xiv, 153, 164-65
Roig de Leuchsenring, Emilio, 159, 160, 161, 164, 167, 172
Roiz Silva, José, 72, 73
Roman Catholic Orphan Asylum, 74, 75, 79, 137
Romay y Chacón, Tomás, 13
Royal Patriotic (Economic) Society, and Espada y Landa, 11-12, 16, 35; reaction in, 93, 122; and social progress, 9-10, 31, 45; and Varela, 29-30, 33, 35-36, 38, 154-56
Royal Society of Friends of the Country. *See* Royal Patriotic Society
Ruiz, Francisco, 27, 39, 114-16, 130-31, 135, 144
Saco, José Antonio, as co-editor with Varela of *El mensagero semanal*, 70, 77, 122; as collaborator on *El Habanero*, 54; and constitutional reform for Cuba, 56, 93, 122-23; as disciple of Varela, 18, 27-28, 121; as editor of *Revista bimestre cubana*, 70, 93; as editor of *La Verdad*, 60, 123; his *History of slavery*, 28, 123, 146; as teacher at San Carlos, 35, 38, 40, 53
Sagra, Ramón la, 70 n
St. Augustine, Fla., church (cathedral) of, 3, 5, 124, 134; devotion of its people to Varela, 124, 134, 141-45, 153; in mid-nineteenth century, 121-22, 124-26, 134; its monument to Constitution of 1812, 18, 121; in Varela's childhood, 2-5; and Varela's remains, 153-56, 166, 168-69, 173; Varela's retirement in, 120-22, 124-33; and Verot, 151-53, 155, 166, 170
St. Domingue, 19
St. Francis de Sales, college, 12

St. James's Church, 99-100, 113, 117, 118, 128
St. Mary's Church, 75, 76, 79-80, 87, 113; new building, 80, 91
St. Mary's Seminary, Baltimore, 113
St. Patrick's (Old) Cathedral, 51, 72, 73, 74, 75, 76, 77, 78; services for Varela in, 135
St. Peter's Church, 51, 72-74, 76, 77, 78, 117, 136. *See also* Power, John
St. Teresa's Convent, 6, 16, 114
St. Vincent de Paul, Church of, 126
St. Vincent's Hospital, 79, 137
Salamanca, University of, 7
Salazar, José María, 67
Salvation outside the Church, 88-89
San Carlos, College and Seminary of, in the Espada era, 13-17, 19, 24, 30, 35-36, 45, 47-48; in the present era, 156, 172 n.; under reactionary governors, 52-53, 93, 122
San Ignacio College and Seminary, 13
San Marcos, Castle of, 2-4, 6, 121
Sánchez, Bernabé, 66
Santiago de Cuba, 10, 151
Santo Domingo, 19
Santos Suárez, Leonardo, 39, 41, 48, 49-50, 93 n
Savannah, Ga., 124-25, 151
Schneller, Joseph A., 78, 86, 99, 101, 107
Scholasticism, 20-21, 163
Schools, free, in New York City parishes, 78
Sentmanat, Francisco, 48, 53, 69
Seton, Elizabeth Ann Bayley, 76
Seventh Presbyterian Congregation, 76
Seward, William Henry, 91, 106
Sheridan, Stephen, 126, 133 nn., 135, 142
Shortell, Edward, 114
Silliman, Benjamin, 54
Sisters of Charity, 76, 79, 87, 91, 137
Sisters of St. Joseph, 168
Slavery, in Cuba, 10, 19, 28, 32-33, 36, 40; in Haiti, 19; and Saco, 28, 123; in St. Augustine, 3, 44; in Santo Domingo, 19; in Spanish Cortes, 44-47. *See also* Cuba; Varela, Félix, and abolition of slavery; Verot
Smallpox inoculation, 11
Smith, John Talbot, 76-77
Sociedad Económica de Amigos del País. *See* Royal Patriotic Society

Socrates, 147
Somaglia, Cardinal de la, 74 n
Someruelos, Marqués de, 11, 12 n., 16, 19
Spain, Age of Enlightenment in, 7-10; and Catholicism in New York City, 72-73; under Charles IV, 33-34; in Napoleonic era, 11, 16, 18, 29; and rediscovery of Aristotle, 20; during reign of Ferdinand VII, 32-35, 39-44, 46-49, 51, 63-64, 67
Stone, William L., 87
Stoughton, Tomás, 60-62, 73
Suárez, Francisco, S.J., 7-8, 48, 51, 163
Tacón, Francisco, 80-81
Tacón, Miguel, 93, 122
Tanco, Félix M., 96
El Telégrafo (Trinidad), 153
Terhykowicz, Lewis, 101
Tolomato, burial place of Varela, 129, 134, 141-45, 155, 168, 173; cemetery, 6, 121, 129; mission site, 2
Tolón, José, 53
Total Abstinence Society, 191
Traconis, Francisco, 5
Transcendentalism, 110
Transfiguration, Church of the, 100-23 *passim*; 127-29; 136-39, 173
Tres-Palacios, José de, bp., 11, 12
Truth Teller, 75, 78, 85-86, 102, 107-09, 149
Uncle Tom's cabin, 147
UNESCO, Cuban National Commission for, 167
United States Catholic miscellany, 113
United States Government, and Cuba, 65-68, 122-23, 154, 157; and Florida, 18, 122; and Monroe Doctrine, 18-19, 49-50, 66; and Spanish American revolutions, 18
Unzueto, Juan Antonio de, 68-69
Urrutia Lleó, Manuel, 172
Ursuline Convent, burning of, 87, 92
Utilitarianism, 115
Valdés Domínguez, Eusebio, 148
Váldez, Gerónimo, 122, 148 n
Valera y Jiménez, Pedro, primate, 23-24
Valerino, José Manuel, 27, 105
Valiente y Bravo, José, 31-32
Valle, Raúl del, vii-x, xiii, xiv, 172 n
Vallejo, José María, 73
Valverde y Maruri, Antonio L., 156
Varela, Cristina, 2

INDEX

Varela, Manuel, 2, 78
Varela, María de Jesús, 2, 16, 18, 102, 112, 120
de Varela, María Josefa Morales, 1, 2
Varela y Morales, Félix:
and abolition of slavery, 3-4, 44-47, 158, 170; and the *aggiornamento*, 173, and Agramonte, 166, 172; and Allo, 129-31; and anti-Catholicism (American Nativism), 83-90; apotheosis of, 146-73; arrival in New York, 49-53; assailed by Spanish officials, 60-65, 80-82, 122; assassination plot against, 59-60; attacked in print by Ferrety, 57-59; and autonomy for Cuba and Puerto Rico, 41-43, 47, 127, 157
benevolence of, 103-04, 139; biographies of, 135-36, 139-40, 147-50, 162-63; birth and baptism, 1; burial in St. Augustine, 134-35, 144
his *Cartas a Elpidio*, 71, 94-98, 164, 171; his *Catholic Expositor*, 110-13, 116, 149, 164; his *Catholic Register*, 107-08, 110, 164; centenary of death, 166-68; centenary of ordination, 155; chapel to, in St. Augustine, 141-45, 151-54, 165-66, 168-69; childhood in St. Augustine, 2-6; his *Children's Catholic Magazine*, 102, 106; and cholera epidemic, 91; at Christ Church, 77-100 *passim*; as constitutional law professor, 35-37; in Cortes of Spain, 41-49
death of, 133, 140, 146-47; his *Despedida*, 38-39; his disciples in Cuba, 27-28, 47-48, 53, 57, 93, 94, 114-16, 131-32; and Dubois, 76-78, 80-83, 90-92, 104-05
early education, 4-5; eulogy of Ferdinand VII, 32-33; eulogy of Valiente, 31; as exile from Cuba, 49-65, 69-71, 93-98, 126-27
and Fidel Castro, 18, 172; flight from Cádiz, 49; and *Freeman's Journal*, 110, 119, 135-36; his friends in New York, 114; his funeral oration for Charles IV, 33-34
his *El Habanero*, 54-65, 159, 164; his Half-Orphan Asylum, 79, 101, 119, 137; and Hernández Travieso, 14 n., 159, 165-66; and Hughes, 106-10, 113, 118, 120, 127-28, 131, 135-37
illness of, 53, 119-21, 127-31; and independence for Cuba, 55-71, 123, 127, 150, 161-63, 167; and independence for Spanish America, 43-44, 158; his *Instituciones de filosofía*, 24, 164; his *Institutiones philosophiae eclecticae*, 24
journey to Spain, 38-40
his *Lecciones de filosofía*, 25-26, 54, 77-78, 113, 114, 164, 166, 172; his library, 138
and Martí, 18, 146, 167; and Martínez Dalmau, 160-63; and *El mensagero semanal*, 70, 77, 122; and Mexico, 68-69; his *Miscelánea Filosófica*, 25, 41, 114, 164; his *New York weekly register*, 78, 86-87, 107
his *Observaciones sobre la constitución de la monarquía*, 35-37, 164; ordination of, 15-16
parentage, 1-2; and parish missions, 102; in Philadelphia, 53-60; philosophy of, 20-26, 114-16, 159-60; and phrenology, 114, 116; and Poinsett, 65-68, 158; and Portell Vilá, 158; and Power, 73-87 *passim*, 105-06, 113; and prelacy of New York, 80-83, 105-06; as priest at St. Peter's, 73-77; his *Propositiones Variae*, 23; his *Protestant's Abridger*, 88-90; as public speaker, 28-34
as "Regenerator of Cuban thought," 27-28, 37; his remains examined and reinterred, 166, 168-71; retirement in St. Augustine, 121-33; and *Revista bimestre*, 70-71, 77; and Rodríguez, 1 n., 24 n., 147-53 *passim*, 165; in Royal Patriotic Society, 29-30, 33
in Savannah, Ga., 124-25; and School Aid Crisis, 102, 106-12; as seminarian at San Carlos, 12-15; and Spanish pirates, 92
teacher at San Carlos, 17-19, 26-27, 35-37; transfer of remains to Havana, 141, 143-44, 154-56; and Transfiguration Church, 100-23 *passim*, 127-29, 138-39; translates *Elements of chemistry*, 69-70; translates *Manual of parliamentary*

procedure, 70; and Tres-Palacios, 12; and *Truth Teller,* 75-76, 78, 86, 149
and *United States Catholic miscelany,* 113
and *La Verdad,* 71; and Verot, 105, 151-52, 165-71; as Vicar General, 71, 78-90, 104-06
his *Young Catholic's magazine,* 102, 113; his *Youth's Friend,* 75-76
Varela y Pérez, Francisco, 1, 2
Varona y Pera, Enrique José, 150, 154, 156, 157
Vásquez, Gabriel, 7
Velázquez de la Cadena, Mariano, 30, 73, 74, 75, 99, 101
Venezuela, 29
La Verdad, 60, 71, 123, 129
Verot, Augustin, bp., and papal infallibility, 89 n., 151-52; at Provincial Council, 105; and St. Augustine, 151-52, 155; and slavery, 151, 170-71; in Varela's tomb, 151-56, 165, 168-69

Victoria, Guadalupe, 69
Villamil, Domingo, 159
Vitier, Medardo, 159
Vitoria, Francisco de, 7, 8 n., 51
Vives, Francisco Dionisio, 52-53, 59, 60, 66, 92
Vives, Luis, 7
Voltaire, François Marie Arouet de, 9, 114
Ward, Henry George, 68
Weekly Register. See *New York weekly register and Catholic diary*
Weld, Thomas, cardinal, 83
Wellington, Duke of, 16, 29
Weyler, Valeriano, 154
Whelan, Richard, bp., 113
Wolff, Christian, 22
Young Catholic's magazine, 102, 113
Youth's friend; El amigo de la juventud, 75-76
Zaquía, Paulo, 14
Zayas, Alfred, 154
Zequeira y Arango, Manuel Tibercio de, 13, 70